To Hasten the Homecoming

TO HASTEN THE HOMECOMING

How Americans Fought World War II through the Media

Jordan Braverman

ROWMAN & LITTLEFIELD
Lanham • Boulder • New York • London

Published by Rowman & Littlefield
A wholly owned subsidiary of The Rowman & Littlefield Publishing Group, Inc.
4501 Forbes Boulevard, Suite 200, Lanham, Maryland 20706
www.rowman.com

Unit A, Whitacre Mews, 26-34 Stannary Street, London SE11 4AB

Distributed by NATIONAL BOOK NETWORK

Copyright © 2015 by Rowman & Littlefield
First paperback edition 2015
Hardback originally published by Madison Books, 1996

British Library Cataloguing in Publication Information Available

Library of Congress Cataloging-in-Publication Data

The hardback edition of this book was previously cataloged by the Library of Congress as follows:

Braverman, Jordan.
    To hasten the homecoming : how Americans fought World War II through the media / by Jordan Braverman.
        p. cm.
    Includes index.
    1. World War, 1939–1945—United States. 2. World War, 1939–1945—Mass media and the war. 3. World War, 1939–1945—Public opinion. 4. Public opinion—United States. 5. Popular culture—United States. I. Title.
    D796.1.B73   1995
    940.54'8673—dc20
    95-4767   CIP

ISBN 978-1-56833-047-1 (cloth : alk. paper)
ISBN 978-1-4422-4874-8 (pbk : alk. paper)
ISBN 978-1-4422-4875-5 (electronic)

∞™ The paper used in this publication meets the minimum requirements of American National Standard for Information Sciences—Permanence of Paper for Printed Library Materials, ANSI/NISO Z39.48-1992.

Printed in the United States of America

First, this book is dedicated to my parents, Morris and Molly Braverman, and my brother, Irwin, who shared the triumphs and tragedies of World War II on Boston's Lorna Road where my father served his country as a civil defense air raid warden and my mother made sure her children bought war bonds and war stamps, planted Victory Gardens, collected scrap, and participated in other wartime activities to hasten the homecoming.

Second, to peoples and their governments everywhere. May you never forget the anguished cry of Kurt Mueller, antifascist underground hero of *Watch on the Rhine*: "Shame on us! Thousands of years and we cannot yet make a world."

CONTENTS

PREFACE

World War II has been called the greatest cataclysm in the history of mankind—with dimensions so vast that decades later its social, economic, and political consequences continue to influence our daily lives. However, this global conflict was not solely a war of physical survival of either nations or the individuals who composed those nations. It was also a war of ideology that sought to capture the heart and soul of men's minds. It was a conflict that would determine whether civilization as we knew it would return to the Dark Ages or continue to evolve and progress to a brighter tomorrow. It was a war in which all of America's resources—human and material—were used to maintain its viability as a free nation and assist those seeking to be free. Among the most important resources the United States and the other warring nations used were the verbal, visual, and technical skills of the communication media. Through the media Americans learned about themselves, their Allies, and their enemies and were reminded of the principles for which they were fighting and what would befall their country and the rest of the world if they and their Allies won or lost the war.

Many books have been and continue to be written about World War II. Some have reassessed the roles of military leaders, and others have reappraised enemy war aims and strategies. This is not such a book. This book presents a portrait of America at war through the words we spoke, read, sang, and heard during those turbulent years when the war's outcome or the events of the postwar world were unknown. This book is a portrait of how Americans perceived and fought the war through the communication media and how the media, in turn, reflected our perceptions of the war. So let us return to the time in our nation's history when the greatest conflict in the history of mankind occurred and changed the course of world history—a time when America reached a preeminence in the world it had never attained before. Let us return to the time known as World War II.

ACKNOWLEDGMENTS

I thank the staff of Madison Books for its assistance in the publication of this book: Jon Sisk, editor, whose enthusiasm for the manuscript was everything an author seeks; Deirdre Mullervy, editor, for all her advice and assistance in guiding the manuscript into the editorial process; Jennifer Ruark, acquisitions editor at Madison who invited me to submit my manuscript for review; and Kelly Rogers, for advice on copyright law.

In addition to the Madison staff, I also thank John L. Jones, Jr., for his advice and expertise on the computerization of the manuscript and other valuable counsel; Arlene Zimmerman for her editorial insights, review, and support; Stephen E. Greenfield, chairman, FMAS Corporation, for past considerations; Betty Hayler, Vice President, CBS Radio, for assistance and counsel; Larry Merritt, Curator, Prologue Room, McDonnell-Douglas Corporation, for his informational assistance on World War II; Leonard Bushkoff, historian, for his observations regarding World War II; Mary Ison, Head, Prints and Photograph Reading Room, Library of Congress, for her assistance on poster art; Claire Johnston, Peer Music Company, for our discussions on wartime music; Ardena Lovelace and Calvin Thomas, Jr., for production advice; and Chris McKinley, who with utmost diligence and technical skills, converted a manuscript of more than several hundred pages into its appropriate computerized format within an extremely short time.

I also wish to express my appreciation to Janet Murrow for allowing me to quote the words of her husband, Edward R. Murrow, about various events of World War II, including the liberation of the Buchenwald concentration camp, so that the world will never forget his personal witness to crimes against humanity; Nanette Fabray MacDougall for providing me with insights about the writings of her husband, Ranald R.

MacDougall; Shirley Robson for background information on the programs her husband, William N. Robson, created and wrote, and for directing me to other appropriate sources regarding wartime radio; and Norman Corwin for our conversations about his writings during the war years.

I want to acknowledge a special remembrance to the residents of Lorna Road during World War II, wherever you now may be—the Starrs, Shumans, Kuppersteins, Thompsons, Rubins, Masons, Slavets, Gordons, Raymonds, Lipsons, Burks, Waters, Ziskinds, Santises, Lerners, Levines, Snyders, Wilsons, Castellines, Samuelsons, Rosenthals, Lapiduses, Sorkins, Claricos, Shermans, Whites, Greens, Figaros, Flaxes, Weiners, Schwartzes and others. Together as families, friends, neighbors, and acquaintances Boston's Lorna Road was more than just the name of a street. It was a communal oasis of friendship and peace in a world torn asunder by war because other peoples in other lands could not live with each other in the same way on their own Lorna Roads.

Finally, I'd like to thank the following individuals and organizations for their kind permission to quote material under copyright.

Excerpts from "The Murder of Lidice" by Edna St. Vincent Millay. Copyright © 1942, 1969 by Edna St. Vincent Millay and Norma Millay Ellis. Reprinted by permission of Elizabeth Barnett, literary executor.

Excerpt from "Back in the Military Closet" by Peter J. Gomes, May 22, 1993 (op-ed). Copyright © 1993 by the New York Times Company. Reprinted by permission.

Editorial, March 1942. Copyright © 1942 by the New York Times Company. Reprinted by permission.

"Fortune Press Analysis," December 1944 *Fortune* © 1944 Time Inc. All rights reserved.

Excerpt from "Thank God for the Atomic Bomb," by Paul Fussell, *New Republic*, 1981. Reprinted by permission of *The New Republic*, © 1981, The New Republic Inc.

Leonard Bushkoff for permission to quote material from his article, "The War that Changed the World" in *The Washington Post*, September 2, 1979 and the identical article that appeared in the *Boston Globe* on the same date.

Mr. Dan Thomasson, Vice President, News, *Scripps Howard* newspapers, for permission to quote from Ernie Pyle's newspaper columns.

© 1941–1945 Newsweek Inc. All rights reserved.

© 1941–1945 Time Inc. Reprinted by permission.

Life Magazine © Time Inc. Reprinted by permission.

National Broadcasting Company for permission to use various excerpts from programs broadcast over the National Broadcasting Company; © National Broadcasting Company, Inc. All Rights Reserved.

Columbia Broadcasting System for permission to use various material from programs broadcast over the Columbia Broadcasting System; © Columbia Broadcasting System. All rights reserved.

For excerpts broadcast over WGAR-FM, the Nationwide Communications, Inc., licensee of WGAR-FM.

WTOP-AM, Washington, D.C., for permission to use an excerpt of Arthur Godfrey's broadcast of Franklin D. Roosevelt's funeral, which was fed over the Columbia Broadcasting System.

WOR-AM, New York, for permission to use WOR-related announcements, analyses, and commentary.

Mrs. Janet Murrow for permission to quote the writings and commentary of her husband, Edward R. Murrow.

Mrs. Shirley Robson for permission to use excerpts from *The Man Behind the Gun*, directed by her husband, William N. Robson, and "Open Letter on Race Hatred," by William N. Robson.

Mrs. Nanette Fabray MacDougall for permission to quote excerpts written by her husband, Ranald R. MacDougall, from *The Man Behind the Gun*, and *Smith Against the Axis*, a play in the radio series *This Is War!*

Mr. Norman Corwin for permission to quote his writings in the *Saturday Review of Literature*, "This Is War!" radio series, "On A Note of Triumph," and "Fourteen August." © Norman Corwin 1945. Renewed 1972.

For the advertisement "The Kid in Upper Four." Reprint permission granted by the Advertising Council.

For the advertisement "Squeeze that Money Brother . . . It's Mine Too!" Reprint permission granted by the Advertising Council.

For the advertisement of "Loose Talk can cost Lives." Reprinted by permission of the John B. Stetson Co.

Ms. Cherie Voris, Public Relations Archivist, Texaco Inc. for permission to use Texaco advertisements: "US Highway Number 1," "Life on a US Warship," and "Don't let your gas ration 'Go up in smoke.' "

Excerpt from *The North Star* by Lillian Hellman. Copyright 1943 Lillian Hellman. Use by permission of Viking Penguin, a division of Penguin Books USA Inc.

Excerpt from the March of Time episode entitled "One Day of War—Russia 1943." Permission to quote from The March of Time courtesy of SFM Entertainment, a division of SFM Media Corporation.

Excerpts from the following motion pictures:
Mrs. Miniver; © Turner Entertainment Co.; All rights reserved.
Nazi Agent; © Turner Entertainment Co.; All rights reserved.
Thirty Seconds Over Tokyo; © Turner Entertainment; All rights reserved.

Excerpts from *Watch on the Rhine*, a play by Lillian Hellman © 1941. Renewed © by Lillian Hellman 1968. Reprinted by permission of Random House, Inc.

Brandt & Brandt Literary Agency for permission to quote an excerpt from Stephen Vincent Benét's *Your Army*, a play in the radio series "This Is War!" © 1942. Not renewed.

Ms. Brook Hersey for the Estate of John Hersey to quote John Hersey's commentary regarding *A Bell for Adano*, a play by Paul Osborn, based on the novel by John Hersey.

Excerpts from the play, *A Bell for Adano* by Paul Osborn, based on the novel by John Hersey. Reprinted by permission of Brandt & Brandt Literary Agency. Copyright 1944, 1945 by Paul Osborn; Copyright renewal (c) 1971, 1972 by Paul Osborn; all rights reserved.

Excerpts from *The Moon Is Down* by John Steinbeck. Copyright 1942 by John Steinbeck. Renewed (c) 1970 by Elaine Steinbeck, John Steinbeck IV and Thom Steinbeck. Used by permission of Viking Penguin, a division of Penguin Books USA Inc.

Excerpts from *The Moon Is Down;* Copyright 1942 by John Steinbeck; Copyright © renewed 1969 by Elaine A. Steinbeck, Thom Steinbeck

Rutherfurd, Jr., Anne Phipps Sidamon-Eristoff and Theodore Jackson as Trustees of God Bless America Fund. International Copyright Secured. All Rights Reserved. Used by Permission.

INTRODUCTION

Long before the wars in Kuwait, Iraq, Afghanistan, Iran, Syria, Lebanon, and Israel; long before the wars in El Salvador, Nicaragua, Chad, Somalia, Ethiopia, and Angola; long before the wars in India, Pakistan, Tibet, Korea, and Vietnam, there was another war. It was a conflict of such proportions that its initiation and outcome have influenced world history ever since and, perhaps, in some instances directly and other instances indirectly, created the political, social, and economic climate that led to those subsequent hostilities. This conflict is called World War II. It was fought at a time when America's self-perception was still innocent as was its perception of peoples in other lands. It occurred in an era when there was no question about the principles for which America stood. It took place in a period when Americans knew that their wars were just and, that despite the terrible Depression of the 1930s, their country was still blessed with the freedoms and bountiful resources that formed the foundations for a better tomorrow. It happened amidst a generation of Americans who saw themselves reflecting the unconquerable will and spirit of their forebears who had tamed a wild frontier and civilized a continent; who believed that their best years, like those of the country itself, still lay ahead. It was fought in an era when Americans knew that right would prevail and wrongdoers would always lose. Simplicity was their quality; hope their strength.

This was the America that learned one quiet Sunday afternoon in December 1941 that naval and air forces of the Empire of Japan had attacked Pearl Harbor in the Hawaiian Islands. This was the character of the country that, during the darkest period of the war in 1942, for itself and its allies, kept on fighting and producing in the years that followed until victory was won. This was the nature of the America that entered the war with the debate over isolationism still ringing in its ears and at war's end, when triumphant, became internationalist in its outlook and assumed its new responsibilities as a world superpower.

Helping to shape the nation's self-perception were the communication media. Books, movies, and music extolled our qualities—positive and negative—as a nation and as individuals. The media initiated and influenced some of the values, behavior patterns, and other characteristics that constitute the cultural fabric of a society. The media permeated American culture in so many ways that perhaps, after a while, the public took the media for granted and became less conscious of the subliminal, but very real, effects the media had on their daily lives. The influence of the media on our society has been substantive, and also inestimable. For this reason, when World War II finally exploded on American shores one Sunday morning in December 1941, the U.S. government called up and drafted the media for the duration of the war.

In viewing how a nation goes to war, this book examines how America fought World War II through the media: their role in wartime America, what they did, what they said, and how they affected the war effort at home and abroad. The United States used the media to fight and win World War II as surely as it used guns, tanks, ships, and people. In some instances (for example, radio) in the beginning, the media were novices in effectively using the resources at their command because they had no prior wartime experiences to call upon; however, by war's end, like the military, they too had become veterans at their craft. In other instances, such as the movies, the media could use the experiences gained from World War I to plan their new wartime activities. In still other instances, such as music, the media were initially perplexed as to how they could contribute to the war effort because the conditions, the implements of war, and the scope of the conflict were so different than World War I. But even they learned to adapt to America at war.

The media, however, were not just another wartime tool to fight the Axis powers; they mirrored the world in which Americans lived. So this book is really a dual story: how a nation went to war through the media and how the media reflected conditions in wartime America. For some readers, many memories may be evoked of what Charles Dickens might have called "the best of times and the worst of times." For others to whom World War II may be part of America's ancient history, I hope the book will reveal a country whose youth and innocence were swept away by an international conflagration or, as Margaret Mitchell might have said, they were "gone with the wind." However, whatever knowledge or new experiences you may gain as a reader, the book has been written in the hope that there will never be another World War II to write about. So let us return to the early 1940s and relive an experience that will never be forgotten in the annals of mankind—an event whose lessons may someday be heeded and allow individuals to live with each other in peace forevermore.

Chapter One

THE HOME FRONT
An Overview

THE CLOCK READS 2:21 P.M. It is Sunday. A day to attend church. A day to relax. A day families get together for dinner or visits. A day to see a movie or attend a sporting event. A day to clean the house or the car. A day that is one day closer to the merriest holiday of the year, the birth of the Prince of Peace. A day on which America is still at peace in a world where the flames of war have begun to consume Europe, Russia, Asia, and North Africa.

That is the way it was on Lorna Road—a street that could have been any street in any town in America, but which was located in Mattapan, Mass., a subdivision of Boston. Here at number seventeen, my family spent that Sunday and the many Sundays that followed. Lorna Road was a cross section of America on that day, a street of mixed creeds and nationalities—Russian-, Italian-, and American-born, and others.

On that particular Sunday, some of Lorna Road's residents were probably in nearby Evans Pharmacy on Morton Street, only a few stores away from Raverby's butcher shop, Oscar's shoe repair store, or Patsy's barber shop. At Evans Pharmacy, they might have been waiting to be served at the counter or buying a 5-cent candy bar, a 10-cent comic book, or a Sunday newspaper such as the *Boston Post*, the *Boston Globe*, the *Boston Herald*, or the *Boston Advertiser*. Or they might have been waiting for the Norfolk Street bus in front of Evans Pharmacy to take them to the Ashmont Street station; there they could board a subway train to the Park Street station in downtown Boston from which they could walk to the Majestic, Wilbur, or Shubert theaters to attend a play.

1

Or, perhaps, they went to see a film at a local movie house such as the Oriental, Codman Square, Franklin Park, or Morton theaters.

Some of the residents of Lorna Road might have been listening to radio. If they had, one minute later at 2:22 P.M. Stephen T. Early, President Franklin D. Roosevelt's press secretary, changed their lives and the lives of Americans on all the country's Lorna Roads. At that moment, the press secretary flashed 22 words to the Associated Press, the United Press and the International News Service—words that would change America's role in world history for the remainder of the 20th century and, perhaps, beyond: "The Japs have attacked Pearl Harbor, all military activities on Oahu Island. A second attack reported on Manila air and naval bases." A few moments later listeners who were tuned to the Columbia Broadcasting System (CBS) unexpectedly heard the voice of newsman John Charles Daly: "We interrupt this program to bring you a special news bulletin. The Japanese have attacked Pearl Harbor, Hawaii, by air, President Roosevelt has announced. The attack was made on all naval and military activities on the principal island of Oahu." Soon those listening to the National Broadcasting Company (NBC) heard Hans V. Kaltenborn, its distinguished commentator, tell his radio audience: "President Roosevelt phoned Secretary Early half an hour ago that the Japanese have attacked Pearl Harbor, the United States naval base in the Hawaiians. The attack occurred at the very moment when Ambassador Nomura and Special Envoy Kurusu were at the State Department discussing the possibility of peace between Japan and the United States. Japan has made war upon the United States without declaring it." Later that afternoon an observer in Honolulu officially confirmed the attack on Pearl Harbor, when he reported over NBC: "We have witnessed this morning a severe bombing of Pearl Harbor by enemy planes, undoubtedly Japanese. The center of Honolulu has also been attacked and considerable damage done. This is no joke. It is a real war."

With these words the greatest international cataclysm of the 20th century was about to unfold. Before it would end nearly four years later, America would mobilize slightly more than 15 million men and women in its armed services. Of this number, 670,000 would be wounded and more than 292,000 would die in battle. Worldwide more than 55 million people—civilian and military—would lose their lives. The nations of the world would spend more than $1 trillion in arming their military machines.

When President Roosevelt went before the Congress on December 8, 1941, little did the residents of Lorna Road and the rest of the country realize the scope and intensity of the conflict to follow as the president declared, in part:

> Yesterday, December 7, 1941—a date which will live in infamy—the United States of America was suddenly and deliberately attacked by naval and air forces of the Empire of Japan. . . . With confidence in our armed forces—with unbounding determination of our people—we will gain the inevitable triumph, so help us God. I ask that the Congress declare that since the unprovoked and dastardly attack by Japan on Sunday December 7, 1941, a state of war has existed between the United States and the Empire of Japan.

When the President arrived at the Capitol, the clock read 12:12 P.M. At exactly 1:00 P.M., the Senate passed the resolution by a vote of 82–0 (there was one vacancy and thirteen senators were not present.) At 1:32 P.M., the war resolution passed the House of Representatives by a vote of 388–1 (the lone dissenter was Jeannette Rankin, a Montana Republican who, on April 6, 1917, also had voted against the congressional resolution that brought America into World War I). At 4:10 P.M., President Roosevelt signed the war resolution in his office. Three days later on December 11, 1941, Germany and Italy declared war on the United States. Germany, Italy, and Japan had signed the Tripartite Pact of 1940, which required each country to defend the other if attacked (although, in this instance, Japan was the initial aggressor). The possibility of war that had hovered over Lorna Road and the rest of the United States since 1939 was finally a reality.

When World War II reached American shores that fateful Sunday, the residents of Lorna Road responded as did the rest of the nation. Some, perhaps, were spurred by a message broadcast on the Jack Benny program, the evening of December 7th:

> Ladies and Gentlemen, a special announcement. Citizen volunteers are asked to go quietly to their nearest police or fire stations and offer their services if they wish to be of help. There is no immediate cause for alarm and coolness will accomplish more than anything else.[1]

The men on Lorna Road who were not eligible for military service either because of age or physical infirmities contacted the police at Station 19 on Morton Street. Donning their white World War I helmets and arm bands emblazoned with the civil defense insignia, and learning first aid treatment at Franklin Field on Blue Hill Avenue, they were soon patrolling the community with gas masks and billy clubs as civil defense air raid wardens. Meanwhile, the women of Lorna Road prepared against possible enemy attack by putting up black window shades or curtains and making sure they had enough buckets of sand in their home in case of fire.

Even the children of Lorna Road were to become participants in the war effort. At the Charles H. Taylor elementary school—named in honor of the founder of the *Boston Globe*—the pledge of allegiance changed from a salute of an arm outstretched toward the American flag to placing of the right hand over one's heart because the former pledge was too suggestive of the way people were saluting in Nazi Germany. These children who pledged allegiance to their country verbally also pledged their loyalty in other ways. With their nickels and dimes, they purchased war stamps and bonds. When the nickels and dimes were counted at Charles H. Taylor elementary school and at thousands of other schools across the country, they added up to a staggering $1 billion for the War Finance Program, an average of $21 for each school child per year. In 1944, our schools financed 2,900 planes, 33,000 jeeps, 600 amphibious jeeps, and 11,600 parachutes.[2] The contribution of children to the war effort cannot be minimized. Going from house to house with wagons, children on Lorna Roads across the country collected tin cans, paper, or whatever a particular war drive required. Some schools established workshops so that children could make simple clothing for children living in war-ravaged lands. During the war, the Boy Scouts collected 3 million books, more than 109 million pounds of rubber, more than 23 million pounds of tin, and more than 370 million pounds of scrap metal; they were also responsible for the sale of $8 billion worth of war stamps and bonds.[3] When the children on all the nation's Lorna Roads got together, the whole country benefited from their efforts.

Thus, war came to Lorna Road. Yet the night of December 7th did not look any different than the previous night when America had still been at peace. Perhaps it looked like the night of January 2, 1915, when the *New Republic* published the following thoughts, which were as relevant in World War II as they were a generation earlier before America entered World War I:

> On any of these clear, cold nights when the stars possess themselves of the sky, is it sentimental to reflect that those same stars wheeled their slow gaze over France, Serbia, Poland, Russia; over trenches, roofless walls, riddled huts, shattered woods, gunswept fields; over a stiffened horse, or a man stretched to heaven, turning eyes that will shine no more toward stars that will shine forever? . . . And as our eyes look, too, do we not feel the simply earthly bond that makes one of all of us, here in peaceful America and there aching in Europe?

A generation later the ache was everywhere, stretching from Asia and the South Pacific to North Africa, Europe, and Russia.

In the ensuing weeks, months, and years, Lorna Road, like many streets across the land, sent its sons to foreign battlefields. As on those other streets, windows in the homes on Lorna Road began to display a flag with a blue star, indicating that a family member was in the armed service. Fortunately, families on Lorna Road never had to replace that flag with one bearing a gold star, meaning that a serviceman or woman had died in service to the country.

As December 7, 1941, became December 8th, and as 1941 turned into 1942 and the years beyond, the two most significant messages delivered on the nation's Lorna Roads were sent by the U.S. government and altered the lives of millions of people. The first was sent by one of 6,175 draft boards established throughout the country and simply began:

> The President of the United States
> To-
> Greetings
>   You are hereby ordered to report for induction into the armed forces of the United States . . .[*]

The families and loved ones of about 292,000 men who had received this message were to receive another—a message containing nothing but sorrow and beginning with four ominous words ". . . regret to inform you. . . ." Its arrival notified everyone that another American had given his life for his country. At the beginning of the war, the names of the dead were posted publicly in many small towns and city neighborhoods—a tradition that went back at least as far as the Civil War. But as the casualty lists lengthened, as the days turned into months and the months into years, many communities discontinued the practice.

Evidence of the war being fought in distant lands and in some cases on American shores was always visible to the families on Lorna Road: the reported sinkings of American vessels by German submarines off the nearby Atlantic coast; Italian prisoners of war being housed in a camp at Boston's Carson Beach; blackouts; search lights, ships being built at the nearby Quincy shipyard; jeep or "baby" aircraft carriers (small escort aircraft carriers used for anti-submarine warfare and amphibious air support) that sailed into Boston harbor for public viewing—their aircrafts' fuselage emblazoned with emblems of the "Rising Sun," indicating the number of Japanese planes they had shot down; or the miniature Japanese submarine on display in downtown Boston to show the public how such craft could penetrate harbor defenses and wreak havoc on American ports.

War came to Lorna Road in many ways. Radio, movie newsreels, books, plays, music, and newspapers were constant reminders. Everyone could hear, see, and read about the daily carnage taking place—stories similar to that of the infantryman who lost his arm in 1944 in Italy's Arno Valley and asked why:

> I wanted to die and fast. I wanted to forget this miserable world. I cursed the war. I cursed the people who were responsible for it. I cursed God for putting me here . . . to suffer for something I never did or knew anything about. For this was hell and I never imagined anything or anyone could suffer so bitterly. I screamed and cursed. Why? Why? What had I done to deserve this? But no answer came. I yelled for medics, because subconsciously I wanted to live. I tried to apply my right hand over my bleeding stump, but I didn't have the strength to hold it. I looked to the left of me and saw the bloody mess that was once my left arm; its fingers and palm were turned upward like a flower looking to the sun for strength.[5]

Why did it have to happen to this infantryman and the more than 50 million other men, women and children who were to die before the war would finally end, especially the civilians, the innocent civilians? The residents on Lorna Roads across the country could find a partial answer in a film playing at their local movie house, a film called *Mrs. Miniver*.

Near the end of the movie, the people of the town are sitting on benches among the ruins of a church whose roof had been partially destroyed by German bombs and listening as the Vicar concludes his sermon.

We in this quiet corner of England have suffered the loss of friends very dear to us—some close to this church . . . The homes of many of us have been destroyed and the lives of young and old have been taken. There's scarcely a household that hasn't been struck to the heart. And why? Surely, you must have asked yourselves this question. Why, in all conscience, should these be the ones to suffer? Children, old people, a young girl at the height of her loveliness. Why these? Are these our soldiers? Are these our fighters? Why should they be sacrificed? I shall tell you why. Because this is not only a war of soldiers in uniform. It is a war of the people, of all the people. And it must be fought not only in the battlefield but in the city and the villages, in the factories and on the farms, in the home and in the heart of every man, woman, and child who loves freedom. Well, we have buried our dead. But we shall not forget them. Instead, they will inspire us with unbreakable determination to free ourselves and those who come after us from the tyranny and terror that threaten to strike us down. This is the people's war. It is our war. We are the fighters. Fight it then! Fight it with all that is in us and may God defend the right![6]

Moving Toward War

It was a people's war. As the decade of the 1930s neared its end, each year that passed seemed to confirm this inevitability. In 1937, Japan and China went to war. In 1938, Hitler occupied Austria and the Sudetenland in Czechoslovakia. In 1939, Italy invaded Albania and Russia attacked Finland as Hitler absorbed the rest of Czechoslovakia and overran Poland. Beginning in April 1940, Hitler invaded and by June had subdued Denmark, Norway, Holland, Luxembourg, Belgium, and France. By the summer of 1940, Great Britain stood alone.

Even then, hope still flickered that someone somewhere might appear to stave off America's involvement in these worldwide conflicts. Perhaps the households living on America's Lorna Roads tried to grasp such hope on May 10, 1940, when they heard Edward R. Murrow, the CBS London news correspondent, describe the man who was succeeding Neville Chamberlain as British Prime Minister:

> Winston Churchill, who has held more political offices than any living man, is now prime minister. He is a man without a party. For the last seven years, he has sat in the House of Commons, a rather lonesome and often bellicose figure, voicing unheeded warnings of the rising tide of German military strength. Now, at the age of sixty-five, Winston Churchill, plump, bald, with massive round shoulders, is for the first time in his varied career as journalist, historian, and politician the prime minister of Great Britain. Mr. Churchill now takes over the supreme direction of Britain's war effort at a time when the war is moving toward Britain's doorstep. Mr. Churchill's critics have said that he is inclined to be impulsive and, at times, vindictive. But in the tradition of British politics he will be given his chance. He will probably take chances. But if he brings victory, his place in history is assured.
>
> The historians will have to devote more than a footnote to this remarkable man no matter what happens. He enters office with the tremendous advantage of being the man who was right. He also has the advantage of being the best broadcaster in the country. Mr. Churchill can inspire confidence. And he can preach a doctrine of hate that is acceptable to the majority of this country. That may be useful during these next few months. Winston Churchill has never been known for his caution and when he has completed the formation of his new government you may expect this country to begin living dangerously. Hitler has said that the action begun yesterday [the Nazi invasion of Holland, Belgium, and Luxembourg] will settle the future of Germany for a thousand years. Mr. Churchill doesn't deal in such periods of time, but the decisions reached by this new prime minister with his boyish grin and puckish sense of humor may well determine the outcome of this war. I now return you to Columbia in New York.[7]

Since 1939, at first slowly and then ever more quickly, hope began to fade that America could avoid entanglement in foreign wars even though neutrality was the law of the land as recently as 1935. First, the Neutrality Act of 1939 repealed the arms embargo for France and England. In September 1940, President Roosevelt agreed to transfer fifty old destroyers to England in exchange for British bases in the West Indies, Newfoundland, and Bermuda. That very same month, the President signed into law the Selective Service and Training Act, the first peacetime military draft in American history. Six months later, in March 1941, the president signed the Lend-Lease Act that transferred food, munitions, shipping services, and other supplies to our allies, especially Great Britain and Russia. A month later, Germany attacked Greece and Yugoslavia. In June, Russia came under the German assault. In August in Placentia Bay, off Argentina, Newfoundland, America and Britain signed the Atlantic Charter, which defined the war aims of the democracies. In November, Congress repealed the Neutrality Law. Three weeks later, the Japanese attacked Pearl Harbor, and four days after that attack, Germany and Italy declared war on the United States. The flames rising at Pearl Harbor not only destroyed our Pacific fleet and the isolationist's argument that two great oceans made America impregnable to attack, but also ended all public debate as to whether America should get involved in the war. The country no longer had a choice. America was in the war to the end—whatever that end might be.

World War II was to be a war in which neither side was to give any quarter. With its war in China during the 1930s, Japan had already given the world a preview of its barbarity. In Europe and elsewhere, the Germans were to provide their own shocks as in June 1941 when they obliterated the Czechoslovakian village of Lidice along with its several hundred inhabitants. The Nazis charged that the villagers had harbored the assassins of Reinhard Heydrich—the Deputy Gestapo Chief and former Reich Protector of Bohemia-Moravia. The massacre was so bestial and senseless that Edna St. Vincent Millay, the distinguished poet, wrote an epic poem entitled "The Murder of Lidice." On October 19, 1942, NBC aired the poem which read, in part:

> The whole world holds in its arms today
> The murdered Village of Lidice,
> Like the murdered body of a little child, . . .
> And moans of vengeance frightful to hear
> From the throat of a whole world, reach his ear—
> The maniac killer who still runs wild . . .[8]

Before the maniac killer and others like him were stopped, the whole world would witness other Lidices whether they were in the guise of mass extermination camps, the wanton slaughter of civilian hostages, or the destruction of numerous villages, towns, cities, and countries throughout the world.

Beginning on that Sunday in December and for almost the next four years, Lorna Road and the rest of the country were to bear witness to this observation by a participant in World War I: "War is waged by men, not by beasts or by gods. It is a peculiarly human activity. To call it a crime against mankind is to miss half of its significance; it is also the punishment of the crime."[9] During the war years and those that followed, this punishment altered American lives on the home front and the role of the United States in the world community in ways no one could imagine on that fateful Sunday.

On December 7th, a new spirit began arising in the land. Perhaps, the change in the masthead of the then pro-isolationist *Chicago Tribune* said it best. Before Pearl Harbor, the newspaper's masthead read "Save Our Republic." On December 8, 1941, the paper responded to the attack on Pearl Harbor with the classic words of Stephen Decatur, an American naval officer, on the masthead: "Our country! In her intercourse with foreign nations may she always be in the right; but our country, right or wrong."

For those on the home front and others overseas, World War II was to become a mosaic—a collage of images and events. The war was to be fought on the seas, under the seas, in the air, in the desert, in the jungles, in cities, out in the countryside, and over mountains. The conflict was to become a variety of places and events passing quickly through the country's thoughts.

Before December 7, 1941, Americans had become accustomed to news about Japan's prolonged war with China, Germany's conquest of Europe and its preparations for the invasion of the British Isles; then suddenly and unexpectedly, the European war veered away from England and toward Russia. As the Germans began to overrun Russia, America's thoughts turned toward the see-saw battles between the British and the German Afrika Korps in the North African desert. Just as the country began to concentrate on that theater of war, there was the sudden attack on Pearl Harbor and attention turned toward the Pacific: the surprise American bombing raid over Tokyo and other Japanese cities in April 1942, the U.S. Navy's stopping Japan's southward advance toward Australia in May at the Battle of the Coral Sea, the U.S. victory over the Japanese Navy at Midway Island in June, the beginning of America's Pacific offensive in August at Guadacanal in the Solomon Islands. In November 1942, the United States invaded North Africa. Americans were just becoming accustomed to the beginning of the nation's offensives against the Germans and Japanese, when their thoughts returned to the siege of Leningrad, Russia's winter counterattack against the Germans and the German defeat at Stalingrad in February 1943. The country was just getting used to the news of the Russian and North African campaigns, when its attention was turned once again to England as the base of the massive Allied bombing raids over Germany and German-occupied lands. Just as America was becoming accustomed to the news of the large-scale bombing raids, its thoughts were turned toward its successes against German submarines in the Atlantic. As the nation considered this U-boat warfare in the Atlantic, it could observe U.S. forces in the Pacific theater of war advancing from the Solomons to the Gilbert Islands, the Philippines, Iwo Jima, and Okinawa with innumerable landings on countless islands in between. On the other side of the world, the country witnessed U.S. forces advancing from North Africa to Sicily, Italy, France, Belgium, and the Netherlands and saw the beginning of the end of the war with the Axis powers.

There were so many places, so many events, so many armies, and so many nations—so many smaller wars taking place within the framework of a global war—all occurring sequentially and simultaneously. The whole world was in upheaval. At any moment, an observer could only catch fleeting glimpses of the conflict.

Exploding Growth of Government

Government by Executive Order

When radio first broadcast that Japanese bombs were falling on Pearl Harbor, Americans not only didn't know the extent to which Hawaii's physical landscape was being altered, but they also had no idea how much the political, social, and economic landscape of the United States would be changed in the ensuing years. The most immediate and most visible change on the home front was the explosive growth of the federal government. Each week, it seemed that President Roosevelt was establishing a new agency to deal with the war. On December 18, 1941, Congress passed the First War Powers Act empowering the president to reassign the functions of government agencies which were established by law. On that same day, Presidential Executive Order 8989 established the Office of Defense Transportation (ODT) to direct and coordinate all domestic transportation systems; it eventually included the use of private automobiles (Executive Order 9156, May 2, 1942). Working with the railroads, this agency became so proficient that it knew the exact location of every freight car in the country and the inventory of materials waiting at the Atlantic Coast ports. Its motto, "Is this trip necessary?" made the home front aware that the movement of war matériel—physical and human—had priority over personal pleasure trips.

The next day, December 19, President Roosevelt issued Executive Order 8985 establishing the federal Office of Censorship, whose mission in wartime was not considered an appropriate activity of the federal government in peacetime. The agency director was authorized to use absolute discretion in censoring all communications that entered or left the country regardless of their form of transmission. To gather useful information from abroad and to prevent the enemy from receiving valuable information, many censorship offices were established throughout the country to monitor international cables, telephone and radio communications, as well as printed matter and personal mail sent from one country to another. Thus, during the war years, many Americans who received letters from abroad found that their mail had already been opened, with some words, sentences, or even paragraphs deleted, and then resealed with a piece of tape that read "Opened by the Censor." This was one of the prices Americans paid to ensure the safety and security of the United States.[10]

If Americans thought that they had seen the rapid expansion of the federal government during the first few days of the war, they hadn't witnessed anything compared with the weeks and months that followed.

On January 12, 1942, the government established its authority in labor-management disputes when the president issued Executive Order 9017, which created the National Defense Mediation Board (NDMB). This agency was given final jurisdiction over all labor disputes and wage and salary rates, except in the railroad industry.

A few days later on January 16, 1942, the president established the War Production Board (WPB) through Executive Order 9024. Under the First War Powers Act, the president was given extraordinary powers to oversee and manage the nation's industrial plants from raw materials to finished products; Roosevelt delegated these powers to the War Production Board. The board was given the authority to allocate materials, establish priorities, ration supplies and output, tell producers what they could and could not make and, in an extreme situation, take over a plant if the management did not cooperate with the president's requests. Thus, the board had the power to decide who could and could not receive such materials as steel, copper, and gasoline, and therefore, stopped the manufacture of more than 300 items that were not considered necessary for the war effort, including automobiles, refrigerators, electric fans, and metal coat hangers. The board could force a company to convert a plant to war production or expand into a new plant at government expense. WPB could even force a stubborn business to accept war orders under the threat of punishment if the business failed to do so. Through various industrial divisions such as autos, steel, aluminum, copper, chemicals, construction, mining, transportation, and fuels, the board had to establish difficult priorities. When the infantry wanted rifles and the artillery needed cannons, who was to get what and how many? How should steel be used—in building steel plants to produce more steel, for armaments, or for domestic transportation such as trains to meet the critical transportation shortage? How much of the country's precious metals could be given to its allies to help them in their war effort? These were the kinds of complex problems that the War Production Board had to confront and solve with the enormous powers it had been given.

On January 24, 1942, WPB Directive 1 empowered the Office of Price Administration (OPA) to ration goods and services because consumer demand in 1942 was expected to exceed the supply by $17 billion as the nation began to shift to a wartime economy and production.[11] When President Roosevelt announced in January 1942 that he wanted 60,000 planes, 45,000 tanks, 20,000 anti-aircraft guns, and 8 million tons of shipping produced in that year, economists expected war expenditures to triple by the year's end and increase inflationary pressures in two ways. First, these production goals could only be achieved by diverting material, labor, and manufacturing facilities from the output of consumer goods and services, thus decreasing their supply. Second, the money spent for tanks, ships, and other war materiel would return to the public in the form of wages, salaries, profits, and dividends, thus increasing the consumer's demand and ability to pay for scarce goods and services. In addition to its rationing power, OPA was to continue its other activities to stabilize prices, eliminate hoarding, and prevent speculation.

Almost two weeks later, on February 7, the president issued Executive Order 9054, which established the War Shipping Administration (WSA). This agency was not only directed to build the Victory and Liberty cargo ships, but also to maintain and operate shipping that the United States owned. In addition, WSA was ordered to allocate all shipping under the U.S. flag and to administer, among its various duties, any shipping priorities that the War Production Board might give it.

Two weeks later, on February 24, 1942, the president by Executive Order 9070, established the National Housing Agency (NHA). This agency brought together under a single administration all government housing, planning, construction, management, and financing agencies. During 1942 and 1943, this agency created more than 1,000 emergency war housing communities with a population of 1.5 million people throughout the United States. Generally located in sparsely settled areas where a plant or military base was suddenly established, these government-built towns were constructed as cheaply as possible. Some consisted of simple dormitories grouped around a mess hall. Others were one- or two-story barracklike structures constructed of plywood or plasterboard with paper-thin walls and minimal comforts in terms of plumbing, heating, and kitchen equipment. The larger towns had a primitive business district with a few stores, a firehouse, a movie theater, and a church. Although these boom towns were not easy to live in, they were essential for maintaining America's wartime production.

Then, on April 18, 1942, the president, by Executive Order 9139, established the War Manpower Commission (WMC), which absorbed the Selective Service System and the U.S. Employment Commission. This new agency was given broad coordinating powers over manpower, employment, and training; it was able to assign workers to industry and had authority over all government agencies that were concerned with the use of labor.

On June 13, 1942, the president issued Executive Order 9182 to establish the Office of War Information (OWI), which was given the explicit powers to oversee the news and information output of all civilian government departments and agencies. The agency also had the power to devise programs through the use of the press, radio, motion pictures, and other communication media to bring about the development of an informed and intelligent understanding of the war effort and of war policies and activities, and aims of the government.

The creation of these new agencies seemed to be as rapid as bursts of gunfire. Every week or two for almost six months President Roosevelt would issue an executive order, and a new government agency was born. The rapidity with which these orders were issued demonstrated how quickly the government could take control of a society at war. In about six months, the federal government had entered into censorship and propaganda activities, entered the field of labor–management disputes, and taken control of war production, rationing, transportation, housing, and shipping. During 1942, the U.S. Congress appropriated $160 billion for armaments and shipping—$100 billion in the first six months. Many times the Congress gave the president and the armed services carte blanche on how they should spend the money.

FIGURE 1-1
Government Decisions on the Home Front

1941
- War Insurance Corporation created in December to provide protection from enemy attacks on private property.

1942
- President orders seizure of all enemy patents.
- Government announces $400 million program to produce synthetic rubber.
- War Production Board freezes labor in war plants to prevent labor pirating.
- President commandeers S. A. Woods Machine Company of Boston for refusing to obey unanimous ruling of National Labor Relations Board.
- War Labor Board adopts principle of equal pay for women.
- War Production Board orders cessation of manufacture of radios, phonographs, and new automobiles.
- Government establishes $150 million fund to purchase new and used tires and tubes from automobile owners.

1943
- Office of Price Administration bans all pleasure driving in 12 of 17 eastern states.

- Government has power to seize plants of employers refusing to comply with War Production Board order.
- Government announces shoe rationing plan.

1944

- President orders War Department to take over seven textile plants idled by strike in Fall River, Massachusetts.
- War Production Board tells Congress 200,000 workers must be shifted to midwestern and western areas of labor shortage.
- War Manpower Commission orders hotels to curtail service.

1945

- War Production Board orders lights of nation's show windows, signboards, and theater marquees to go out after February 1st to save 2 million tons of coal a year.
- Consumer goods returning to market in reconversion period to be sold at 1942 price levels.
- War Production Board gives automobile manufacturers permission to make 200,000 cars by end of year, if they can get materials. President Truman orders abolishment of the board, effective November 3, 1945.

New Government in People's Lives

The Office of Civilian Defense (OCD) and the Office of Price Administration (OPA) are examples of two agencies that affected everyday life on the home front. Established in May 1941, the OCD gave 8–10 million men who did not enter the armed forces because of age, physical limitations, or other reasons an opportunity to participate in the war effort and help make their country secure. As air raid wardens, they guarded first aid stations, community installations such as reservoirs, and public air raid shelters, which were established in schools, subways, and public buildings. About one-half million Americans served as aircraft spotters, scanning the skies for an enemy never destined to appear. However, in case the enemy did invade, American cities practiced with blackouts, dim outs, search lights, and air raid sirens in order to be prepared. One way Americans blacked out their cities was by darkening the headlights of their automobiles. The community air raid warden, organized down to the neighborhood block level, made sure everyone participated in and did not violate these civil defense safeguards. As part of civil defense, Americans also protected themselves by learning first aid and by converting their home basements into air raid shelters and stocking them with food, water, and medical supplies. Finally, Americans could help protect their country by participating in civil defense-sponsored rubber, tin, paper, aluminum, and other salvage drives. Through various activities, the OCD provided an opportunity for millions of Americans to contribute their time and effort toward winning the war.

The Office of Price Administration (OPA), established in April 1941 as the Office of Price Administration and Civilian Supply, had a daily impact on life. (The agency's name was shortened after some of its functions were transferred to other government units.) On the home front, World War II was a war of potential inflation and shortages of consumer goods and services. Aware of these domestic inflationary dangers, the Congress enacted the Emergency Price Control Act of 1942 in January. This law gave the OPA administrator the power to impose price ceilings on a range of consumer goods, except food; however, by October 1942, all foodstuffs except fresh fruits and vegetables came within the OPA's price-setting jurisdiction. As inflation and the cost of living continued to rise, the president created a new Office of Economic Stabilization in an effort to bring inflation under control. By the end of the war, at least 8 million items had a price ceiling attached to them.[12]

No matter what the item, it was likely to be in short supply during the war years. On Lorna Road, for example, homes without electrical refrigerators used ice boxes. Residents knew which families had ice boxes by the cards placed in the home's front window informing the iceman how much ice to deliver that week. Other goods and services in short supply on the home front included butter, cheese, sugar, alcohol, hair curlers, apartments, boarding house and hotel rooms, coal, oil, radios, lawn mowers, coffee, cameras, beer mugs, and automobiles. As a result of these and other shortages, OPA was compelled to take certain measures to ensure, if possible, a fair distribution of goods and services. Having the power to set rent controls in areas where the presence of defense industries might create a housing shortage, OPA established rent controls nationwide by the end of 1942. The OPA limited civilians to two pairs of shoes a year.

At the beginning of 1942, the home front had about one-half-million new cars in stock; however, OPA took title to all of these automobiles, stored them in warehouses for the duration of the war, and made them available only on a priority basis to those truly in need. By July 1944, only 30,000 cars—equivalent to a 3-day supply during peacetime—remained in government warehouses. It was common during the war to observe vehicles such as milk wagons being drawn by horses in urban areas; there was an increased use of bicycles; and people did careful maintenance of prewar automobiles that were still operating. As a final example, in March 1943, OPA reduced the availability of meat—each person was limited to 28 ounces a week, with a similar reduction in the availability of hard cheeses. At the government's request, the public endured meatless Tuesdays and Fridays, as eggs and fresh fish became popular substitutes.

In essence, OPA limited the amount of goods each person over 16 years of age could purchase monthly. Beginning in April 1942, ration books of coupon stamps were issued to each family by the local OPA office. The consumer was issued a booklet with a 6-month supply of ration stamps; each stamp had a "point value" based mostly upon the availability of the product. The consumer not only had to pay the seller with cash but also with a certain amount of stamps. According to local economic conditions of supply and demand, at regular monthly intervals OPA declared what the price ceilings would be for a whole host of consumer goods, ranging from bread to peaches. The local OPA office was responsible for keeping these prices up-to-date and making sure that the sellers observed the price regulations, and OPA officials had the power to take any violators to court. Two kinds of stamps were used: red for meats, butter, and fats; blue for processed foods and certain other items. The stamps were coded to show their point value and the length of time they were valid. As the supply of goods varied, so did the point values, and, as a result, the number of required stamps for each purchase varied from month to month. Thus, a pound of steak might cost two points at one time and four points at another. Local OPA officials established the point values, which were regularly posted in stores and advertised in newspapers. Hoarding of stamps was prohibited so that if a buyer did not use all the red stamps one month, she could not purchase twice as much of the item the next.

Gasoline is another example of how complex the system of government rationing was to become. Automobile owners were issued a booklet of stamps each worth a certain amount—a 2.5-, 3-, or 5-gallon purchase, but the person had to display on the windshield a letter indicating the weekly gas allowance for that car: A for general use, B for commuting to work, C for use at work, and E for emergency vehicles such as police cars, tow trucks, and fire trucks; clergymen, journalists, and elected public officials were also given the "E" category. Although this system may sound straightforward, the owners of E stickers could obtain as many ration stamps as they wished, whereas owners with C stickers had to explain their needs to the local OPA board. The owners with a B sticker had to calculate the exact number of miles between their homes and work sites before receiving the appropriate number of stamps, but they could also obtain A stickers for pleasure driving. So consumers were able to apparently obtain more than their fair share of stamps.

The OPA, administered at the local level by volunteer-operated War Price and Rationing Boards, was able to systematize prices and rationing. However, black markets were destined to appear in a system where rationing and an overabundance of spendable income existed, as the defense industry virtually eliminated unemployment and wages rose as war contracts increased the demand for workers. When the understaffed OPA caught black marketers, they charged thousands of dollars in fines. However, these fines were not a deterrent. Whenever there was an opportunity to circumvent the OPA program, whether the black market involved gasoline, nylons, meats, or other items that were in demand and hoarded, someone was willing to make the effort.

Whatever problems Americans faced on the home front, they could always blame "Uncle Sam." If there wasn't enough gas for their cars, blame OPA. If they couldn't buy a steak that week, blame OPA. If they encountered public transportation problems, blame the Office of Defense Transportation. If there was a shortage of workers in their community, blame the War Manpower Commission. If there was a shortage of weapons overseas, blame the War Production Board. Whatever the problem or complaint, somewhere there was a government agency that civilians on the home front could blame rightly or wrongly. No matter what kinds of goods or services were in short supply, citizens always heard the same reason for the situation: "Hey, don'tcha know there's a war on?" After hearing this enough times, they certainly did.

FIGURE 1-2
Life on the Home Front—1942

- New Year's Day Rose Bowl football game transferred to Durham, North Carolina. Pasadena officials fear huge crowd tempting target for Japanese air attack. Oregon State beats Duke, 20-16.
- Complete blackout ordered on Texas coast due to presence of German submarines.
- French luxury liner *Normandie* burns and sinks at New York pier.
- Edward V. Rickenbacker, World War I pilot ace, found in South Pacific with seven Army men after drifting 23 days in a lifeboat; plane went down while on special government mission.
- Congress votes conscription of boys 18 years of age and over for military service.
- Fire starts in artificial palms at Boston's Coconut Grove nightclub; of 800 people in nightclub, 487 die, including Buck Jones, movie cowboy; and scores injured. Cause of fire centers on busboy's match or short circuit in a ceiling lamp.
- Show business luminaries George M. Cohan and John Barrymore die.
- Sale of heavy cream stops, ending whipped cream era.
- Government orders ten large industrial firms holding large war contracts to cease discrimination against available workers because of race or religion.
- Eight Nazi spies and saboteurs landing at Amagansett, Long Island and Jacksonville, Florida captured by FBI; all tried, two jailed, and six executed in electric chair.
- National Geographic Society and California Institute of Technology begin joint project at Mount Palomar to photograph 500 million stars.

Changing Culture

The war years on the home front were not only to be defined by the explosive growth of the federal government, but also by cultural changes and the reemergence of racial tensions. Cultural changes assumed many guises. For example, fads developed in language, music, and fashions. High-school girls began to wear rings of jet black to show that a friend was now a soldier. When teenagers got together in a group discussion, they called it "just messing around." Also, "In like Flynn" became a popular expression of reassurance from one person to another after actor Errol Flynn was acquitted on statutory rape charges during the winter of 1942–1943. A mysterious character kept leaving his calling signature wherever he could write it—on sidewalks, fences, buildings, and other places—that "Kilroy was here." A new expression of approval of something or someone came from a song entitled, "Dig You Later-A Hubba-Hubba-Hubba," as everyone began saying hubba-hubba-hubba. But, when Americans sang another tune called "Mairzy Doats," they really wondered what the lyrics meant. However, it did not seem to matter whether or not the lyrics could be understood, for the song had record sales, including 100,000 copies in one day.

New expressions had many sources. Public and private organizations reminded the home front that "loose talk sinks ships," "it's no crime to kill a rumor," and "free speech does not mean careless talk." Meanwhile, the military developed their own expressions such as "snafu," which tactfully means "situation normal, all fouled up"; while from England came its superlative form, "tarfu," which means "things are really fouled up." Snafu occurs when parts ordered for one kind of vehicle arrive for another, or the supply vessel arrives and the material that should have been packed at the top of the ship's hold is at the bottom.

Wartime circumstances influenced more than language. They also were to affect fashions. Women began to wear hats copied after the British Commando berets or the hats of the U.S. Women's Army Corps (WACs). The design inspiration for evening wraps or blouses with drawstring waists came from Eisenhower jackets, and dresses disappeared in favor of slacks. As ordered by OPA, hemlines rose above the knee, and women's tailored suits had padded shoulders. Women wore their hair swept up and covered by bandannas at work for safety, by turbans in leisure moments when permanents were not possible, and by a loose net called a "snood" for shopping. Because silk and nylon were now diverted for military use, a suntan substituted for hosiery in the summer. Some women even had their legs spray-painted and a seam painted down the calf. Meanwhile, adolescents mismatched their shoes and socks, popularized the wear of blue jeans, and wore sweaters called "Sloppy Joes." Adolescent girls began to wear short socks and came to become known as "bobby soxers." Some men continued to wear zoot suits until OPA stopped the waste of such fabrics. Often identified with criminal-type individuals, the zoot suit consisted of a long double-breasted and wide-lapeled suit jacket, which fell below the hips; the individual also wore large-collared shirts, big ties, wide pants, and a vest with a heavily chained watch.

Calling All Women

Fashions and language were not the only social changes on the home front during the war years. The relationships of Americans with each other also changed. As millions of men entered the armed services, women in greater numbers than at any time in the country's history entered the labor force—women who might not have gone to work had there been no war. They were encouraged to enter the labor market by government radio messages such as the following, which was broadcast on the Office of War Information's "Victory Parade":

> Friends, it would be impossible for me or anyone else to overemphasize the importance of women in this war. Actually, millions of American women are working now in aircraft factories and war plants of all kinds. But even more of us women are needed. The fact is women are needed for all kinds of jobs in many parts of the country.[13]
>
> Thank you,
> Kate Smith

In response to those needs, millions of women found employment in jobs ranging from welders and machine setters to taxi drivers, railroad conductors, and farm workers. They learned to operate punch presses, grinders, buffers, drill presses, and lathes. In fact, between 1940 and 1945, the number of female workers rose from 12 million to 18 million—5 million of them in industrial plants—increasing from one-fourth to one-third of the nation's work force. In shipyards alone, they represented 17 percent of the total number of workers.[14] About a quarter of a million women entered the armed forces when all the services established special women's branches during 1942. These included the WACs, the Navy's WAVES (Women Appointed for Volunteer Emergency Service), the Air Force's WAFS (Women's Auxiliary Ferrying Squadrons), the Coast Guard's SPARS (representing the Guard's Latin motto and its translation *Semper Paratus*—Always Ready), and Women Marines (1943).

FIGURE 1-3
Life on the Home Front—1943

- Jack Benny's violin, a $75 imitation Amati nicknamed "Old Love in Bloom," auctioned off at war bond rally for $1 million.
- Frank "The Voice" Sinatra's appearance at Paramount Theater in New York causes riot among 30,000 fans; 41 officers and 20 patrol cars respond.
- Declaring "there can be no one among us—no one faction powerful enough to interrupt the forward march of our people to victory," President Roosevelt orders U.S. Interior Department to seize control of coal mines, as almost ½-million miners strike.
- J. P. Morgan, the financier; Serge Rachmaninoff, the composer; and Lorenz Hart, lyricist with Richard Rogers, die.
- Errol Flynn, movie actor, acquitted of sex assault charges.
- FBI reports that juvenile delinquency on rise—arrests 17 percent higher than in 1942.
- War Production Board announces birth rate about 25 percent higher over prewar years and orders more baby carriages, single and double.
- Chicago's first subway inaugurated.
- Shortage of tin cans forces Campbell's to stop sponsoring "Amos 'n' Andy"; show canceled after 4,000 performances and 15 years on radio.
- George Gershwin's *Porgy and Bess* opens on Broadway as does Richard Rogers and Oscar Hammerstein's *Oklahoma!*
- Supreme Court finds American Medical Association to be in violation of antitrust laws for attempting to block health cooperatives.

Simmering Racial Prejudice

However, not all Americans were heartily welcomed into the armed services or the work place on the home front. Racial and ethnic prejudice simmered within a society that was supposed to be united in its efforts to defeat nations that were racist in their treatment of other races or ethnic groups. Until President Harry S. Truman integrated the armed services by executive order in 1948, the military reflected the segregated environment of civilian society. Although 100,000 black soldiers had joined the Army by the time of Pearl Harbor and many more were to follow either by choice or the draft, they were generally placed in support units rather than combat units; in other words, they were assigned menial work.

Despite the mounting pressures after the attack on Pearl Harbor to integrate the services, the resistance was fierce. For example, three days after the sneak attack, Texas Congressman W. R. Poage wrote to Secretary of the Navy, Frank Knox, to argue for the continued segregation. "In this hour of national crisis," he said, "it is much more important that we have the full-hearted cooperation of the 30 million white southern Americans than that we satisfy the National Association for the Advancement of Colored People." He concluded, "To assign a Negro doctor to treat some southern white boy would be a crushing insult and, in my opinion, an outrage against the patriotism of our southern people." In 1942, Secretary Knox asked the General Board of the Navy to consider "enlistment of men of colored race in other than mess-man branch." In its report to the Secretary of the Navy, the board asked, "How many white men would choose, of their own accord, that their closest associates in sleeping quarters, at mess and in the gun's crew should be of another race? . . . The General Board believes that the answer is 'few, if any' and further believes that if the issues were forced, there would be a lowering of contentment, teamwork and discipline in the service." The report summarized the three reasons for discrimination: "The white man will not accept the Negro in a position of authority over him"; "the white man considers that he is of a superior race and will not admit the Negro as an equal"; and "the white man refuses to admit the Negro to intimate family relationships leading to marriage."[15] Despite the racial flare-ups between white and black service trainees on and off the bases, especially in the South, the Army Air Force did train an all-Negro fighter squadron, the 99th, which distinguished itself in combat after the invasion of Europe. In 1943, the Navy joined the Army in commissioning its first Negro officers.

The rationale that supported segregation in the armed services was not dissimilar to that which helped maintain segregation in civilian society. Although America's survival during World War II required that the nation mobilize all of its available work force as a team regardless of race or religion, the nation could not change its prejudicial attitudes toward the American black even in time of crisis and welcome this minority into the mainstream of society. As the war opened up new employment opportunities in various parts of the country, persons of all races migrated to the cities seeking jobs in defense plants. Suddenly, people who were not used to working together in defense plants or associating with each other in housing projects had to do so and were confronted with their own racial prejudices and conflicts.

As one war year merged into another, socio-economic conditions on the home front began to release forces that would alter such prewar relationships. One force was the attempt by blacks to get rid of the restrictions that the white society had placed upon them even as the war created new job opportunities for them and other minority groups. Another force came from members of the white society who championed the black cause because they believed that there was no difference between fighting Hitler and his racial ideas "over there" and fighting racial inequality "over here." Still another force came from the groups in white society who did not want to see any change in the blacks' societal status. As these diverse forces began to converge, tensions and frictions began to build between majority and minority groups.

The racial explosions finally came in 1943. In early June, 3,000 rioters severely beat and mistreated nearly 100 people in Los Angeles, most of whom were Mexican-American youths, American citizens. Then, on June 20–21, race riots exploded in Detroit. Twenty-five blacks and nine whites were killed, 700 people were injured and 1,000 persons were arrested; the property damage amounted to hundreds of millions of dollars. Across the country in Harlem, New York, another riot broke out when a rumor spread that the police had shot a black soldier. Six blacks died in the riot, and property damage was in the millions of dollars. For a moment, the war seemed very distant as Americans began to ponder how could they fight the Axis powers to preserve democracy and the freedom it represents and then turn on their fellow citizens who wanted the same ideals for themselves.

As a result of these riots, interest developed in improving race relations. Integration of public and private establishments, especially in the North and Midwest, began to increase gradually. Though still segregated, the armed services increased their enlistment of blacks whose outstanding effectiveness in combat impressed their fellow white servicemen. The American Council on Race Relations was established in Chicago. Many labor unions began to enroll blacks and develop programs and projects to deal with the racial issue. Police training programs also began to educate law enforcement officials on race relations as did schools and civic organizations. The membership of the National Association for the Advancement of Colored People (NAACP) increased from 50,000 to 500,000 during the war years.

While much of the activity on the home front to improve race relations was sporadic and uncoordinated, the conditions that fostered such improvements taught America a lesson. People became more aware of the inconsistency between the American ideals they were fighting to preserve and their own racial beliefs and practices, which were the antithesis of these ideals. The measure of understanding that developed among regions of the country about each other's racial beliefs brought some degree of calm to the country during the last two years of the war.

FIGURE 1-4
Life on the Home Front—1944

- In December, government bans horse racing throughout the United States; government believes sport causes high absenteeism from wartime jobs and the use of automobiles to reach race tracks might violate gasoline and rubber conservation.
- Worst circus fire in history claims 107 lives and injures 412 people, when Ringling Brothers and Barnum & Bailey Circus catches fire during performance in Hartford, Connecticut.
- U.S. Supreme Court upholds right of blacks to vote in state primaries.
- Mild influenza epidemic called "cat fever."
- Louis "Lepke" Buchalter, head of Brooklyn's "Murder Incorporated" dies in electric chair at Sing Sing prison for the killing of Sol Rosen, a clothing trucker.
- Mrs. Herbert Hoover, wife of ex-President; William Allen White, editor; Wendell Willkie, 1940 Republican Presidential candidate; and Al Smith, New York state governor, die.
- Roosevelt beats Dewey for fourth term.
- Charlie Chaplin acquitted of Federal Grand Jury indictment of violating Mann Act.
- Chairman of Montgomery Ward in Chicago forced out of building after refusing to turn company over to the government; company seized on Roosevelt's orders as a result of labor dispute.

- Coca-Cola Company manufactures one billionth gallon of Coca-Cola syrup.
- Nation's first eye bank formed through combined efforts of twenty hospitals in New York City.
- Tennessee Williams publishes *The Glass Menagerie*.
- Signing the GI Bill of Rights, (officially known as the Servicemen's Readjustment Act), President Roosevelt states, "It gives emphatic notice to the men and women in the armed forces that the American people do not intend to let them down." New law provided housing and educational assistance for returning war veterans.

Rounding Up American Citizens

However, the blacks were not the only group toward whom ethnic and racial prejudice was directed. Others included Italian-Americans, Jews, Mexican-Americans, Slavic and Chinese communities to name but a few, and last but not least, Japanese-Americans. The bombs that fell at Pearl Harbor did more than destroy America's Pacific fleet. For one minority group and their immigrant forebears, the bombs destroyed their constitutional rights as American citizens. Swept by a post-Pearl Harbor hysteria that portrayed every ethnic Japanese person, both in the United States and the territory of Hawaii, as a potential saboteur, the federal government took an action without precedent in American history: It interned behind barbed wire 110,000 of its own citizens, more than two-thirds of whom had been born in the United States. At the urging of politicians and the Army to remove the large Japanese-American population settled on the West Coast, President Roosevelt signed Executive Order 9066 on February 19, 1942, authorizing the War Department to remove "all persons" from designated military areas. Congress made it a federal offense to defy the Army and established the War Relocation Authority to oversee the transfer.

Aside from fears that Japanese-Americans might engage in espionage and sabotage, the chief reason given for the evacuation at the time was the government's fear that mob violence might be directed against the Japanese-Americans if the Japanese attacked the West Coast. Four days later, the Japanese submarine I-17 ineffectually bombarded an oil field near Santa Barbara, California—which only heightened the fears. However, oil officials believed that the attack was more an act of revenge because the submarine's captain in prewar days, when a tanker captain, suffered an embarrassing moment in front of some American workers and was heard to vow that one day he would avenge his humiliation. Japanese-Americans who lived in the territory of Hawaii during the war years were not incarcerated. The U.S. military did not consider them a threat to the islands; they had been culturally part of the territory for many decades; and because of their large population their internment would have impacted upon the territory's economic viability. In addition, Japanese-Americans living in the eastern part of the United States were free to come and go as they pleased. Even if the Japanese on the East Coast were aliens, they did not have to submit to the same restrictions as those on the West Coast.

Within two months, Japanese-Americans were herded into temporary camps—soon to be replaced by permanent ones. The Nisei (American-born citizens), never given a trial and thus without any hope of a pardon, lost their homes, businesses, schoolwork, and constitutional rights. They were sent to ten relocation centers located in out-of-the-way and generally arid areas of Arizona, California, Idaho, Wyoming, Colorado, Utah, and Arkansas. These centers consisted of tar-papered barracks (one room per family) surrounded by barbed-wire fences and guard towers with armed soldiers on duty day and night. Guards were instructed to shoot anyone who tried to leave. All this took place even though no criminal charges had been filed against the Issei (the immigrant parents) or Nisei. In fact, not a single Japanese-American citizen was ever convicted of sabotage or espionage during the war nor were any acts of sabotage performed when Pearl Harbor was bombed—the pretext that served as the rationale for this mass evacuation. Despite their mistreatment, Japanese-Americans were to prove their loyalty to the United States when in 1943 the Army allowed young Nisei men to serve in the military. Some 17,600 joined the armed forces. Units such as the 100th Infantry Battalion and the 442nd Infantry "Go for Broke Battalion," consisting entirely of Japanese-American men, achieved outstanding records of gallantry in Europe.

Over time camp conditions improved, and in 1944 many Nisei Japanese-Americans were allowed to leave for points East. On December 18, 1944, the U.S. Supreme Court upheld the constitutionality of the procedure under which this mass evacuation took place as a proper exercise of the power to wage war. On the other hand, the Supreme Court held that nothing in the executive order of the president, or the orders of the War Department, or acts of Congress justified the detention of American citizens against whom no charges had been filed and whose loyalty was not questioned after removal from the areas they had to evacuate. The day before this Supreme Court decision, the government's attitude toward minorities became a little more liberal when President Roosevelt signed a bill repealing the Chinese Exclusion Law of 1882, giving the Chinese an immigration quota and making Chinese residents in the United States eligible for American citizenship.

On December 17, 1944, the War Department lifted the ban against the return of loyal Japanese-American evacuees to California, Oregon, and Washington State. Most had been financially ruined, some $400 million in total. Although Congress allowed some $30 million of that which was lost to be made up in individual claims beginning in 1948, the victims of relocation and their descendants did not receive across-the-board monetary compensation until Congress finally authorized such payments in 1989.[16] The entire episode was so inimical to the principles for which the United States stands that it continues to be remembered as one of the most shameful acts of the American people toward their fellow citizens in war or peace.

FIGURE 1-5
Life on the Home Front—1945

- Henry J. Kaiser builds 247 Liberty cargo ships in first 212 days of year.
- Basketball bribe-taking scandal rocks Brooklyn College.
- Army B-25 bomber, flying from New Bedford, Mass. to Newark, N. J., crashes into 77th floor of Empire State Building; ten people in building and three airplane occupants killed; plane piloted by war veteran unfamiliar with New York area.
- FBI reports 1,500 Axis spies have been rounded up in North and South America.
- Ernie Pyle, noted newspaper correspondent, killed on island of Ie in the Pacific battle for Okinawa.
- A "dim out" is ordered for the entire United States to combat fuel shortage.
- House of Representatives votes to establish temporary Committee on Un-American Activities as permanent body.

- President Roosevelt dies of stroke in Warm Springs, Ga.
- President Truman announces unconditional surrender of Germany.
- Federal government orders reduction in military aircraft after Germany surrenders.
- Atomic bombs dropped on Hiroshima and Nagasaki; Japan surrenders unconditionally.
- Voluntary news censorship ends August 15th.
- WORLD WAR II IS OVER!

Newspapers Go to War

Regardless of the nature of events on the home front or overseas, one of the principal sources of information was newspapers. All kinds of newspapers were published during the war years. Some devoted themselves primarily to news reporting, whereas others used assorted gimmicks to increase their circulation. Some tried hard to remain unbiased and report the news objectively, and others did not care if they exposed their biases in their news columns. Some published the news without fear or favoritism; others headlined their fears and demonstrated their favoritism. During the war, the nation's newspapers published according to the dictates of their own consciences and interests and printed what they wanted to print, attacked who they wanted to attack, and reported with accuracy or distortion— that is, they acted like a free press.

Yet, the newspapers were being published and had to report events of the day within the constraints of a censorship code which the Office of Censorship had established and to which they voluntarily adhered. At the beginning of the war, the Office of Censorship asked newspapers and other publications not to publish the following categories of information unless released by appropriate authorities: troops—character and movements; planes—locations, strength, and movements; fortifications— locations and nature; ships—locations, movements, construction, launchings, and shipyard details; production data; weather forecasts not issued by the Weather Bureau; photographs and maps; premature disclosure of diplomatic negotiations or conversations; casualty lists; movements of senior government officials—civilian and military; information about damage to military and naval objectives or transportation of munitions or other war materials; and new locations of national archives and other treasures of country.[17]

Despite these constraints, most newspapers, publishers, and editors were patriotic and presented news and comments meant to inform. However, a small minority of newspaper owners and executives were viewed as promoting divisiveness and undermining morale over wide areas of the country. This situation became so serious that on April 20, 1942, the *New Republic*, a liberal periodical, announced the establishment of a new department within its publication as follows:

Enemies at Home

They're not only the out and out fascists. They're not only the anti-Semites, the open enemies of Democracy, the professional Anglophobes. They're not only the familiar names that occasionally make the front page. They're also the enemies who are more effective and insidious than any of these; they're the big circulation newspapers who know how to manipulate news and angle their editorializing; they're the dollar-a-year men who "consciously or unconsciously undermine the war effort"; they're the office-holders who are out to beat Roosevelt and his administration first. One and all they are enemies to be watched when they are known and to be searched out and exposed where they are not.[18]

In terms of specific newspapers or publishers, those considered most divisive comprised the New York–Washington–Chicago axis as well as William Randolph Hearst, the West Coast newspaper publisher. In New York, Captain Joseph Medill Patterson's *New York Daily News* told its vast tabloid readership that Congressional elections might not be held in the fall of 1942, despite assertions to the contrary.[19] In an editorial on the federal Office of Facts and Figures, the *New York Daily News* commented that the activity of that federal information agency was beginning to make many people suspicious that the Roosevelt Administration was establishing a propaganda agency similar to that in Nazi Germany to use both during and after the war. Based on this conjecture, the *New York Daily News* went on to speculate that, perhaps, the administration would be operating some kind of totalitarian government either before or after the war ended and was prudently getting ready for the same.[20] In a subsequent editorial, the *New York Daily News* noted that the government's bicycle freezing order was the latest totalitarian prohibition, adding that the continuation of these petty tyrannies should make them an issue in the November elections—if those elections were held.[21] Meanwhile, Colonel Robert R. McCormick's *Chicago Tribune*, another anti-Roosevelt newspaper, very pro-isolationist and severely critical of the administration, implied that the administration was composed of Communists or half-wits, or both, and hinted strongly that the administration was to blame for Pearl Harbor. In Washington, D.C., Eleanor Medill Patterson's *Washington Times-Herald* echoed those sentiments. On the West Coast, William Randolph Hearst, in words that followed the Axis line, told his newspaper chain readership that the British were swindlers, the Russians were worse, and America, as usual, was being taken advantage of by her supposed friends and comrades-in-arms.[22] Because these newspapers reached millions of readers, many Americans believed that the newspapers were aiding the enemy by attacking the administration and its foreign policies. It should be noted that the newspapers themselves never failed to proclaim their own patriotism.

Newspapers also attacked each other. In the fall of 1943, the *New York Herald Tribune*, the country's leading Republican newspaper, attacked the *Washington Times-Herald*, the *New York Daily News*, and the *Chicago Tribune* as being ceaseless in their efforts to undermine Allied unity. The accusation arose after the *Washington Times-Herald* published a report that had originated from the Hearst-owned International News Service. The story implied that the president's top advisers were secretly planning to promote General George C. Marshall, Chief of Staff of the Army, to a powerless command over Anglo-American forces so that the Army's production skills could be used as a political tool to further the president's reelection bid in 1944. The *New York Daily News* counterattacked on behalf of its sister newspapers and the Hearst press by stating that the president, when asked about the story at a news conference, made it an issue so as to make the nation's publishers servile to his will to further his ambitions for a fourth term in 1944.

Newspapers and the President

These newspapers were not the only publications to attack the Roosevelt Administration. In the spring of 1942, almost six months after Pearl Harbor, the *Detroit Times* stated editorially:

Well, that is what the American navy is for, is it not? That is what the American people built the navy for—to defend America.

That is what it was always supposed to do until our present alien-minded government came along and sent it to defend England and Russia and Africa and *"all parts of the world."*[23]

Thus, two years after the war began, deep divisions still existed among some of the nation's press regarding President Roosevelt, whether it was his conduct of the war or his political aims at home.

Newspaper attacks on the president and his administration were not too surprising. The majority of the press opposed his initial election in 1932 and his reelections in 1936, 1940, and 1944. Despite this opposition, a survey by *Fortune* magazine in 1944 revealed that the popularity of the president among the nation's editorial writers varied according to the role he assumed. As commander-in-chief, President Roosevelt's approval rating seemed to follow the unwritten law that wars, if won, are won by armies in the field, but, if lost, are lost by the commander-in-chief. When the Japanese took the Philippines, Java, and Singapore, President Roosevelt's level of support among the editorial writers fell from 80 to 60 percent. However, with the Japanese defeats at the Battle of the Coral Sea and Midway and the invasion of North Africa, newspapers were ecstatic and gave the president an approval rating of 80 percent. Once American forces achieved victory in Tunisia in 1943, Roosevelt had established himself as commander-in-chief among the nation's press and editorial comments on this issue were no longer paramount.

The press, on the other hand, had varying opinions about the president's ability to handle diplomatic affairs. In general, newspapers supported the Roosevelt Administration's foreign policies. Until the invasion of North Africa in November 1942, the country's preoccupation with the war plus censorship made foreign policy problems manageable or kept them under the surface. In 1943, Roosevelt's editorial support ranged from a low of 47 percent to a high of 72 percent as Sumner Welles resigned as Under-Secretary of State; Roosevelt met Churchill and China's Chiang-Kai-shek in Cairo and Stalin at Teheran; Congress began to concern itself with a postwar world organization; and U.S. forces invaded Sicily. In 1944, the president's support among the nation's editorial writers ranged from a low of 30 percent when Henry Morgenthau Jr., Secretary of the Treasury, proposed the permanent dismantling of

Germany's heavy industry (a policy Roosevelt soon questioned at election time) to a high of 60 percent as eventual victory became more and more apparent.

As a domestic leader, Roosevelt gradually lost support between 1941 and 1944. After peaking at 70 percent at the time of Pearl Harbor, newspaper support fell to a low of 25 percent during the presidential elections in 1944. In the interim, 32–62 percent of the nation's press supported his actions in 1942 as he announced censorship rules for the communication media, his anti-inflation program, and other wartime measures. In 1943, newspaper support declined to an average of 30–40 percent when the mine workers went out on strike and Roosevelt seized the mines. The downward drift of his presidency in terms of domestic affairs seemed to result from an accumulation of minor complaints rather than any deep-seated change in feelings. During the war, the nation's editorial writers had confidence in President Roosevelt as commander-in-chief, generally sided with him in the realm of foreign policy, but more than once questioned his domestic policies and opposed many of them.[24]

FIGURE 1-6
Presidential Election of 1944

August—Thomas E. Dewey warns forthcoming Dumbarton Oaks Conference on international organization against proposing domination of world by four great powers (United States, Russia, Great Britain, and China); Secretary of State Cordell Hull denies such proposal.

September—In response to whispering campaign that he dispatched a destroyer to pick up his pet scottie, Fala, left behind in the Aleutians, Franklin D. Roosevelt attacks Republicans by saying, "These Republicans have not been content with attacks on me or my wife or my sons. Not content with that, they now include my little dog Fala . . . I think I have a right to resent, to object to libelous statements about my dog."

Truman tells Detroit workers that Democratic Party will protect laborers and their interests in reconversion to peacetime economy.

Dewey declares chief blame for wartime strikes goes directly to White House and War Labor Board.

October—Dewey charges that Communists are backing Roosevelt because the New Deal is developing its own form of corporate state. Roosevelt answers, "I have never sought and I don't welcome the support of any person or group committed to Communism or Fascism or any other foreign ideology which would undermine the American system."

Dewey asserts, "We cannot achieve our objectives under an Administration too tired and worn out to bring order out of its own chaos either home or abroad."

Roosevelt backs idea of establishing a world security organization before war ends.

Roosevelt blunts criticism about his health and vigor by touring New York City in open car in rain.

November—Roosevelt charges that Republican Party is threatening "to build a party-spite fence between us and peace" unless a Republican is elected.

Roosevelt beats Dewey, carrying 36 states, getting 25,602,504 popular votes and 432 electoral votes to 12 states, 22,006,285 popular votes and 99 electoral votes for Dewey.

The Press and Misinformation

Criticisms about irresponsible journalism were not confined to the editorial pages. Editors and their headline writers were also severely criticized for the size and shock of their headlines, which were written to sell the newspapers but, which upon closer examination, did not represent the story they purported to tell. On August 19, 1942, the *New York Post* ran a full-page headline "YANKS INVADE EUROPE" when, in fact, the story referred to a small group of American ranger observers who accompanied a Canadian force that unsuccessfully raided Dieppe, France.

The national frustration and disbelief that can result from this kind of headline writing, when repeated often enough, were not confined to the United States. In 1942, London's *New Statesman and Nation* published the following verse which is relevant to any newspaper regardless of national origin:

> The public has wit to perceive
> A rather acute contradiction
> Between facts it is bound to believe
> And the newspapers' rose-colored fiction.
> On Monday our forces advance;
> On Tuesday the foe has retreated;
> On Wednesday, prepared for this chance,
> Our fortunate feats are repeated;
> On Thursday we strike a hard blow,
> Our moves are completely effective;
> On Friday, however, the foe
> Has somehow obtained his objectives.
>
> The experts have never found out
> That nothing so daunts and depresses
> As news of an actual rout
> After series of rumored successes.
> Though for the duration content
> Not to ask for the rhyme or the reason,
> We thus humble petition present
> (though it may be regarded as treason)
> That they ban as a public abuse
> All boasting, bamboozling and bluffing.
> We know we are merely a goose—
> But we beg to dispense with the stuffing.[25]

Many reasons were given for misleading newspaper accounts, especially in the war's early stages. Some critics thought that the press had assigned to itself the mission of arousing America's support—almost as if the press were fighting the war itself as the country stood aloof—with journalists giving unlimited praise and limited facts and description about their visits to training bases, dockyards, and munition plants, or even their firsthand accounts of land or sea battles.

Other critics believed that the military was responsible for the misinformation the press reported. Faced with the dilemma of reporting the real state of a battle while suppressing facts that might aid the enemy, most generals found it difficult to state the complete truth in a report or in public. Few were as forthright as Lieutenant General Joseph W. "Vinegar Joe" Stilwell, Sr., whose area of responsibility was the China-Burma-India theaters of war and who served as the American Chief of Staff to Generalissimo Chiang-Kai-shek until October 6, 1944. After the Japanese had conquered almost the whole of Burma by May 1942, Stilwell declared: "I claim we got a hell of a beating." Military information was also subject to the censorship of public relations officers who withheld certain facts from correspondents or released some facts and not others, thus creating a distorted view of an event. As a result, no one was served—neither the troops engaged in bitter fighting that correspondents reported as a mild engagement, nor the public on the home front whose support and understanding was so vital for the successful prosecution of the war. On occasion, the home front failed to realize how horrible the war actually was—the significance of the fighting in many sectors, how great the odds were of winning, the relative importance of any given military operation, or the immensity of the task the military faced to achieve final victory. However, as the war progressed communiqués and news stories became more sound and closer in tone and fact to the actual situation taking place. By war's end, the speed with which news transmissions reached American shores improved. For example, radio immediately reported the invasion of Iwo Jima in February 1945—a place where, in the words of Admiral Chester W. Nimitz, Commander-in-Chief of all naval forces in the Pacific, "uncommon valor was a common virtue"—and film of the battle took less than a day to reach the United States. At that time, the film transmission was a record-breaking event. In contrast, on-the-spot reporting of the U.S. invasions of Guam and Saipan in the Mariana Islands during the previous summer reached the United States one to two weeks after they had begun because the news was being brought back by courier.

Compared to the current era of satellite transmissions and instantaneous worldwide communications, the transmission of World War II communications seems primitive; but journalists recognized the constraints under which they worked. Arthur Krock, the distinguished columnist of the *New York Times*, noted that, in general, because war news came from either sources or independent press reports that had to be submitted for censorship, "the consequence is that except for headlining and placement of the news within the paper, the news of the war is a government product."[26]

The Press Outside of Censorship

Despite censorship rules, many press freedoms were not curbed. There was no censorship review of syndicated columns, editorial pages, interpretation of the news by military experts and technical specialists, or the comments pouring forth every day from Washington correspondents and feature writers. Thus, although all Washington news relating to foreign affairs and national defense was essentially and factually the same every day in all newspapers, censorship did not affect variations of these news items in terms of volume, interpretation, emphasis, and timing.

The federal Office of Censorship whose code affected the nation's press was directed by Byron Price, a former executive news editor of the Associated Press. Price had his own views of a newspaper's obligation, which he enunciated in a speech at the Library of Congress in early 1945, a few months before the war ended in Europe. Price stated, in part:

> A free press is obligated by its birthright to be a competent press, produced by competent men. The press neither does its duty nor fulfills its destiny if it poisons its news columns with propaganda and private opinion; or is careless of its facts; or swayed by hearsay; or publishes misleading advertising or vicious and sensational gossip from whatever source.[27]

As outlined by Price, the responsibilities of the press, especially in wartime, were very grave. Because newspapers spoke to millions of people daily, the press was an appropriate vehicle for reducing the divisiveness and antagonism the Axis powers tried to sow among all Americans, whether it was management against labor, Catholic against Protestant, Christians against Jews, or white against black.

In general, the criticisms by the press were constructive and designed to bolster rather than sabotage the war effort. Newspapers paved the way for the public's acceptance of President Roosevelt's tough posture on the issue of inflation. The press prepared the country for Congress to lower the draft age. They smoothed the way for nationwide rationing. Newspapers fought against members of Congress who were hampering the war effort. The press bolstered support of scrap drives when such efforts bogged down. They lifted the nation's morale when the course of the war was in the enemy's favor. Newspaper publishers donated millions of dollars of advertising space to the government for its own use.

They kept the pressure on Roosevelt to appoint one person to be in charge of wartime production. The press exposed the rivalry between the Army and Navy and prepared the way for the Joint Chiefs of Staff. They successfully fought Attorney General Francis Biddle's proposal in February 1942 that Congress make it a criminal offense for officials to reveal the contents of any government document marked "confidential." Any minor or major officeholder could not conceal any malfeasance from journalists, investigators, or others by simply labeling records as "confidential." Voluntarily adhering to the nation's censorship codes and receiving guidance from the U.S. Office of Censorship, newspapers kept thousands of items out of print that might have revealed the development of the atomic bomb, the invasion of North Africa in November 1942, or the invasion of Europe at Normandy in June 1944.

Perhaps, the press's role in World War II was best stated by Thomas Jefferson when he wrote: "To the press alone, as chequered as it is with abuses, the world is indebted for all the triumphs which have been gained by reason and humanity over error and oppression." In the hindsight of history, these sentiments were certainly true as newspapers told their readers about one of the greatest events of the twentieth century—the story of World War II.

Nightfall, December 7, 1941

When the residents on all the country's Lorna Roads retired at evening's end on December 7, 1941, little could they anticipate the events that were to occur in the ensuing years of war. Little could they visualize how their personal lives were about to be altered by the bombs that had fallen at Pearl Harbor only a few hours before. Little could they forecast the social, economic, and political forces that these bombs were about to release at home or the way these bombs were to change America's role in the world for the remainder of the twentieth century. Before Pearl Harbor, many Americans held isolationist views about the entanglement of the United States in the affairs of other countries. These political views were reflected in an address Charles A. Lindbergh delivered in Des Moines, Iowa, on September 11, 1941, as reported in an Associated Press dispatch in newspapers of September 12:

> The three most important groups which are pressing this country toward war are the British, the Jewish and the Roosevelt Administration . . .

They planned, first to prepare the United States for foreign war under the guise of American defense; second, to involve us in the war, step by step, without our realization; third, to create a series of incidents which would force us into actual conflict. Only the creation of sufficient "incidents" yet remains; and you see the first of these already taking place, according to a plan—a plan that was never laid before the American people for their approval.[28]

At the war's beginning, when America's bravado was high and ignorance of the war's future ferociousness not yet dispelled, the words of Civil War General William Tecumseh Sherman at a Union Army convention on August 11, 1880, bore much truth:

There is many a boy here today who looks upon war as all glory, but, boys, it is all hell. You can bear this warning voice to generations yet to come. I look upon war as a horror.[29]

During the course of the war, many Americans would come to agree with the sentiments of General Dwight D. Eisenhower:

I hate war as only a soldier who has lived it can, only as one who has seen its brutality, its futility, its stupidity.[30]

At the war's conclusion when the world could finally view the dimensions of its barbarity, Americans were certainly in accord with the words of President William McKinley who, in 1898, stated:

You understand, Messrs. ambassadors, when we go to war it will be for humanity's sake.[31]

If war must have a noble purpose, then nothing can be much higher than for the sake of humanity and, as history was to reveal, World War II certainly proved to be the verity of this ideal.

Notes

1. Jack Benny program, National Broadcasting Company, December 7, 1941.

2. Anna M. Wolf and Irma Simonton Black, "What Happened to the Younger Children," in Jack Goodman ed., *While You Were Gone: A Report on Wartime Life in the United States* (New York: Simon and Schuster, 1946), 74–75.

3. Ibid., 75.

4. Cabell Phillips, *The 1940s: Decade of Triumph and Trouble* (New York: MacMillan Publishing Company, 1975), 74–75.

5. Paul Fussell, "Hiroshima: A Soldier's Story," *New Republic*, August 22 & 29, 1981, 30.

6. *Mrs. Miniver*, Metro-Goldwyn-Mayer, 1942.

7. Edward R. Murrow, "A Reporter Remembers—The War Years," British Broadcasting Corporation, February 24, 1946 and as originally broadcast, Columbia Broadcasting System, New York, May 10, 1940.

8. Edna St. Vincent Millay, *The Murder of Lidice*, (New York: Harper & Brothers, 1942) and as aired by the National Broadcasting Company, New York, October 19, 1942.

9. Fussell, 30.

10. Robert Humphreys, "How Your News is Censored," *Saturday Evening Post*, January 26, 1943, 114.

11. U.S. Bureau of the Budget, "The United States at War," Washington, D.C., 1946, 235–37.

12. Clark G. Reynolds, *America at War 1941–1945: The Home Front*, (New York: Gallery Books, 1990), 11.

13. Ibid., 14.

14. "World War 2," Sounds of History: American Radio Mobilizes the Home Front, National Archives, Washington, D.C., 1980.

15. "Back in the Military Closet," *New York Times*, June 22, 1993, 19.

16. Reynolds, 9.

17. Humphreys, 114.

18. "Enemies at Home," *New Republic*, April 20, 1942, 551.

19. As quoted in Virginius Dabney, "Press and Morale," *Saturday Evening Post*, July 4, 1942, 5.

20. "Enemies at Home," 441.

21. Ibid.

22. Dabney, 5.

23. As quoted in "Enemies at Home," *New Republic*, May 11, 1942, 638.

24. "Fortune Press Analysis," *Fortune*, December 1944, 286, 288, 291.

25. "Lost in the War—News Wonderland," *Reader's Digest*, December 1942, 69.

26. T. H. Thomas, "The Shape of the News," *Atlantic Monthly*, August 1942, 63.

27. As quoted in "The Censor Takes a Look," *Time*, March 5, 1945, 63.

28. George Seldes, *The Great Quotations*, (New York: Pocket Books, 1969), 963.

29. Ibid., 969

30. Ibid., 958

31. Ibid., 966.

Chapter Two

OWI
What Shall We Tell? How Shall We Tell It?

WHEN AMERICA OFFICIALLY entered World War II, the federal government created a new agency whose specific purpose at home and abroad was to tell the public what was happening in this international conflict—the U.S. Office of War Information (OWI). The need for such an agency was manifold. World War II was not just a war of military machines and personnel. It was also a war of propaganda—a term the dictionary defines as "ideas, facts, or allegations that are spread deliberately to further one's cause or damage an opposing cause." Though never a replacement for military strength or extensive resources for waging war, this weapon did assume an important role for the Allies and their enemies during World War II. According to Victor Margolin, "in its broadest sense, World War II propaganda was just about anything that influenced or confirmed the feelings or behavior of all involved, both toward their own country's efforts and those of their enemies."[1]

"Truth, it has been said," wrote Liam O'Connor in 1943, "is the first casualty of war, and the propagandist is the assassin." According to this view, the propagandist is essentially a liar; he uses the lie to mislead the enemy, to deceive his own people, to secure the aid of neutrals and allies. He has one aim, according to Joseph Goebbels, "the conquest of the masses. Every means that serves this end is good."[2] "Adolph Hitler [was] in full agreement with his Minister of Propaganda and Public Enlightenment." He thought "that the propagandist should not only qualify as a liar but be as big a liar as possible. Hitler's Principle of the Big Lie is stated in *Mein Kampf* (My Struggle)" where he wrote "that it is a very sound principle" that "a definite factor in getting a lie believed is the size

43

of the lie . . . for the broad mass of people in the primitive simplicity of its heart more readily falls victim to a big lie than to a small one.' "[3]

Two days after Pearl Harbor, President Franklin D. Roosevelt outlined America's policy on war information; it was the opposite of the Axis powers. In a radio address to the American people, the president stated, in part:

> We are now in this war. We are all in it all the way. Every single man, woman and child is a partner in the most tremendous undertaking of our American history. We must share together the bad news and the good news, the defeats and the victories—the challenging fortunes of war.
>   . . . This Government will put its trust in the stamina of the American people, and will give the facts to the public as soon as two conditions have been fulfilled: First, that the information has been definitely and officially confirmed; and second, that the release of the information at the time it is received will not prove valuable to the enemy directly or indirectly.[4]

The dissemination of information to the public at home and abroad played a vital part in winning the war. On the home front, information had to keep 130 million Americans working at full speed to bring the war to a successful conclusion whether they were carrying a rifle, piloting a plane, producing food, working in a factory, or sitting at a desk. Overseas, information had to keep the United Nations working together with maximum effort toward common goals. In the long run, information had to convince the world that the United Nations could not be defeated and that only an Allied victory assured a fair peace.

America faced a variety of informational problems when its own participation in the war became official. Some segments of the public believed that a defensive rather than an offensive war ought to be waged. Americans had a tendency to underestimate the enemy and the magnitude of the war job. They also had considerable distrust of the British and the Russians as well as a lack of faith in their future cooperation. The public was ignorant of the economic controls that were necessary to regulate the cost of living and did not understand that excess buying power had to be reduced to prevent inflation. Different groups in society such as labor and management did not have much confidence in each other. A substantial minority of the public believed that the government was not releasing sufficient information about military and naval events.

On the foreign front, the United States was fully engaged in trying to counter enemy propaganda at home and abroad. The Germans, Italians, and Japanese tried as hard as possible to sow the seeds of disunion between the United States and its allies. Axis shortwave radio sought to create distrust between England and the United States, tried to portray the Nazi attack on Russia as a crusade against Communism, and attempted to spread the view in America and in Asia that England and America were engaged in a racial war against the colored peoples of the earth. Soon after Pearl Harbor, a Nazi broadcast to the United States shouted: "British naval circles are finding encouragement in the defeat suffered by the United States."[5] German broadcasts charged that the landing of American troops in Northern Ireland in January 1942 was timed "to coincide with Roosevelt's gradual absorption of Australia and Canada," that "American foreign policy is dictated from Downing Street rather than from Washington and will leave America holding the bag," and "the British Empire is dissolving like a lump of sugar into Roosevelt's tea cup."[6] The Axis also made special efforts to disrupt Western Hemisphere relationships by accusing the United States of having imperialist aims in Latin America.

The pessimism, intolerance, and apathy among American people proved fertile soil for Axis propagandists. While the majority of Americans recognized the seriousness of the war, were determined to win it, and approached postwar problems with a high measure of idealism, certain groups in the country sought to undermine public confidence in the good faith of the United States. This situation at home was so serious that on April 13, 1942, *Life* magazine published an article entitled "Voices of Defeat." In this article, *Life's* editors and correspondents exposed the activities of many of these groups to show who they were, what they were like, and what they were saying so as to prevent them from sapping America's morale by spreading Hitler's propaganda through their lies and hate. The editors noted that "there are always a certain number of yapping dissidents about the feet of a great nation marching to war."[7] *Life* presented the following examples:

On December 24, 1941, the *Nationalist Newsletter* of the Michigan-based National Workers League announced: "The Asiatic war indicates the probable defeat of Great Britain and the U.S.A. within 60 days."

On February 9, 1942, the pro-isolationist *Chicago Tribune* of Colonel Robert R. McCormick editorialized: "It is time that those who willed the war were driven from their hiding places and sent to the front where they can share some of the agony they created."

On February 21, 1942, the *X-Ray* attacked the American Red Cross volunteer blood bank program that was saving the lives of hundreds of wounded men on the battlefronts with this headline:

BLOOD CONTAMINATION
IS THIS "BLOOD BANK" SCHEME FOR TRANSFUSIONS A JEW SCHEME
TO MIX THE BLOOD OF THE RACES?

On March 16, 1942, the front page of *Social Justice*, a publication of Father Charles E. Coughlin, asked "WHO STARTED 'SACRED' WAR?" On page three, readers found the Coughlin answer: Jews. "Soon nine years will have elapsed since a worldwide 'sacred war' was declared on Germany, not by the U.S., not by Great Britain, not by France, not by any nation; but by the race of Jews. Guilt for the present war belongs to the Jews who organized a boycott against their Nazi tormentors in 1933. We repeat that for the persecutions suffered by 600,000 Jews in Germany the world was catapulted into a 'sacred war' of economic boycott. The object of the war was to destroy Germany's export trade upon which her 'very existence' depended. Only an irrational man would deny that such an economic war would inevitably lead to a bloody, physical war."[8]

These were the kinds of anti-Semitic, anti-American, and anti-Ally propaganda that some American citizens were disseminating during the early months of the war, which impelled *Life* magazine to state: "This is crackpot talk of course. But in time of war, especially an all-out war for national existence, crackpots who spread enemy propaganda are a dangerous luxury."[9] *Life* magazine went on to say, "*Life's* editors and correspondents . . . have prepared this article, not to frighten Americans with bugaboos, but to make them mad enough to see to it that their officials take the necessary action."[10]

Handling Wartime Information

Two months after *Life* published this article, the federal government acted. On June 13, 1942, President Roosevelt established the Office of War Information to counteract enemy propaganda at home and abroad. The idea for such an agency could be traced to World War I when President Woodrow Wilson delegated George Creel, a well-known journalist, to be chairman of the Committee on Public Information, being careful, however, not to label it "propaganda."

Creel's Committee, established in April 1917 by Executive Order 1, developed rules for the voluntary censorship of the press and was the central source of all war information emanating from government agencies. Creel decided which government agencies could say what and silenced the others. His slogans, posters, publications, and campaigns so inflamed the American people that they dealt roughly with dissenters. He organized the Four-Minute Men who made street corner speeches based on committee-prepared material, produced motion pictures, and sent abroad a corps of high-powered experts to strengthen the morale of the Allies and shatter that of the enemy, chiefly by having pamphlets distributed behind enemy lines. America helped win the war ideologically and on the battlefield with such slogans as "making the world safe for democracy." Nevertheless, as soon as the war was over, the committee was disbanded and its funds withdrawn.

During its short existence, some members of Congress, most American diplomats, and the Secretary of State regarded the Committee on Public Information with distaste. There was even less call for such an agency in the isolationist period between the wars. Americans were disillusioned with the results of World War I; they thought that the Treaty of Versailles which ended the war may have led to the rise of dictatorships in Europe; and they believed that British propaganda such as "the fate of Western civilization is at stake" and false stories about German troop atrocities in Belgium tricked America into entering World War I. Consequently, when Great Britain and France went to war with Germany in 1939 following the invasion of Poland, a majority of Americans believed that the United States should stay out of the European conflict and were suspicious of propaganda from either side.[11]

Early Efforts

As the European war began in 1939, the United States was the only major power that did not have an agency devoted to propaganda. Before the year ended, however, the federal government did establish the Office of Government Reports, the first of several major information agencies which, among other duties, sampled, and analyzed public opinion about such issues as war production, price controls, and rationing. In June 1941, the Division of Information of the Office of Emergency Management was given the task of keeping the American public informed about the country's defense program.

A month later, in July 1941, the Office of the Coordinator of Information was created to collect and assemble all information and data that might bear upon America's national security. This agency's mandate was the entire world, except for Latin America, which came under the jurisdiction of the Coordinator of Inter-American Affairs in the Office of Emergency Management. The purpose of the Coordinator of Information was to give policy makers a centralized and reliable source of information upon which they could make decisions. To do so, the agency not only sent agents to the four corners of the world to gather information, but also sought to bring together information from the files of other government agencies such as the War, Navy, and State Departments. Through its Foreign Information Service, the agency disseminated information to other countries, except those in Latin America. Other departments could prevent the agency from collecting their information, and the agency could not live up to its expectations.

In an attempt to create a more uniform information policy, the president established in the summer of 1941 the Office of Facts and Figures, under the leadership of Archibald MacLeish, poet and Librarian of Congress. The agency's purpose was to ensure that proper information about the government and the American defense effort was made available to the American public and that the public received as many facts, good and bad, about the war as the White House, Army, and Navy thought it should have. However, the Office of Facts and Figures could not compel the release of those facts; it could only coordinate existing channels of information on a voluntary basis because there was never any intent to limit the information freedom of other departments. As a result of its weak authority, the Office of Facts and Figures could not straighten out the public information problems in Washington, because it could not prevent other agencies from going their own way if they chose to do so.

In addition to these super-information agencies, other agencies like the Treasury Department and the Selective Service System were also disseminating public information on the home front. The result of all these activities was that public information was being managed by no one in particular, and by many government officials in general. The various agencies wallowed in conflict and duplication of effort. The agencies were supposed to inform; they sometimes practiced censorship. They were often inefficient and slow, and they sometimes contradicted each other. So did many of the department press offices. For example, the War Production Board, the Army, and the Navy all covered news of the wartime output; whereas the War Production Board wanted to release information for the sake of morale, the military services suppressed the same information because they thought it aided the enemy.

The failure of these various war information agencies was not the fault of their leaders. The problem was that their functions overlapped and their powers were not clearly defined; even the names of the various agencies were misleading. The Coordinator of Information did not coordinate information; that was the duty assigned to the Office of Facts and Figures, which did not issue facts and figures. These came from the Division of Information in the Office of Emergency Management and from the Office of Government Reports, which did not issue government reports. Domestic radio was under the aegis of the Office of Facts and Figures, European and Asian radio was under the Coordinator of Information, and Latin American radio came under the Office of the Coordinator of Inter-American Affairs, which also was in charge of movies for Latin America. Domestic films were under the Office of Government Reports, except that the Treasury Department, the Office of Facts and Figures, the Army Signal Corps, and the Division of Information also had a role in making or approving them.[12] As the United States entered its first full year of the war in 1942, the federal government was once again faced with the problem of trying to develop a coordinated and uniform policy for disseminating wartime information on the home front and abroad.

Creation of OWI

Proponents for a superpublic information agency argued that the United States ought to send the same information abroad that it released at home because under democratic conditions of free speech it was impossible to separate both operations. It was also argued that both programs should be based on a strategy of truth, and civilian rather than military authorities ought to share control of the information policy. Those who opposed the creation of a superagency argued that domestic and foreign information should be separate because each required a different administrative approach to its aims and methods. They believed that foreign intelligence ought to be used as a weapon of war and effectively allied with the military services, and that any linkage between domestic and foreign information agencies would endanger security and impair the effectiveness of psychological warfare.

The president studied both viewpoints. Then, agreeing with the former, the president issued Executive Order 9182 on June 13, 1942. This directive merged most of the previously mentioned information agencies into one large superagency—the Office of War Information (OWI)—under the direction of Elmer Davis, a highly respected newscaster. OWI was responsible for overt or "white" propaganda. The Office of Strategic Services (OSS), another new agency and forerunner of the U.S. Central Intelligence Agency, was established, in part, for covert or "black" propaganda.

As a news analyst for the Columbia Broadcasting System (CBS) and a former reporter and editorial writer for the *New York Times*, Davis brought a great deal of public affairs experience to his position. After taking office, Davis outlined the purpose of OWI:

> Our job is to give the American people the fullest possible understanding of what this war is about—a war which our enemies, for more than two years past, have called a world revolution, and which they have been conducting as a world revolution for their world supremacy, far more than as a war of the old-fashioned type. But really it is a counter-revolution against the ideas and principles which first appeared in this country in 1776 and spread from here over most of the world. So it is the job of the OWI not only to tell the American people how the war is going, but where it is going and where it came from—its nature and origin, how our Government is conducting it, and what (besides national survival) our Government hopes to get out of victory.[13]

To achieve these goals, the president's executive order authorized OWI to record, clear, and approve all proposed radio and motion picture programs that federal agencies sponsored and to serve as a contact for the radio broadcasting and motion picture industries in their relationships with federal departments and agencies concerning these governmental programs. The agency was also supposed to coordinate the war information activities of all federal departments and agencies to ensure that an

FIGURE 2–1
The War Overseas—1942

January—Japanese occupy Manila; Axis forces retake Benghazi; Chiang-Kai-shek named Commander-in-Chief of all Allied troops operating in China; First contingent of American troops lands in Northern Ireland.

February—Singapore surrenders to Japanese; President Roosevelt orders General MacArthur to leave the Philippines and transfer his headquarters to Australia.

March—Japanese invade New Guinea and control Dutch East Indies.

April—Japanese capture Bataan; British RAF bombs Hamburg and Augsburg; Lieutenant Colonel J. H. Doolittle leads first American air raid on Japan with sixteen B-25 bombers taking off from carrier *Hornet* to bomb Tokyo, Kobe, Yokohama, Nagoya, and Yokosuka.

May—Japanese occupy Mandalay; Corregidor surrenders; U.S. Navy stops Japanese southward advance to Australia at Battle of Coral Sea.

June—U.S. Navy defeats Japanese Navy at Battle of Midway Island; Japanese landing in Aleutian Islands off Alaska; Tobruk, North Africa, falls to Axis forces.

July—British attack Axis forces at El Alamein, 70 miles away from Alexandria, Egypt; Axis bombers hammer Malta.

August—American forces land in Guadacanal in Solomon Islands, South Pacific; Dieppe, France, raided by Allied forces consisting of mostly Canadian and British forces with some American Ranger observers and a few Free French.

September—Battle of Stalingrad rages; Stalin presses British and Americans to open up second front.

October—U.S. War Department undertakes to arm and equip thirty more Chinese Divisions; Convoy of vessels for Operation "Torch," the landing in North Africa, begins to assemble in Clyde of Firth.

November—American forces land in North Africa; Algiers surrenders to American forces; Germans repulsed at Stalingrad; Germans make full retreat in Egypt; German troops invade unoccupied France.

December—British RAF, based in Egypt, bombs Naples; Munich heavily bombed in RAF night raid.

accurate and consistent flow of information reached the public and the world. In addition, the OWI was to formulate and carry out information programs to increase an understanding of the war by using the press, radio, and motion pictures; it also was to maintain a liaison with the information agencies of the United Nations so as to relate our information programs to theirs. Finally, OWI was to obtain, study, and analyze information about the war effort and to advise agencies about the best way to keep the public informed—in addition to performing other duties the president might authorize.[14]

On one hand, OWI was to disseminate propaganda overseas to the Allies and Axis alike. On the other hand, the agency was to interpret the frequently ill-defined goals and programs of the government to the public with a degree of unified control and direction that such agencies had never achieved. Outside OWI's jurisdiction was handling news to Central and South America, which was still the responsibility of the Office of the Coordinator of Inter-American Affairs, and censorship, which was handled by the Office of Censorship, created for this purpose on December 19, 1941.

By the fall of 1942, OWI was prepared to declare that all federal agencies had to clear their national news releases through its staff, except for local or regional agency offices that could deal directly with the press on local and regional issues. OWI could place what the government wanted the people to think into every newspaper, school, movie theater, radio, and magazine and on every public platform. The vast opinion-making machinery of American democracy was never so totally mobilized. The need for such a mobilization was underscored by a government poll taken in midsummer of 1942. The poll revealed that

- almost one-third of the American people would be prepared for a negotiated peace with German army leaders.
- Nearly 50 percent of the people confessed they were not clear what the war was all about.
- The topic about which they felt they knew the least was "What would happen if the Axis won the war?"[15]

In view of these results, OWI faced an almost impossible task of keeping the public informed of all pertinent war information while publicizing administration policies.

The Role of Propaganda

The use of psychological warfare in conjunction with military forces is not new; it can be traced as far back as the armies of Genghis Khan and beyond. His victories were preceded by secret agents who worked on the populations of the countries he was about to attack. Spreading defeatism and division, the agents demoralized the populaces so that they had less heart to fight fiercely when the Mongol armies advanced. Centuries later after World War I, based on the intense emotionalism of the war years and the confessions of European propagandists that stories of the mutilation of women and children and crucifixions were just manufactured as "part of the game" to incite hatred and the "will to win" against the enemy, Americans viewed propaganda as just another evil weapon in the arsenal of war. Having learned the lessons of the previous war, Davis recognized the necessity for truth in public information:

> We even intend to see to it that the enemy peoples are truthfully informed, because we believe that truth is on our side, not only as to the nature and issues of the war, but as to who is going to win it. We cannot profess that we are going to tell the whole truth, because some things must be held back on the ground of military security; but we are going to tell nothing but the truth, and we intend to see that the American people get just as much of it as genuine considerations of military security will permit. . . . We are going to use the truth, and we are going to use it toward the end of winning the war. . . .[16]

The opposing views of America and Germany had a philosophy behind them. Thomas Jefferson stated the conflict clearly:

> Men by their constitution are naturally divided into two parties. Those who fear and distrust the people, and wish to draw all power from them into the hands of the higher classes. Secondly, those who identify themselves with the people, have confidence in them, cherish and consider them as the most honest and safe, although not the most wise depository of the public interests. In every country these two parties exist, and in every one where they are free to think, speak and write, they will declare themselves.[17]

The Fascists did not attempt to hide their contempt for the common man. Joseph Goebbels said, "The ordinary man hates nothing more than two-sidedness, to be called upon to consider this as well as that. The masses think simply and primitively."[18] To Goebbels, the secret of propaganda was to simplify complicated ideas, to make them as simple as possible, so simple that even the less ingenious people could understand what he meant. Simplicity and repetition are the secrets of modern propaganda. Hitler could not have agreed more with Goebbels's view. In *Mein Kampf*, he wrote: "The intelligence of the masses is small; their forgetfulness is great. Effective propaganda must be confined to a few issues which can be easily assimilated."[19]

Modern propaganda basically has four objectives: To mobilize hatred against the enemy, maintain the friendship of allies, gain the cooperation of neutrals, and demoralize the enemy. When carrying the war into the enemy's homeland, propaganda also has several virtues, including being corrective, instructive, and suggestive. In counteracting enemy propaganda in Axis and occupied countries, the activities of OWI had to have these qualities.

Propaganda owes its development to various fields, including technology, psychology, and ethics. Radio allowed countries to target their propaganda to other nations via shortwave broadcasts, and the airplane allowed soldiers to drop millions of leaflets over enemy territory. Psychologically, each of the European countries had its own profile which Allied propagandists had to know how to address. In the area of ethics, the propagandist had to decide how much good news versus bad news ought to be given out—a decision that would affect the morale of the audience. Also, where does the rearrangement of facts depart from the truth into actual misrepresentation?

Meeting OWI's Challenges

Propaganda is more difficult to organize in democratic countries than in dictatorships where the people have been conditioned to accept decisions without hesitation. In democratic countries, lies are more easily revealed, and the big lie cannot be easily repeated or it will become laughable and have the reverse effect.[20] The U.S. Office of War Information had tremendous challenges at home and abroad—on the home front, to energize the public's will to win the war despite privations and sacrifice; overseas, to help sap the enemy's will to fight, while helping to preserve the Allied coalition and the neutrality of the neutral nations. To achieve these goals, OWI was organized into three broad branches—Domestic, Policy Development, and Overseas.

The Domestic Branch, which coordinated and disseminated war information in the United States, consisted of six bureaus whose areas of responsibility were the press, radio, motion pictures, publications, campaigns, and such special operations as community services and public inquiries. The branch had three principal functions: To seek the release of as much news as possible from the military fronts and on the military's progress in the war; to obtain and circulate news about the operations of all the government agencies involved in the war; and to make all the news available to the public as quickly as possible. The Policy Development Branch was responsible for straightening out conflicts among federal agencies about information policy.

The Overseas Branch was eventually the largest division of the agency, with the most employees and funding. Its purpose was to disseminate propaganda overseas by shortwave radio, posters, and pamphlets. Its audience consisted of the enemy, America's allies in the free and occupied lands, neutral nations, and the American armed forces outside the United States. Introducing itself as "The Voice of America," the Overseas Branch used shortwave along with medium and longwave broadcasts from transmitters located strategically along the Atlantic and Pacific Coasts of the United States as well as in Europe and Asia. The branch broadcast news and entertainment shows to troops stationed overseas. Allied and occupied nations were told about American production, what America was doing in the war and plans for a second front; they were reassured that America would not be defeated. Enemy countries were told America was going to win. The Overseas Branch dealt in official announcements and did not attempt to scoop the regular news services. If the government officially reported bad news, OWI had to report it along with good news. The agency could not afford to say anything that the enemy could disprove. In addition to using radio, the Overseas Branch also cabled news to Allied and neutral nations via telegraphic code and transoceanic wireless. The cables were sent to favorably influence public opinion about the United States, especially in the neutral countries that could as easily have tilted toward the Axis powers as toward the United Nations.

The Overseas Branch also distributed pamphlets that spoke of America's war aims as announced in government policy statements and leaflets that planes dropped over enemy and occupied lands. The leaflets were important as physical evidence to others that America was there. In 1944, for example, propaganda leaflets over Germany and occupied lands were being dropped at a rate of 73,500,000 per month; no fewer than 12 million leaflets were dropped on D-Day when Allied forces landed on the beaches of Normandy. During the war, the leaflets served many purposes. Some told simply what was happening in the war—the territory gained by the Allies, the progress of the war in various theaters. The leaflets represented factual news without commentary to either contradict what the enemy might have been telling the people or inform the people of what the enemy was not saying. Leaflets also were used to warn people of forthcoming bombing raids, so they could evacuate the area. At Monte Cassino, Italy, leaflets warned citizens who were sheltered in the monastery that a bombing raid was to occur in 24 hours. Leaflets also served as "safe conduct" passes for enemy soldiers, enticing them to desert with promises of good treatment and illustrations of the kind surroundings they would inhabit. The "safe conduct" passes always contained a box written in English to instruct the American soldiers whom the enemy approached with leaflets: "The man who carries this leaflet is no longer an enemy. Under International Law, you will ensure that he is guaranteed personal safety, clothing, food, living quarters and, if necessary, medical attention." Other leaflets were counterfeit ration cards, stamps, coupons, and currency.[21] The Overseas Branch also distributed propaganda in magazines, movies, soap, matches, shoe laces, puzzles, baby diapers, and needle and thread—all packaged to contain a message.

In short, the Office of War Information used every means at its disposal to tell America's friends and enemies, and the neutrals that the United States was coming, was going to win the war and the world would be far better off because of a United Nations victory. OWI conducted its foreign information activities in conformity with the foreign and military policy of the United States.

FIGURE 2–2
The War Overseas—1943

January—Roosevelt and Churchill end Casablanca Conference; Roosevelt declares terms of Axis surrender are "unconditional."

February—Germans defeated at Stalingrad; Japanese abandon Guadalcanal; Germans seize and then lose Kasserine Pass, Tunisia, to U.S. forces.

March—Eight Japanese transports and four Japanese destroyers sunk in Battle of Bismarck Sea by U.S. and Australian forces.

April—Massacre of Jews in Warsaw Ghetto; Joint Anglo-American command set up to plan a European landing.

May—Organized resistance by Germans in Tunisia ends; Americans capture Attu in Aleutian Islands; Council of National Resistance founded in Paris.

June—Allied bombings of Sicily continue without respite.

July—Allied forces invade Sicily; Syracuse falls; Fascist Grand Council passes no-confidence vote in Mussolini, who is jailed; Marshal Badoglio invited to form new government; Roosevelt announces terms of Italy's surrender are "unconditional."

August—Messina, Sicily, falls; Sicilian campaign over in thirty-nine days; Japanese withdraw from Kiska in Aleutian Islands; Italian government declares Rome an Open City to avoid further destruction by bombing; Americans wipe out last pocket of Japanese resistance on New Georgia, Solomon Islands.

September—Italy surrenders unconditionally to General Eisenhower; Germans chased off Sardinia; Germans occupy Rome.

October—Italy declares war on Germany and acquires hybrid status among Allies as "co-belligerent."

November—Roosevelt and Churchill meet Stalin at Teheran; American forces land on Bougainville Island in the Solomons; Tarawa and Gilbert Islands pass into American hands despite heavy losses.

December—General Eisenhower appointed Supreme Commander of Allied Expeditionary Force to invade Western Europe.

The primary objectives of conducting political warfare overseas were to invade the enemy's mind before invading his territory, to destroy his self-reliance and confidence in victory before delivering the military blows, to decimate his following before doing the job physically, and to explode the myths the enemy pounded into the world's ears through his own propaganda machine. Because psychological warfare was a new endeavor to the Americans, OWI had set up a training center in Long Island, New York. There, the agency conducted an intensive three-week course ranging from studying the nature of the enemy to commando techniques.

Psychological warfare had to be adapted for the particular country toward which it was aimed, and there was much variety in the messages OWI sent. For example, an OWI agent in South Africa reported that anti-German stories made little impression on a large area settled by German people, but these people feared the Japanese; therefore, news sent to that area was full of true stories of Japanese atrocities. An OWI agency in Chungking, China, learned that the Chinese were not impressed by money; a story about a $50 billion production program was meaningless because the Chinese already believed that America was a fabulous land. However, when that same story was translated into ship, plane, or gun production, it was widely read. American psychological warfare special-ists learned that peoples in conquered lands would not accept the confi-dence and stories of a country that had never felt the crushing impact of a blitzkrieg. They wanted help, not advice. They wanted straight news, not news of what America intended to do because their attitude was "we'll believe it when we see it." As a result, rather than teaching these people how to sabotage the enemy, OWI reported incidents of sabotage that already had occurred; an incident in Norway would be described fully to the people of Poland and an incident in Poland would be told to the people of Norway. Political or psychological war became like the publication of multilingual newspaper to the peoples of the world.

The Use of Publications

The Domestic and Overseas Branches each had a publication bureau. The OWI's publication output was enormous. For the home front, the OWI published such items as *Tale of a City*, which told about Warsaw's experience during the Nazi occupation. The booklet's message was that Germany was "at war with the human spirit—the spirit of decent men crying out for release from tyranny and demanding for themselves and their children a world of justice and hope."[22] In *Negroes and the War*, the booklet spoke about Negroes in American life, dramatizing their stake in democracy. The publication highlighted the hypocrisy and purposes of those who attempted to persuade Negroes that they could not expect anything if America was victorious in this war. Although the booklet did not attempt to gloss over the Negroes' problems in America, the publication did emphasize that their hopes were inseparable from the survival of free America. In the *Unconquered Peoples*, OWI told what was known about the European resistance to Nazi rule. The booklet described a mighty groundswell that was gathering strength and direction, although the publication was careful to note that the full story would not be told "until the United Nations by military action have joined hands with the patriots in final battle for ultimate victory."[23]

The OWI list of publications was prodigious and varied. For example, during the week of April 26–May 3, 1943, OWI mailings included a Department of Interior release on how to store coal as a hedge against possible transportation shortages; "Dates with Your Government," a list of deadlines on rationing from the Office of Price Administration; a report on wartime problems in Baltimore, Md.; "Some Revealing Facts Showing the Great Difference Between This War and the Last One"; a release about the Civil Air Patrol; an item about Negroes in shipyards; an item noting that shrimp production had decreased by 20 percent; a release stating that thirty-two Chinese engineers had arrived at the expense of the Board of Economic Warfare to learn American production secrets; and another release stating that baby scale production would be lower in 1943 than in 1941.[24]

Overseas, OWI distributed such publications as *U.S.A.*—a pocket-sized journal of reprints from American periodicals; and a magazine named *Victory*, which was created to counter Axis propaganda publications being issued in neutral countries such as Turkey. "A tabloid newspaper produced by the OWI called *L'Amerique en Guerre* (America at War) . . . described factually war production figures, the weapons and ships being turned out daily, hourly, by the most powerful industrial nation in the world. It listed Allied advances with names of places in North Africa, Sicily, and Italy. . . . By D-Day, 1944, 7 million copies of this journal were being dropped weekly in France. Similar newspapers were distributed in Norway, Spain, and Ireland. . . . Later, a news tabloid *Sternebanner* (The Star-Spangled Banner) was dropped weekly on German cities. On the lines of *L'Amerique en Guerre*, it too was strictly factual—so factual that it occasionally contained news unfavorable to the Allies."[25] Although high Allied military circles raised objections to this reporting, German readers found *Sternebanner* believable because, as OWI had espoused, credibility could not be achieved without objectivity.

A Controversial Agency

In carrying out its mission at home and abroad, OWI constantly faced economic and political problems. Congress had misgivings about the agency's creation because it wielded large powers domestically and internationally. The information bureaus of other war agencies viewed OWI as a rival. OWI found it difficult to satisfy the demands of the press, radio, and motion picture industries. The agency also had internal organizational problems because it was an amalgamation of prior information agencies. Despite these problems, however, OWI, along with the Office of Censorship, did a great deal to bring some coordination, control, and direction to the information services of the federal government during the war years.

Conflict with Other Agencies

OWI faced a great deal of friction in its relationship with the military. The armed services resented Davis's demands for facts and figures about defeats, casualties, and victories, and his desire to discuss the necessity of peacetime reconversion as the war progressed and victory seemed more of a reality. The Army and Navy competed with each other over who was to receive credit for what in their communiqués; for example, both claimed the victory at the Battle of Midway. For a full year after the event, the military had suppressed the details of the Doolittle raid over Tokyo and other Japanese cities in April 1942.

Although Davis, in theory, had the power to order and supervise such military releases, in reality the military refused to allow any civilian to decide what could or could not be released and what was secret information. Rather than being present when the military chiefs gave the president daily reports and advising on the spot what portions of the reports should be instantly released, OWI officials found themselves at the mercy of the public relations officers of the war agencies. Even though Davis appealed to the president in September 1943 about the situation and succeeded in having a presidential directive issued, his victory was short-lived. Essentially, the directive gave Davis the authority to decide when, where, and how all war news should be released, but any department had the ability to appeal to the president as an arbiter about any news whose early release might endanger national security. One immediate result was that when the Navy attacked the Japanese at Marcus Island (Minami-Tori-Shima, northeast of the Northern Marianas) from the land and sea, the news was announced while the attack was in progress. A few months later, everything reverted to the predirective era; the issue was the "March of Death on Bataan."

In November 1943, the OWI first learned of the Japanese atrocities to American prisoners in what has come to be known as the "March of Death on Bataan." The agency tried to break the news but failed. Fourteen months later, in February 1944 and two years after the event itself, the Army and Navy finally released a communiqué, based upon eyewitness non-hearsay accounts of three Americans who escaped Japanese imprisonment. Their stories shocked a complacent nation. As reported in *Time* magazine, according to Lieutenant Colonel William Dyess, an eyewitness, the following incidents, in part, were the fate of the American and Filipino prisoners:

> In groups of 500 to 1,000 men, the prisoners were marched along the national road off Bataan. Those marchers who still had personal belongings were stripped of them; the Japanese slapped and beat them with sticks as they marched along without food or water on a scorching hot day. . . . None were permitted to eat. Those who had Japanese tokens or money were beheaded. A Japanese soldier took my canteen, gave the water to a horse, and threw the canteen away. Men recently killed were lying along the roadside; many had been run over and flattened by Japanese trucks. . . . Finally, a Japanese soldier permitted us to drink water from a dirty carabao wallow. . . .
>
> Our guards repeatedly promised us food, but never produced it. . . . American and Filipino prisoners fell out frequently and threw themselves moaning beside the roadside. The stronger were not permitted to help the weaker. We would hear shots behind. . . .
>
> We were introduced to a form of torture which came to be known as the sun treatment. We were made to sit in the boiling sun all day long without cover. We had very little water; our thirst was intense. I made the march in six days on a mess kit of rice. . . . The Japanese dragged out the sick and delirious. Three Filipino and three American soldiers were buried while still alive.
>
> (At Camp O'Donnell) . . . (The usual diet was a) watery juice with a little paste and rice. . . .
>
> Hundreds of Americans lay naked on the bare floor without covering

of any kind. Some afflicted with dysentery remained out in the weather near the latrines until they died.

Men shrank from 200 pounds to 90. They had no buttocks. They were human skeletons. . . .

The Americans and Filipino soldiers would not have surrendered if they had known the fate in store for them.[26]

The news of these horrendous atrocities was only a forerunner of the news of even more heinous crimes that the Axis powers had perpetrated against humanity and which Americans and the rest of the world would learn about in the ensuing years.

The Office of War Information also had a frictional relationship with the Department of State. When OWI was established, its executive order directed the agency to perform its functions in a manner consistent with the foreign policy of the United States. However, the executive order never specified how OWI was to know what was America's foreign policy. OWI officials contended that the nation's foreign policy was determined by presidential speeches and other announcements, which they were just as capable of interpreting as the State Department. In other words, OWI was reluctant to concede to the State Department that agency's traditional role of enunciating U.S. foreign policy. Friction soon developed on both sides. OWI officials believed that the State Department did not keep OWI fully informed about developments abroad. Similarly, State Department officials felt that OWI disregarded their directives and used confidential State Department information for propaganda purposes for which the information was not intended. In addition, OWI chafed under U.S. passport regulations and censorship of materials that traveled by diplomatic pouch. For example, the State Department could prevent OWI personnel and leaflets from going abroad.

An excellent example of the friction that existed between OWI and the State Department occurred on July 25, 1943, the day on which the fall of Mussolini was announced. Top officials of OWI's Overseas Branch never hid their outspoken criticism of America's friendly foreign policy toward Vichy France, General Franco of Spain, and the King of Italy. So on that day, OWI sent a shortwave broadcast to Europe announcing Mussolini's fall, but also described typical American reactions. An unidentified broadcast announcer who called himself the "Voice of America" quoted *New York Post* columnist Sam Grafton on King Victor

Emmanuel as follows: "The moronic little King, who has stood behind Mussolini's shoulder for twenty-one years has moved one pace. This is a political minuet and not the revolution we have been waiting for."[27] According to *Time* magazine, "the OWI [then] added an epithet of its own: Marshall Badoglio, a high-ranking Fascist, has been named successor."[28] OWI also stated that the overthrow of Mussolini "changes nothing," that while the news of Mussolini's resignation is welcome to Americans, it is not regarded here as an event of great importance.[29] In contrast, the Berlin correspondent of the Stockholm *Dagens Nyheter* wrote: "Nobody can deny that it is the biggest shock of this war for the Germans."[30]

Thus, OWI missed a propaganda opportunity of historic proportions. In belittling the anti-Fascist pretensions of King Victor Emmanuel and Marshal Badoglio, OWI also ended up belittling the greatest political event of the war to that date. Although the president rebuked the agency for the two-day broadcast, OWI was not entirely at fault for its transmission. Its Overseas Branch officials were not aware of negotiations taking place between the United States and the King of Italy and, according to *Time*, "the propaganda agency . . . never had a clear explanation of U.S. foreign policy from either Franklin Roosevelt or his State Department."[31] In addition, "neither he (Roosevelt) nor the State Department, nor OWI's overseas chief, Robert Sherwood, had authorized such statements. . . . Said Sherwood: "Regrettable slip."[32] Critics believed that OWI failed to recognize history in the making, namely, that the fall of Mussolini hailed the beginning of the end of Fascism.

FIGURE 2–3
The War Overseas—1944

January—Russian forces drive into Poland; Allied troops land at Anzio, Italy; Marines consolidate position on Cape Gloucester, New Britain; Russians announce complete lifting of siege of Leningrad; Invasion of Marshall Islands begins.

February—American forces land in Admiralty Islands; Kwajelein atoll in hands of U.S. forces; U.S. aircraft bomb Monte Cassino, Italy.

March—Germans complete occupation of Hungary and also Rumania by agreement with Rumanian government.

April—Japanese launch last big offensive against nationalist China; King

Victor Emmanuel of Italy abdicates in favor of his son, Umberto;
General George S. Patton says destiny of America and England to rule
world, later amending statement to include Russia.

May—Germans abandon Monte Cassino.

June—Rome falls to U.S. Fifth Army; Allied forces invade Europe at
Normandy, France; England attacked by "robot planes" described
by Germans as their "first secret weapon" of war; U.S. forces begin
invasion of Saipan in Marianas.

July—Unsuccessful attempt to assassinate Hitler in Rastenburg in East
Prussia; U.S. forces land on Guam; U.S. Fifth Army reaches Arno
River between Florence and Pisa, Italy; Japanese high command re-
places Premier Hideki Tojo with General Yoshijiro Umeza.

August—Paris is liberated; New German "jet" fighter seen in action
over Germany; India cleared of Japanese soldiers; Rumania declares
war on Germany.

September—Finland ceases fire on all fronts; Russians invade Hungary
and Czechoslovakia; Allied and Rumanian Armistice signed; Hungary
declares war on Rumania.

October—American forces land at Leyte in the Philippines; Bulgaria
signs armistice with United Nations.

November—Liberation of Greece completed.

December—Germans launch powerful counterattack through Ardennes
Forest; Bastonge, Belgium isolated; German drive stopped almost 50
miles away from Belgium border.

Internal Conflicts

The Overseas Branch had a collision of wills between its director,
Robert Sherwood, a distinguished author and playwright, and Elmer
Davis, director of the OWI. By 1944, the Overseas Branch had 97 percent of OWI employees and 90 percent of its budget. By the end of the
war, the Overseas Branch had outposts throughout the world and 8,400
employees and was America's voice overseas. It is not surprising that
with such global responsibilities the Overseas Branch director would
have liked the branch to have been an autonomous unit within the OWI,
not subject to the wishes or orders of Davis. This situation affected the
everyday activities of the OWI in carrying out its wartime mission.

Personnel problems were not confined solely to OWI's overseas operations. They also affected the OWI's home front operations. First, there

was a frequent turnover in the Office of Director of the Domestic Branch because the men who accepted the position did so on the condition that they would only stay a year or less. This policy impeded any continuity or stability in the branch's leadership. Under one of the directors an influx of advertising personnel led to a mass resignation of fifteen writers who stated that the agency was trying "to soft-soap the American public." They noted

> there is only one issue—the deep and fundamental one of honest presentation of war information. We are leaving because of our conviction that it is impossible for us under those who control our output to tell the full truth. No one denies that promotional techniques have a proper and powerful function in telling the story of the war. But as we see it, the activities of the OWI on the home front are now dominated by high-pressure promoters who prefer slick salesmanship to honest information. . . .[33]

The advertising executives began to adopt new methods of selling the war to the American people, including the idea that the only way to appeal to the public in wartime was through the selfish question, "What's in it for me?" In asking people to plant Victory Gardens and share their food, the answer to "What's in it for me?" would be the pleasure, taste, and health benefits of all the fresh vegetables the public may want. If merchants helped the government promote Victory Gardens, "What's in it for me?" would be an increase in business income from the sales of attractive garden clothes. Although the writers who resigned questioned whether the appeal to a person's selfish motivation was the correct approach in motivating the American people, advertising did induce many millions of Americans to buy war bonds, save rubber, refrain from hoarding, and take other domestic measures that were necessary for waging war. It was not the medium of advertising itself that caused dissension within OWI. The issue was the motivation behind the appeals that were being directed at the American people and whether or not they were being told the whole truth about the war—the bad news as well as the good—or just information that some elements within the government wished them to know so as to build rather than harm the nation's morale.

Conflict with Congress

The OWI's problems were not limited to working with other federal departments, or carrying out its foreign propaganda activities, or even the dissension within the ranks of its own personnel. The agency also had major problems with the Congress. Some members of Congress began to regard the agency as a public relations instrument for President Roosevelt and the New Deal; some Southerners resented its praise of the blacks' contribution to the war effort; still others became very critical of the quality of its propaganda journals. Some members even viewed the OWI as the principal refuge of radical and subversive elements within the government—in other words, supporters of the president—and these potential traitors had access to the confidential files of Army Intelligence.

As the Congressional attitude toward OWI worsened, the agency received no support from the White House or the president who was busy with military and international affairs. Even the internal bickering within OWI that led to the resignation of the fifteen writers displeased Congress. The net effect of all this political antagonism toward OWI was that in June 1943 Congressional opponents were successful in cutting OWI's appropriation for the following fiscal year. Davis was forced to close all forty-six domestic regional offices, ending OWI's domestic propaganda. Gone were the Domestic Branch's motion picture documentaries, posters, pamphlets, and news service. The Domestic Branch essentially became an agency that coordinated campaigns on war needs with other government agencies and the private communication media. The Overseas Branch continued until victory, but the Army generally was in charge. When Japan finally surrendered in August 1945, the President by executive order dissolved the Office of War Information and several other war emergency agencies.

In its brief wartime history, the Office of War Information had to confront many charges, including that it had been overrun by Communists, foreigners, and draft dodgers; that it was inefficient and unnecessary and wasted the taxpayer's money; that it attempted to dictate foreign policy and campaigned for a fourth term for President Roosevelt. Elmer Davis answered most of these charges as they arose; others were answered in Congressional debate.

FIGURE 2–4
The War Overseas—1945

January—Russians capture Warsaw; Hungary signs armistice with United Nations; Russians liberate Auschwitz concentration camp in eastern Poland.

February—Roosevelt, Churchill, and Stalin meet at Yalta in the Crimea; Turkey declares war on Germany and Japan after Allies announce that only nations at war with Axis powers can participate in San Francisco World Security Conference; American forces land on Iwo Jima; Allied aircraft firebomb Dresden, Germany.

March—American, British, and Canadian armies cross Rhine River at several points; new German weapon, a 13½-ton rocket, hitting southern England and London area; Argentina declares war on Germany and Japan; General MacArthur declares on Corregidor: "Hoist the colors . . . and let no enemy ever haul them down again."

April—American forces land on Okinawa; Russians open all-out drive to Berlin; Russia denounces neutrality pact with Japan; Death of President Roosevelt at Warm Springs, Georgia announced to world; Hitler takes over defense of Berlin; Italian patriots execute Mussolini at Lake Como; United Nations Conference on International Organization opens in San Francisco; American and Russian forces link up at Elbe River at Torgau; unconditional surrender of all German troops in Italy; Hitler commits suicide in the Chancellory Bunker.

May—Admiral Karl Doenitz succeeds Hitler as head of German state; Germany surrenders unconditionally; Rangoon, Burma falls to British Third Army.

June—U.S. bombers begin series of violent raids against 23 major Japanese towns, all with populations between 100,000 and 250,000; Okinawa captured; Brazil now in war.

July—Norway declares war on Japan; Truman, Churchill, and Stalin meet at Potsdam, Germany; United States, Great Britain, and China issue unconditional surrender ultimatum to Japan lest it suffer "prompt and utter destruction"; United States ratifies United Nations Charter; Italy declares war on Japan; Liberation of Philippines completed.

August—Russia declares war on Japan; Atomic bombs dropped on Hiroshima and Nagasaki; Japan surrenders unconditionally.

September—Japanese sign instruments of surrender on board U.S.S. *Missouri* in Tokyo.

OWI's War Record

The OWI had some successes. Its leaflets were effective with the enemy and in occupied and neutral countries. In North Africa and Sicily, enemy troops surrendered as a direct result of the "leaflet offensives"; there were even cases of Japanese soldiers surrendering with OWI "safe conduct" passes in their hands. Under Davis's direction, OWI energetically tried to coordinate war information and tell the public as much as possible about the war. There is evidence that Davis pushed as hard as he could to get government agencies to resolve their policy differences and give out consistent information about the war effort.

Domestically, OWI found itself under tight restrictions. It could not tell the American people about the government's war aims until policy makers enunciated them. The agency never tried to mislead the public or to force the press to accept the administration's views. By refusing to stir up anger against the Axis powers by fabricating atrocities, OWI went so far in the opposite direction that the real atrocities were approached as if they were horrors that should not be publicly discussed. In general, except for the brief time when advertisers attempted to take over the agency, OWI used common sense and patriotism in making its appeals to the American people. The agency furnished no Four-Minute Men speakers in American communities as the government had done in World War I to incite the public emotionally to take direct action against others on American soil. OWI provided a central source of information, especially for newspapers, in contrast to the many information agencies that had preceded it.

If critics believe that it was OWI's purpose to raise the public's morale, then on this point, OWI's record would be a failure. The agency did not alter the complacent state that developed between labor and management in the country as the war began to be won. Although the OWI tried to improve race relations, it could not prevent riots in Los Angeles or the Ku Klux Klan-instigated strike in Detroit in opposition to the hiring of blacks. World War II did generate ill feeling on the home front. People were overworked and fatigued; they had to stand in line; they could not travel where they wished and buy what they wanted. Although these frustrations ought to have been directed against the enemy, the enemy was too far away. Too often on the American home front the anger and frustration were directed against other Americans—Jews, Negroes, Mexicans, Congress, or the administration. OWI did not have authority to try and dispel such animosities.

OWI also had other failures in terms of public morale. Black markets existed during the war and the public did not do much to get rid of them nor could the OWI arouse the public to do so. There was a feeling in many places that "I'm going to get mine while the getting is good." However, Congress had indicated that it was not the purpose of OWI to improve public morale; thus, the agency's Domestic Branch confined itself to more achievable, but indispensable tasks: bringing order and a system into government information; persuading the Department of War and the Navy to be more informative in their releases; and bringing sound advice to magazine editors, book publishers, radio announcers, and motion picture producers who wanted to promote the national interests. The agency prevented disputes among government officials by reviewing statements and speeches before they were delivered. OWI explained government policies and helped the public understand what government agencies were doing.

Although Congress's funding cuts reduced OWI's Domestic Branch to just a small group in Washington, the Overseas Branch continued to fulfill an important purpose in the war. Its contribution was so important that correspondents like Quentin Reynolds and William L. Shirer cabled the U.S. Senate during the appropriation process in June 1945 after the House of Representatives severely reduced OWI's funding after Germany's surrender. Their message stated, in part, that if OWI was destroyed, the field would be open to the enemies of democracy. Decades after Congress received these words, the government in its wisdom has continued to operate the "Voice of America" of the Overseas Branch in today's U.S. Information Agency. The enemies of democracy still don't have a clear field to voice their propaganda because the counterforce established in 1942 as the Office of War Information continues to speak today on behalf of freedom and all those who still yearn to be free.

Notes

1. Victor Margolin, Foreword to *Propaganda: The Art of Persuasion, World War II* by Anthony Rhodes (Secaucus, N.J.: Wellfleet Press, 1987), vii.

2. Liam O'Connor, "The Strategy of Truth," *Commonweal*, July 9, 1943, 293.

3. Ibid.

4. U.S. Bureau of the Budget, "The United States at War," Washington, D.C., 1946, 203.

5. Ibid., 204.

6. Ibid.

7. "Voices of Defeat," *Life*, April 13, 1942, 86.

8. Ibid., 86, 90–91, 93–94, 97–98.

9. Ibid., 88.

10. Ibid., 86.

11. Rhodes, 139.

12. "A Job for Elmer Davis," *New Republic*, June 22, 1942, 847.

13. Michael Darrock and Joseph P. Dorn, "Davis and Goliath," *Harper's Magazine*, February 1943, 226.

14. Ibid., 230.

15. Stanley High, "It is Not a New Deal War," *Reader's Digest*, November 1942, 25.

16. As quoted in O'Connor, 294.

17. As quoted in O'Connor, 294.

18. As quoted in O'Connor, 294.

19. George Peel, "The Science of Propaganda," *Contemporary Review*, November 1944, 270.

20. Rhodes, 144.

21. Ibid., 146–147.

22. Norman Cousins, "The Big, Bad OWI," *Saturday Review of Literature*, March 13, 1943, 10.

23. Ibid.

24. "A Week with OWI," *Nation's Business*, June 1943, 62.

25. Rhodes, 147.

26. "The Nature of the Enemy," *Time*, February 7, 1944, 52, 54.

27. "The Strange Case of John Durfee," *Life*, August 9, 1943, 31.

28. "Opportunity Lost," *Time*, August 9, 1943, 86.

29. "History Unrecognized," *Nation*, August 7, 1944, 144.

30. "Opportunity Lost," 86.

31. Ibid.

32. Ibid.

33. "Struggle in the OWI," *New Republic*, April 26, 1943, 551.

Chapter Three

RADIO
The Programs We Heard

Although World War II was America's second war in the twentieth century, it was radio's first. The existence of radio is taken for granted today, but commercial radio was only two decades old at the time of the attack on Pearl Harbor. Radio had no prior model for its wartime role, especially in a conflict of such international proportions; it had to make many adjustments in adapting to its new responsibilities.

Whether in peace or war, radio has a unique power to marshal the spiritual and ethical forces of a nation because it so easily enters into millions of homes, work sites, and other locations. Each day radio informs the listener of local, national, and world events by broadcasting news, public affairs discussions, and informational programs. At the same time, it entertains with drama, sports, comedy, music, and other formats that attract and hold the listener's attention.

Compared with the print media, radio offers the advantage of listening, which requires less effort than reading, and has a timely immediacy unlike newspapers with limited circulation and necessarily delayed reporting. However, radio does not operate in a vacuum. Although the print media can report on events in far greater detail and can serve as the source of radio pronouncements, the information radio provides can stimulate listeners to purchase and read the print media to get more details about a story. Radio has tremendous power to influence a society; the speed with which invading armies attempt to take control of radio stations when conquering a country attests to this fact.

During the war years, the scope and character of radio resembled current television programming—dramas, comedies, public affairs,

71

news, quiz shows, concerts, daytime "soap operas," sports, special
events, commentary and educational broadcasts. Through these and
other programs, radio could continuously instruct, inform, and beguile
its listening audience. The U.S. Treasury Department sold war bonds
and stamps through radio advertising. When necessary, the president
enunciated national policies and decisions with radio addresses. Civil defense instructions were broadcast over radio. Through this medium, the
public was able to tour military bases and attend ship launchings and
other military events. One of radio's greatest contributions to the war
effort like that of other forms of media was helping the nation maintain
its morale through these terrible days and years.

As World War II officially began for the United States, many debated
the role of radio in this conflict. One of the clearest voices to enunciate
radio's purpose and function was that of Norman Corwin, the noted
radio writer:

> The duty and responsibility of American radio is obvious and simple and
> urgent: to explain the nature of fascism and why we are fighting it; to
> explain what we stand to lose by defeat and gain by victory; to face
> squarely the issues of war instead of ducking them; to hammer away at,
> to reiterate, to follow through with the truth no matter how many ap-
> peasers and editors and weary intellectuals resent and resist the truth;
> to inform the people instead of selling, coaxing, upbraiding or exhorting
> them.
>
> I believe that if people are brought to understand the origins of fascism,
> its accomplishments and goals, they will be more activated by something
> more affirmative than Hate; by a rational as well as emotional abhorrence
> of fascism, together with the conviction that they are fighting for a just
> cause and for the future of limitless good possibilities.[1]

To those who still might question these convictions, Corwin added:

> The tragedy of the situation can be measured only against the contrasting
> clarity of the enemy on all these points. Nobody knows better than they,
> alas, how vast the power of radio—a power far exceeding that of the
> press. The painful truth is that neither our government nor the industry
> of radio itself seems fully awake to the potentialities. One can only hope
> that the complete awakening will not be as late, or as rude, as it has been
> elsewhere.[2]

Axis Radio Propaganda

Corwin's comments raise the question as to what was the enemy's understanding of the power of radio? How did the Axis powers use radio against America and its allies? How did this country respond? The answers to these and other questions enabled American radio through its programming efforts at home and abroad to make significant contributions to the war effort.

Corwin's fears about America's ignorance of radio's influence are underscored by the many preposterous stories and rumors that spread throughout the United States as the war progressed. Americans heard the following kinds of tales.

- The British didn't have rationing like the United States and were joyriding throughout England on American tires and gasoline.
- The Red Cross didn't really need human blood because animal blood was just as effective.
- America promised to feed Russia and England even if its own babies had to starve.
- President Roosevelt and the U.S. Treasury Department had no intention of ever redeeming war bonds and stamps.
- There were 120,000 British agents in the United States and some of them were sabotaging factories to create fifth-column hysteria.[3]

When traced back to their original source, each of these rumors was the result of shortwave radio propaganda broadcasts that the Germans, Japanese, or Italians directed at America. Regardless of enemy origin, the basic principles of the Axis propaganda were the same. Their own successes were praised to the skies. If possible, they portrayed United Nations' successes as their own. If not possible, they lied away the significance of such successes. In addition, they rigidly adhered to the black-and-white technique: what the Axis powers accomplished was always white, what the United Nations did was always black, and no intermediate tones were allowed. The Axis propagandists also believed that lies could not hurt unless they hurt the enemy. Finally, the Axis powers underscored their own invincibility and, in increasing doses, the fact that the price of ultimate victory was sacrifices, privations, and a long war.[4]

When the previous principles were translated into Axis shortwave radio propaganda, they resulted in three kinds of programs. First, the Axis transmitted distorted news summaries and frank persuasive talks by Americans and others who betrayed their own countries for the Axis cause. Second, they sent coded messages to Axis spies and saboteurs in America embedded in programs that on the surface seemed to be extraordinarily inept propaganda. For example, if a program—often in the form of a skit—sounded ridiculous, and if the speaker or characters frequently referred to numbers, then it was a safe assumption that the program contained coded messages. Third, the programs told Axis sympathizers what rumors to spread in the United States. Such programs often consisted of dialogues in which one speaker mentioned to another what Americans weren't being told because of censorship. Frequently, they were light and lively talks that supposedly offered the inside information by means of news flashes, discussions, and arguments. For example, some actual Axis transmissions reported:

> Flash! From Gary, Indiana! British seamen who have deserted their ships in United States ports are applying in ever-increasing numbers for jobs on boats plying on the Great Lakes.

> Flash! From San Francisco! Public health officials state confidentially they may have to stop the flow of Mexican labor pouring in here to replace Japanese labor, now interned. The Mexicans are bringing many contagious diseases, causing epidemics, which was not the case when Japanese labor was available.[5]

These flash reports were the source of the most disruptive and subversive rumors in America. These programs were never intended for the average American listener. The Axis propaganda chiefs knew that very few Americans listened to their programs except for some laughs or, perhaps, out of passing curiosity, and most of these listeners would neither believe or repeat the Axis stories they heard. The most dangerous qualities of Axis propaganda were its highly developed ability to mix truth with untruth and its skill for distortion. Sometimes the most outlandish lies were mixed so brilliantly with a few odds and ends of truth that the whole story acquired a believable flavor; at other times, true facts were exaggerated and exploited to the fullest; and plain facts were never presented as such.

The enemy technique was designed so that the average American would hear the story from a neighbor, a relative, or a friend—someone the person trusted. The Axis sympathizer knew that he was being instructed to spread as rumors the false stories being broadcast. So as not to call attention to himself he mentioned them half-jokingly, perhaps, at his workplace or wherever people gathered socially such as a barroom or a lodge meeting. His wife made the same comments in a neighborhood store. A bystander was almost certain to repeat them to a friend as a joke or as gossip. By the time half-a-dozen people repeated the joke or story, it took on a life of its own. It began to travel quickly and sometimes was believed because now it was being circulated by people who could not be suspected of treason and had no idea they were doing exactly as the Axis had wished.

German Propaganda

The Germans used shortwave radio in other ways to promote divisiveness in America. Familiar with the skip and the bounce of shortwave radio waves between the Earth and the ionosphere, they would insert such phrases as "over there" (referring to Europe) in their pronouncements. In this fashion, they were hoping that listeners would believe that the broadcast was of American origin rather than from their own European radio station whose call letters were D-E-B-U-N-K, "the station of all free Americans."

Axis radio hammered away at every possible wedge to create disunity among the American people. Rumors asked, "have you heard that there are only fifty anti-aircraft guns to protect the entire United States because the rest were sent to Russia? Do you know that the English are underselling Americans in South America with our own Lend-Lease goods?" Of course, Axis radio did not overlook racial hatred toward minorities. Radio programs accused the Jews of starting World War II, claiming that the Jews as international financiers were seeking to exploit the common people or, as Communists, were trying to destroy capitalism.[6] Nazi radio tried to exploit American regional differences such as those between the North and the South by stating that a pleasure yacht, full of soldiers from New Orleans, was bombed by a Navy officer from Boston, Massachusetts. The program continued warning all Americans to beware "not only of Jews but also those sly, shrewd, sharp Yankees, loving money and trade above all else, and who are the real villains in this world tragedy."[7] Axis radio also made appeals to Hungarians,

Rumanians, Italians, and above all, to those of German descent living in the Americas. "Blood is thicker than water," one Nazi announcer declared repeatedly, "Why not give your German cousins a break?"[8]

Some Nazi radio propagandists were more well known than others such as Axis Sally (Mildred Gillars, an American) and Lord Haw Haw (William Joyce, an Englishman). Others who were born in America and broadcast for the Nazis used such pseudonyms as Paul Revere, Mr. Guess Who, Mr. O.K., Bingo Bill, White Oak, and Mr. Everybody. In July 1943, a Federal Grand Jury in the United States indicted them for treason to their country under their real names of Fredrick W. Kaltenbach, Robert H. Best, Douglas Chandler, Edward Delaney, Constance Drexel, Jane Anderson, Max O. Koischwitz, and Ezra Pound, the poet and only American in the group to defect to the Italian cause.[9] After the war, all the American radio broadcasters who were brought to trial were found guilty and incarcerated in a federal facility.[10]

The cardinal principle upon which the Nazis based their propaganda was to appeal to the emotions of the masses. By using their technique of repetition, German broadcasts to America stressed the war's hopelessness—the inevitable defeat of the Allies; terror—the United States alone in a hostile world; and as already noted, American societal dissension—the arousal of class against class, race against race, isolationist against interventionist, and everyone against the press. Even before the United States officially entered the war in December 1941, America heard these kinds of pronouncements. On September 9, 1941, Paul Revere (Douglas Chandler) broadcast the following message (in part) to the United States over Radio Berlin:

ANNOUNCER: From the heart of Hitler Germany, your messenger Paul Revere greets you again.
PAUL REVERE: Countrymen, friends, foes, Jew haters and Jew servers . . . Tonight we are on the eve of the third birthday of the Axis Pact . . . For 3 years the Axis partners have marched from victory on every front . . . military, diplomatic, economic. For 3 years, the democratic opponents of world progress, led by Churchill the charlatan and Roosevelt the renegade, have sought to substitute deeds, little deeds, with words. All their futility, all their shameful incompetence these men have tried to cover behind an impenetrable smokescreen of lying words . . . Dear friends, keep in mind that your betrayer in the house that once was white is a graduate of Harvard. That revered alma mater in Cambridge by

Boston has to bear its own share of the blame for Roosevelt's anti-American deeds. . . . [11]

Italian Propaganda

Italian radio programs were not as insidious or as coordinated to a party line as the German's. The Italian formats varied from boring, long-winded analyses of military campaigns and geopolitics to just plainly bloodthirsty diatribes. For example, an eloquent speaker on one of Radio Roma's programs declared:

> Today we face the enemies themselves, breast to breast. Our sword hunts among their barbaric ribs for the right place for the *coup de grace*. Here we have the ruddy breast of England, flaccid with whiskey, wrinkled with age, covered with pustules from overeating. Here is the young but obese breast of the U.S.A., fat rather than muscular. . . . Between the spirit of Rome, which above all things is idealism and justice, and the spirit of the U.S.A. which is gold and arrogance, there is no possibility of negotiation.[12]

Another speaker told the Italian people that Americans were so filthy rich that they discarded their dirty shirts rather than launder them.

On occasion, Berlin and Rome disagreed with each other. Berlin, for example, insisted that England got America into the war to save its own hide; Rome, apparently forgetting that the German broadcast was beamed to America, stated that President Roosevelt intended to take over the British Empire. "As things stand at present," Radio Roma said one day, "Great Britain is fighting for ancient economic security, while the United States tries to filch it from her under a scheme designed as friendliness."[13] Meanwhile, Ezra Pound informed the English-speaking world that Benito Mussolini had made fascist Italy the heir of ancient Rome and the pioneer of a better, more modern world order in contrast to British and American statesmen who were leading their countries to destruction by involving them in a war with the Axis powers.[14] Or as Ezra Pound said one day on radio in his own vernacular: "You have been hugger-muggered and scarum-shouted into a war and you know nothing about it."[15]

Japanese Propaganda

Radio Tokyo was the third major Axis organ. The station, especially at the beginning of the war, relied upon alleged statements by American prisoners for its broadcasts to the United States. Their voices were rarely heard. On occasion, when a prisoner was heard on the air, it was painfully obvious that he was speaking against his will. According to Radio Tokyo, the United States was a hotbed of plutocrat profiteers, black-market bootleggers and hijackers, recalcitrant draftees, millions of resentful blacks, labor agitators, and plotting Communists who were indifferent to the war. In addition, all Americans ever thought about was swimming, hay rides, mountain climbing, and they certainly did not have any inclination to fight.

In bragging about the moral superiority of the Japanese, Radio Tokyo reported one day that "the American Navy has special ships which follow the maneuvers of their fleet. These ships carry the wives of Navy men. This has its roots in the fact that many American women ask for a divorce if they are separated from their husbands for more than three months. Thus, the American Navy recognizes the validity of their selfishness. What a way of thinking that is! What a contrast to the ideals and thoughts of the Japanese."[16] Almost every 15 minutes with a trumpet fanfare, Japan would announce over shortwave radio: "This is the Broadcasting Corporation of Japan." The Japanese broadcasters boasted a great deal about the power and strength of Japan compared with that of the United States. Their English-speaking broadcasters had names like "Ann the Orphan," dubbed by the GIs as "Tokyo Rose;" their programs consisted of music, insults, taunting memories of home, and the latest news from America, which was almost always bad—announcements of strikes, crimes, floods, and other troubles. What did these programs sound like? Well, over Radio Tokyo on August 14, 1944, "Tokyo Rose" (Iva Ikuko Toguri D'Aquino)[17] told our GIs in the Pacific:

> Hello, you fighting orphans in the Pacific. How's tricks? This is "after-her-weekend-Annie" back on the air, strictly under union hours. Reception O.K.? Why, it better be because this is all request night. And I've got a pretty nice program for my favorite little family, the wandering boneheads of the Pacific islands. The first request is made by none other than the boss. And guess what? He wants Bonnie Baker and "My Resistance Is Low." My, what taste you have sir, she said . . . [18]

Confronting Propaganda at Home

The United States was confronted with the problem of how to counter the enemy's propaganda that reached the United States. One way was through radio. For example, in August 1942, the Columbia Broadcasting System (CBS) began to air a program called "Our Secret Weapon." Rex Stout, the author and creator of Nero Wolfe, the fictional detective, hosted the program. According to *Newsweek*, "each week Stout would review some 30,000 shortwaved Axis words, select pertinent lies, dig up the truth, and write an exposing script."[19] A typical exchange would be:

ANNOUNCER (German accent): "The best soldiers and officers in the United States Army are Germans. So are all the best baseball and football players."

STOUT (with sarcasm): "As you can see they've got the facts, no getting away from it. Take the six leading batters in the major leagues: Williams, Gordon, Wright, Reiser, Lombardi, Medwick. Some bunch of Germans. Also, the great German prize fighter, Joe Louis."

By December 1942, after five months on the air, the show was such a success that orders for scripts were running as high as 6,000 a week.

The show even began to annoy the German Ministry of Propaganda. In recognizing the program about that time, German radio stated: "A new propaganda organization has been set up in Washington recently, consisting of some 3,500 writers, headed by Rex Stout, well-known detective and pulp magazine writer. . . . Now we have the explanation why so many of the war stories released in Washington have so strong a flavor of Chicago gangsterism." Stout answered on another program: "Goodness, I hope these little broadcasts I do aren't bothering Dr. Goebbels. I am a man of good will. I wish him the best. I hope he is boiled in the very *best* oil—none of that ersatz stuff." Sometimes, the program dramatized German, Italian and Japanese speeches with actors playing the roles of Hitler, Mussolini, and Hirohito. The series was a direct counterforce to the strategy of German Propaganda Minister Joseph Goebbels, who was filling the airwaves with claims of German, Italian and Japanese superiority and American ineptness.

Censoring American Airwaves

Axis propaganda was founded on Nazi geopolitics, the close scientific study of each regional audience of the earth, its interests and susceptibilities. The Axis powers used every trick in their propaganda book to assault the United States and its allies, and they were very formidable in their craft. They were assaulting a nation that until the attack on Pearl Harbor lacked any kind of organization that could effectively fight back or even prevent valuable information from reaching the Axis powers because the American government did not regard censorship as a proper peacetime function. However, the First War Powers Act (December 18, 1941) did confer on the president the authority to establish censorship activities; and, on December 19, 1941, in accordance with this legal authority, President Roosevelt by Executive Order 8985 established the federal Office of Censorship. In announcing its creation, President Roosevelt stated:

> All Americans abhor censorship, just as they abhor war. But the experience of this and all other nations has demonstrated that some degree of censorship is essential in wartime, and we are at war.
>
> The important thing now is that such forms of censorship as are necessary shall be administered effectively and in harmony with the best interests of our free institutions.[20]

The Office of Censorship had two principal objectives. The first was to prevent the transmission of information, within or outside of the United States, that might be useful to the enemy such as that relating to sabotage, espionage, and subversive activities and to block the entrance of harmful propaganda. The second objective was to obtain information from examined communications that might be of value in fighting the war; that is, communication intercepts about conditions in enemy countries, attempted evasion of export and import regulations, enemy shipping information, new industrial developments of military importance, and financial transactions related to the war. It should be noted that in April 1941, under a directive inspired by the State Department, the Federal Communications Commission had established the Foreign Broadcast Intelligence Service to listen in on, digest, and report on all foreign shortwave broadcasts, no matter where they were aimed or by whom.

Two of the new agency's responsibilities concerned radio and the domestic press. But the censorship of these media was voluntary and not authorized by the executive order that had created the agency. On January 27, 1942, President Roosevelt wrote a letter to the agency director in which he stated:

> As President of the United States and Commander-in-Chief of the Army and Navy, I hereby authorize and direct you in your capacity as Director

of Censorship to coordinate the efforts of the domestic press and radio in voluntarily withholding from publication military and other information which should not be released in the interest of the effective prosecution of the war.[21]

To achieve such censorship goals, the government published codes that noted what material might and might not be stated. In January 1942, the government issued the censorship codes for radio:

• Ad libbing is out. Informal interviews in public places, where the group is small and arrangements cannot be made to investigate the participants' backgrounds, are banned. On-the-scene reporters must be careful not to broadcast information to the enemy. No one on quiz shows of the audience-participation variety should be guaranteed a chance to take part.

• No telephone or telegraph requests for musical numbers are permitted, for they can easily transmit coded messages. Information on lost persons, animals, or objects also is out. A given request for a specified broadcasting time is to be avoided. In this way, no chances are taken on prearranged signal communications.

• Programs must steer clear of attempts to portray the horrors of combat. Sound effects which might be mistaken for air-raid alarms are forbidden.

• Approved newspaper material cannot be aired, unless further censored.

• News of sinkings and other reverses from unidentified sources is banned.

• Weather information must be approved by the Bureau. Any reference to weather conditions in on-the-scene broadcasts of special events must be avoided.[22]

The major networks promptly approved the regulations and issued instructions to avoid forbidden subjects. The Office of Censorship proved so skillful in administering the radio and press codes that there were few complaints about them from the public. Although the censorship agency appeared to be the supreme authority regarding this activity, every government information agency also had the powers to decide what to issue and how.

In addition to the previous radio codes, 205 U.S. foreign language radio stations in May 1942 established the Foreign Language Radio War-time Control which adopted a code calling for advance approval of all scripts by the stations, monitoring of all programs, extensive investigation and fingerprinting of all personnel, and each station's assumption of full responsibility for program content and loyalty of employees. Shortly thereafter, these codes were incorporated into those of the Office of Censorship. Until these codes were formulated, the government was worried what these U.S. foreign-language stations were telling their 14 million listeners who were either foreign-born or first-generation Americans.

American Propaganda

In the fall of 1942, the government took another major step in organizing its propaganda war against the Axis powers. The Office of War Information (OWI) and the Office of the Coordinator of Inter-American Affairs, led by Nelson Rockefeller, announced that they would begin to lease or purchase air time on a full-time, 24-hour-a-day basis from the fourteen shortwave stations then in operation. To ensure that the radio stations told the same story about America to listeners overseas, the government began to coordinate all shortwave propaganda efforts and adopted the policy that broadcasts should present incontrovertible facts plus appeals to the decent instincts of audiences within the Axis regions. Until that time, the government only supplied each station with program material, and each station's broadcasters rewrote or edited the proffered programs with such diverse judgments that they frequently contradicted each other in expressing the government's viewpoints.

During the first year of operation, the government's shortwave propaganda efforts against the Axis powers were not very successful. In the summer of 1943, Italian underground agents reported that when America broadcast its Italian-language programs to their country, the broadcasts sounded indecent, arrogant, demagogic, oratorical, and offensive. The Italian antifascist listeners could not understand why the United States was unable to demonstrate with hard evidence that democracy was superior to dictatorship as a way of life. They also wanted to be told how resistance groups in Nazi-dominated lands were faring and be given practical information about how these groups were carrying out their clandestine activities.

If America's propaganda broadcasts were not initially successful, it was not from want of trying. By September 1943, the Atlantic radio barrage of the Office of War Information reached 2,600 programs per week; with repeats and duplications, about 6,000 shows per week were being transmitted to Europe. While some were beamed to provide entertainment to the armed forces overseas, the majority were directed to Nazi-occupied Europe itself. In addition, OWI developed a network of local radio stations in such friendly countries as Sweden, Egypt, Iran, Lebanon, and Palestine, to which it beamed its broadcasts. The typical program was identified as the "Voice of America" (OWI was never mentioned), fifteen minutes in length and introduced by a brisk chorus of "Yankee Doodle." Typically, the broadcast was a straight newscast, perhaps slightly altered in subject matter to fit the country to which it was transmitted. Other programs might include music such as a series on American symphony orchestras or other lighter subjects.

By 1944, the quality of shortwave propaganda directed against the Axis powers began to improve. *Life* magazine described the various programs and techniques of one such shortwave radio station, known as Radio Luxembourg, after its capture by U.S. forces. This station, according to *Life*, "with its entrée into virtually every home in Germany" provided a variety of programs. *Life* noted "one program consists of excerpts from letters captured from the Germans before they could be mailed or delivered. Another gives "inside" news from Germany, stories of scandals and corruption. A third broadcasts recordings made by German prisoners describing how well they are treated. But, the station's staff considers the jokes told on many of its programs as perhaps the most effective propaganda of all . . . the quality of many of the jokes . . . are designed to appeal to the heavy handed sense of German humor. . . ."[23] They were delivered as follows:

> "Why did Grandpa join the Volssturm (Home Guard)?" one voice asked. "Because he had no one to take care of him now that Grandma's in the Luftwaffe (Air Force)," replied the other.

> "Our brave SS divisions are advancing toward Russia and France. Those in Russia are advancing toward France and those in France are advancing toward Russia."

The jokes covered a variety of topics from Germany's military situation and the status of its military personnel and equipment to Germany's political leadership and other subjects. But, as *Life* observed, the various broadcasts " . . . are designed to sap German morale and lure German soldiers into surrendering."[24] Irrespective of their location along the Pacific or Atlantic Coasts of the United States or in strategic areas of Europe or Asia, whether the government built, leased, or used captured facilities, the radio transmitters beamed their broadcasts continually to undermine the enemy's morale and bolster that of the United Nations.

Bringing the News Home

The war created a new kind of radio program and it created radio's newest star—the radio news correspondent who brought the home front listener to battlefields all over the world and in the process became a household name. To name but a few, they included Edward R. Murrow, Eric Sevareid, Charles Collingwood, William L. Shirer, Robert Trout, and George Hicks. Reporting from such trouble spots as Cairo, London, Singapore, Normandy, and Rome, these men brought the vividness and immediacy of the global struggle back to the home front. Not all reporting was vigilant. Soldiers were known to have huddled in foxholes under heavy aerial bombardment, while their radios were telling them that U.S. forces had complete control of the skies in their battle sector. Cognizant of these and other potential abuses where the news did not match the reality of events, radio did try to maintain a vigil over slack reporting.

Radio did many jobs in various theaters of war, large and small. At home, right after the attack on Pearl Harbor, radio commentators—neither commiserating nor acting as cheerleaders—did much to reassure an uneasy nation. Raymond Graham Swing was one such commentator, who said over WOR-Mutual and other stations:

> We have been the safest-minded people on earth. And we have indulged to the full the extravagance of underestimating our opponents. . . . There is, however, one mercy in this grievous situation. . . . Our defeat has come at the beginning. . . . We can outproduce the Axis. And we can out-will the Axis.[25]

The rise of a news program as a popular radio feature was a wartime phenomenon. In times of crisis, commercials were interrupted for bulletins or canceled entirely to make way for special pickups from the home front or abroad. Key stations remained on the air throughout the night just in case special events had to be reported; they presented news summaries each hour. The news programs became so popular that several advertisers would cosponsor a single program. In 1944, the National Broadcasting Company (NBC) estimated, for example, that news programs accounted for more than five times as many network hours as in 1939. CBS estimated that news programs constituted almost 39 percent of the network's total program hours from the time of Pearl Harbor to V-E (Victory in Europe) Day.

One of the first news broadcasts in which the United States was involved as a direct wartime participant gave home front listeners much to think about as they listened to a description of the Japanese bombing of Manila on December 8, 1941. Bert Silen, the local radioman for NBC, and Don Bell, his relief announcer, reported the attack in the following fashion:

> We are trying to locate the exact place of the tremendous fire that is raging and turning the sky absolutely crimson . . . In the vicinity of Nichols Field there is a terrific fire that looks very much as though a gasoline dump or something is burning over there . . . Ladies and gentlemen, there is one thing we definitely found out at the present time; the Japanese came over with the idea of hitting a definite target, and they have hit that target . . .[26]

Those who survived the Japanese attack on Pearl Harbor not many hours before would have agreed with that last point. Although the broadcast was obviously useful news to the Japanese about the success of their air raid, it was also useful to the United States. The report dispelled once and forever the prevalent and dangerous notion that existed until that time, namely, that the Japanese pilots couldn't see straight and their bombing was inaccurate.

Radio news correspondents also brought the war a little closer to American shores as on the Sunday in February 1942 when Dave Driscoll on board a Navy patrol boat described the havoc that German submarines were wreaking on American ships off our Atlantic Coast. In his WOR-Mutual radio broadcast, [Dave] "Driscoll summed up his impressions and dubbed in some of the nerve-tingling recordings [that had been] approved by the Navy":

Over the graveyard of the torpedoed destroyer *Jacob Jones*: "Upon our arrival we discovered two large oil slicks . . . Overhead are three United States Army Flying Fortresses and a Navy blimp . . . Our ship has gone into action. She is going full speed and our guns are being loaded and the depth-charge racks are manned, ready to make an attack, I believe. I am remote from the bridge, staying away from where I will be in the way . . . Just a moment, I see something on the surface . . . I am wondering whether or not that boat that I see is a submarine or patrol boat."

Alongside the sinking tanker *R. P. Resor*: "I can see a great spurt of flame . . . The stern is enveloped in a big cloud of smoke . . . We are now over on the windward side of this tanker around in the heavy smoke . . . and if my voice sounds muffled it is because I am working very close to this microphone as the wind is whipping across this deck . . . Now the bow seems to be slipping under. It is. There she goes. There goes the tanker . . . slipping beneath the waves, the flames dying away from the big mass and licking over the surface of the water."

Because of censorship, Driscoll's reporting could not be as unconstrained as newscasters may have liked, but it demonstrated that the armed services "could arrange for a new kind of coverage with the drama and spontaneity that only on-the-spot reporting affords."[27]

Such was the situation during the first twenty-four hours of what has come to be known as D-Day, June 6, 1944, when under the Supreme Command of General Dwight D. Eisenhower, the Allied Expeditionary Force began its invasion of Europe at Normandy, France. Home front listeners fortunate enough to be tuned to radio throughout that first night had a broadcasting experience they were unlikely to forget. They could listen to the voices of history such as General Eisenhower announcing the invasion:

People of Western Europe, a landing was made this morning on the coast of France by troops of the Allied Expeditionary Force. This landing is part of a concerted United Nations plan for the liberation of Europe made in conjunction with our great Russian Allies . . . The hour of your liberation is approaching.[28]

Before dawn had broken over the Eastern United States, U.S. correspondents such as NBC's Merrill Mueller, CBS's Richard Hottelet and Mutual's Larry Meier began filing their eyewitness reports over American radio. They described the shipped-packed English Channel, told of the landings on the coast of France, and recreated the mood and appearance of General Eisenhower's headquarters.

One of the most memorable reports came from George Hicks, London news chief of the Blue Network. It was an account of the Nazi bombing of the U.S. flagship (U.S.S. *Ancon*), which Hicks was aboard during the Channel crossing. His calm description of the scene was accompanied by the sound of the ship's ack-ack guns, the gunfire from nearby ships, the calling of all hands to General Quarters, the excited comments of the gun crew making their first kill, and the sound of a German plane shot down and crashing into the English Channel. The following excerpt from his report, supplemented by the listener's imagination, made his home front audience a participant in the invasion of Europe on that fateful day:

Our own ship is just sounding the warning (*siren sound*) and now flak is coming up in the sky with streamers from the warships behind us . . . Now the darkness has come on us. These planes you hear overhead are the motors of the Nazis coming and going in the cloudy sky . . . (*an explosion*). . . . That was a bomb hit. Another one! Fire bursts and the flak and streamers going out in a diagonal slant (*sound of ack-ack*) right over head. . . . Flares are coming down now. You can hear the machine gunning . . . Here's heavy ack-ack now (*loud firing and shouts of crew*) . . . Here we go again! Another plane has come over (*sound of engines*). . . . The cruiser right alongside us is pouring it up (*sound of ack-ack*]. . . . Something burning is falling down through the sky and circling down. It may be a hit plane (*machine gun fire*). Here we go. They got one! They got one! . . . (*Gun crew voices: "We made it look like polka dots!"*) The lights of that burning Nazi plane are just twinkling now in the sea and going out . . . It was the first kill for this gun and the boys were all pretty excited about it . . . They're already painting a big star on their turret. Meanwhile, the French Coast is quieting down and there appears to be no more shelling into it and all around us there is darkness and no light or no firing . . . It's now ten past twelve, the beginning of June 7, 1944.[29]

The excitement that the battle reports from Normandy generated in America was in stark contrast to the solemnity of the prayers being offered for the fighting forces seeking to gain a foothold on the European continent. President Roosevelt spoke for each American when he uttered the following prayer over radio:

My fellow Americans, I ask you to join with me in prayer.

Almighty God: Our sons, pride of our Nation, this day have set upon a mighty endeavor, a struggle to preserve our Republic, our religion and our civilization, and to set free a suffering humanity . . . The road will be long and hard. The enemy is strong . . . Success may not come with rushing speed, but we shall return again and again. And we know that by Thy grace, and by the righteousness of our cause, our sons will triumph. They will be sore tried, by night and by day, without rest till victory is won . . . Some will never return. Embrace these, Father, and receive them, Thy heroic servants, into Thy kingdom . . . Thy will be done, Almighty God. Amen.[30]

As Americans listened to the news about D-Day, they knew very little about the mechanics of how it was being transmitted to their country. About a week after the invasion had begun, Edward R. Murrow, European news chief of CBS, gave the nation a brief insight when he described the small cramped space—without windows or ventilation—in the basement of the British Ministry of Information, from which the quickest and most dramatic news of the invasion emerged.

Reporters come in fresh from planes and landing craft, the dust of Normandy still on them. As they sit down at a typewriter, you notice that they look more healthy than the people who have worked in this hotbox since D-Day . . . There are no filing cabinets down here, no desk, just a long table ringed with typewriters. There aren't enough chairs. It's a triumph of cooperation between American networks that no man has yet been forced to write his copy standing up.[31]

From this location the large American networks—Mutual, Blue, NBC, and CBS—put aside their rivalries and reported the biggest story of the war: the invasion of Europe. It was one of American radio's outstanding moments; and it had succeeded at its job.

Bringing Radio to the Soldiers

Via shortwave, radio could even reach Bataan and the beleaguered forces of General Douglas MacArthur and to whom it sent news and recorded programs such as Jack Benny and Bob Hope. In March 1942,

WGAR, a radio station in Cleveland, Ohio, broadcast to Bataan, "Te Deum," composed by Zoltán Kodály in 1936 to celebrate the 250th anniversary of Budapest's emancipation from Turkey. Artur Rodzinski, conductor of the Cleveland Symphony Orchestra, introduced the live program and dedicated it to MacArthur and his men with the words: "To you, our salute and our prayers." Said commentator Kay Halle: "In such moments a hymn of praise and thanksgiving can say more than any words . . ."[32]

In the winter of 1943 after OWI learned that Marines in the Southwest Pacific wanted more news, personal and actual, than they were receiving from home, the agency began to air a program called "Tell It to the Marines," which was broadcast five days a week, fifteen minutes a day. Along with news, music, and gossip, OWI sent the Marines all kinds of personal messages such as

- "Corporal Jones says he will collect that $14 from you. However, if you care to settle in another manner, it's OK. Fourteen Japs will do the trick."
- "Captain Smith went to Springfield to deliver your Navy Cross to your mother . . . just before Christmas."
- "Daddy finally got his new teeth, but instead of wearing them, he carries them around in his pocket."

In addition to the major networks, the armed forces could listen to the Armed Forces Radio Service (AFRS), which was a branch of the Army Morale Division. By 1944, AFRS had established 100 radio stations from Greenland to China. As *Time* magazine noted, "what such programs can mean to GIs was suggested . . . by an AFRSman who had helped set up the Indian network":[33]

I don't care whether you're a highly educated technical officer or the most ignorant draftee. You're sitting in nowhere after a hard day and you have nothing to read but a couple of old magazines you've read ten times. It's raining solidly, so there aren't any movies. The Indian radio is full of Urdua and Hindustani and that monotonous music which drives Caucasians crazy. So you go out and get yourself a bottle and a woman. This may sound silly or sissy or something, but when you turn on your set and hear good old corny Jack Benny and stuff like that, well you might, just might lie back on your cot and relax.

To the men and women abroad, radio was theater, the daily newspaper, and the postman bringing a letter. Radio brought variety shows like "Command Performance," sponsored by the U.S. government and featuring Hollywood and other star performers requested by members of the armed forces. Its master of ceremonies signed off the program in various ways as the singer, Al Jolson observed: "So the Japs want more room. We'll give 'em all the space they want; we'll give 'em hell."[34] Radio carried shows with swing music like "G.I. Jive" and "Downbeat" and other musical programs called "Melody Roundup" and "Personal Album"; and sports programs such as "Sports Review" and "Sports Parade." A counterpart to "Tell It to the Marines" entitled "Calling the Navy" informed its audience of naval activities on the far flung battlefronts. Radio brought "News from Home," a series of national and local news programs.

For security reasons, almost all of these programs were prerecorded because airwaves of the world were wide open and any slip of the tongue could mean a catastrophe. Recorded programs could be played many times, at any time of day. The networks also recorded their own programs to be aired overseas—boxing matches, quiz shows, or radio detective adventures. On the home front, the networks also aired shows produced at service camps or about the military like "The Army Hour," "This is Fort Dix," and "Cheers from the Camps," which originated each week at different military camps and served as a sort of letter to the folks at home and a report to servicemen who were in training elsewhere. By 1943, local radio stations were broadcasting more than 600 camp shows a week. Radio through its various programming efforts became one of the more important elements bonding the American people together at home and abroad during this period of international strife.

Radio Drama

During the early years of the war, especially at the beginning, radio was faced with a basic dilemma. What would make a listener say, "This war must be won. This is my war. I must help win it. I must fight to win it."[35]

Norman Corwin

Within a year after the war began, almost every major network within a space of 24 hours had at least one effective broadcast to raise the nation's morale. Some of these originated from the creative brilliance of Norman Corwin. In a distinguished career that was to span radio, books, films, and television, Mr. Corwin received some of the most honored awards given to any American writer, including a Radio Hall of Fame statuette, an Oscar nomination by the film industry for *Lust for Life*, an Emmy Award (the television industry's equivalent of the Oscar), and two George Foster Peabody Awards for outstanding achievement in broadcasting—the industry's equivalent of the Pulitzer Prize. Though generally regarded as radio's foremost dramatic writer, Norman Corwin was also a director. For example, for drama Corwin directed the thirteen plays of "This Is War!" for the four major networks—CBS, NBC, Mutual, and Blue. The programs had such titles as "The Enemy," "America at War," "Your Army," "The United Nations," "Your Navy," and "Smith Against the Axis." Each week 20 million listeners tuned in. At war's end, just after the surrender of Germany, Mr. Corwin produced a special documentary for V-E Day entitled "On a Note of Triumph," which earned him several prizes for excellence, including the 1946 Wendell Willkie One World Award. The program began with words of jubilation:

> So they've given up.
> They're finally done in, and the rat is dead in an alley back of the Wilhelmstrasse.
> Take a bow G.I.
> Take a bow, little guy.
> The superman of tomorrow lies at the feet of you common men of this afternoon.
> This is It, kid, this is The Day, all the way from Newburyport to Vladivostok.
> You had what it took and you gave it, and each of you has a hunk of rainbow round your helmet.
> Seems like free men have done it again . . .

Sixty minutes later the program ended with a prayer, the conclusion of which read:

Lord God of test-tube and blueprint
Who jointed molecules of dust and shook them till their name was
     Adam,
Who taught worms and stars how they could live together,
Appear now among the parliaments of conquerors and give instruction
     to their schemes:
Measure out new liberties so none shall suffer for his father's color or
     the credo of his choice:
Post proofs that brotherhood is not so wild a dream as those who profit
     by postponing it pretend:
Sit at the treaty table and convoy the hopes of little peoples through
     expected straits,
And press into the final seal a sign that peace will come for longer than
     posterities can see ahead,
That man unto his fellow man shall be a friend forever.[36]

The possibility of the arrival of that day when human beings could live as friends in peace forevermore became more of a reality on August 14, 1945 when Japan accepted the United Nations' terms of unconditional surrender. Once again, Corwin celebrated victory when he wrote and CBS aired on August 14, 1945 the documentary, "Fourteen August," while noting the uncertain future that lay ahead as the world ushered in its newest era, the atomic age ("God and uranium were on our side . . . The wrath of the atom fell like a commandment, and the very planet quivered with implications . . ."). In postwar radio, Corwin was to write one of his very best plays entitled "Document A/777," produced for United Nations Radio in 1950, and which represented his very strong plea for an International Bill of Human Rights.

Office of War Information

"This Is Our Enemy," sponsored and produced by OWI, is another example of the kind of radio drama that aired on the home front and spoke about the war. "We cannot win our war or make our peace unless we understand the character of the enemy we are fighting." The show purported to present the Nazis as they really were, dramatizing their inhumanity and the outrages they committed. The propaganda message of the program was quite clear: "Nazis despise the common man . . . to have such people resist is an affront to them . . . it is not in their pattern of order and obey . . ."[37] Each program promised to add something to the listener's knowledge of the enemy.

Robson and MacDougall

When radio drama during the war years is discussed, two of its most innovative creators must be mentioned—director William N. Robson and writer Ranald R. MacDougall. Together they brought home front listeners to battlefields around the world, be it the British Royal Air Force and the Battle of Britain or the story of the U.S.S. *Boise*. Although a light cruiser, the U.S.S. *Boise* on the night of October 11–12, 1942, sank six Japanese ships, including three Japanese heavy cruisers and two Japanese destroyers in less than 35 minutes in the Battle of Cape Esperance at Guadacanal in the Solomon Islands, before suffering nearly fatal damage herself. In postwar radio, Robson created, directed, wrote, and produced adventure series "Escape," and directed "The CBS Radio Workshop," and "Suspense." MacDougall wrote at least forty screenplays in Hollywood, including *Objective, Burma!*, and he later served as the president of the Screen Writers Guild. The writing genius of Corwin, Robson, and MacDougall is all the more remarkable in that MacDougall was only in his twenties and Robson and Corwin were in their thirties when they created these award-winning radio dramas.

The first collaborative effort of Robson and MacDougall was at CBS and was called "The Twenty-Second Letter," which stood for "V" for victory; it was a series of dramatizations about the underground in occupied countries of Europe. When the series ended, MacDougall created, again with Robson as director, one of the most memorable programs broadcast during World War II—"The Man Behind the Gun." For this program, Robson and MacDougall won the George Foster Peabody Award. In regard to Robson, it was the first of six Peabody Awards he was to receive in his distinguished broadcasting career. Covering the global conflict, the show stated that it was dedicated to the fighting forces of the United States and the United Nations and was presented to inform the American public how their armed forces were waging battles against the Axis aggressors.

But "The Man Behind the Gun" was more than just another wartime radio dramatization. With his keen ear for dialogue and creative inventiveness, MacDougall introduced a new writing style in radio. In this series, he began writing in the second-person singular. For example, when "The Man Behind the Gun" was the skipper of a motor torpedo (PT) boat named "Prep Joe" (which was ordered into action off Savo Island near Guadacanal one night in 1942), MacDougall wrote, in part,

> The boat [PT] snaps around on a dime with a nickel left over and you
> head back toward the [Jap] destroyer. As you turn, you see a tremendous
> blast of flame at the destroyer's waterline. One of your torpedoes hit home
> . . . You go by the destroyer at 40 knots and you can see that she's done
> for. The Jap is split open . . . and she's beginning to roll over. Men are
> jumping into the sea . . .

MacDougall's use of "you" enabled the program's narrator to involve
the radio audience in the story on a very personal level, a style of writing
that was to be emulated by other radio shows in the postwar era.

However, the war not just overseas. Another kind of war was being
fought by and among Americans on the home front and at the heart of
this war was racial prejudice. When wartime drama is mentioned, one of
Robson's programs cannot be ignored because the message it bore is as
relevant today as it was in 1943. The program "Open Letter on Race
Hatred" was inspired by the Detroit race riots of that year, aired over
CBS and won Robson his second Peabody Award. The letter began:

> Dear fellow Americans. What you are about to hear may anger you. What
> you are about to hear may sound incredible to you. You may doubt that
> such things can happen today in this supposedly united nation. But we
> assure you, everything you are about to hear is true. And so, we ask you
> to spend thirty minutes with us facing quietly and without passion or
> prejudice a danger which threatens all of us—a danger so great that if it
> is not met and conquered now, even though we win this war, we shall be
> defeated in victory and the peace which follows will be for us a horror of
> chaos, lawlessness and bloodshed. This danger is Race Hatred! . . .

and closed thirty minutes later:

> We hope this open letter about the irreparable damage race hatred has
> already done to our prestige, our war effort and our self respect will have
> moved you to make a solemn promise to yourself that, wherever you are
> and whatever is your color or your creed, you will never allow intolerance
> or prejudice of any kind to make you forget that you are first of all an
> American with sacred obligations to everyone of your fellow citizens.[38]
>   Sincerely yours, The Columbia Broadcasting System

The program may not have eliminated racism from America's social
fabric, but it certainly warned the nation about the threat such intoler-

ance posed to its social, political, and economic stability, both during the war years and those following its victorious conclusion.

Literary Drama

Radio drama was not only presented in prose but also poetic verse. In addressing the war against totalitarianism, Archibald MacLeish's "Air Raid" warned the democracies that they would have to fight for freedom. Louis MacNeice's "Alexander Nevsky" praised the Russian victory over the Germans, and Edna St. Vincent Millay's "The Murder of Lidice" lashed out against Nazi brutality. When the words of radio drama were good, they were something that the listener could hear, feel, and respond to but could not describe as in these lines of Norman Corwin:

> The stone beneath our feet was good French stone; the wind that drove the rain was a west wind blowing over the fields of France; the sky was a French sky; the rain was a French rain; only the bullets were German.[39]

Sometimes the material was so factual that the listener knew that the added grace of the word, and nothing but the word, made the writing come alive as it was spoken and as the following examples from the "This Is War!" series illustrate. One quotation is an excerpt from George Faulkner's "The United Nations" expressing praise for the Chinese people:

> Could we lose Pittsburgh, and then *move* Pittsburgh under fire to Denver, and go on producing and fighting? Could *we* lose New Haven and Cambridge, and then *move* Yale and Harvard to Salt Lake City, and go on *learning* and fighting?
>
> Could *we* lose New York and New Orleans and then, under fire, cut us a new road through hell and high water to Hudson's Bay—and go on producing and learning and fighting? Could we see *that* road lost and start to build another . . . and another? The Chinese people have accomplished tasks just as hard, with their bare hands, their bowed backs, their tough minds.
>
> To the Chinese people! The Chinese people in the might of their meekness. The Chinese people in the glory of their courage. The Chinese people in the everlasting glory of their utterly unconquerable will to victory.[40]

Or the following piece from Stephen Vincent Benét's "Your Army":

Would you come up to the mike a minute, soldier with the blue hat-cord and the crossed rifles on your collar? Who are you and what's your job?

Infantry: I'm infantry. I'm Private Dogface, private one million, draft number 2985, dog tag number 893,247. Otherwise, I'm just the guy who occupies ground. They land me in planes from the air and they shoot me up to the front in trucks and scout cars . . . but a lot of the time, still, I walk—yes, even with all the wheels and machines of modern war . . . I walk and I creep and I dig and I burrow and I wiggle ahead. I take cover and I creep from cover and hold the line. I hide all day in the foxholes under the bombings, and last out.

I marched with the Continentals and I marched with the Army of the Valley, and in France I went ahead through the wheat, and I'm still marching.

I'm blind without planes and you've got to give me planes—I can't fight tanks with my hands and you've got to give me tanks—I'm not artillery and you've got to give me guns—but when all's said and done, I'm the guy who holds the ground.

I'm not just a foot-slogger with a rifle in this new army—I'm a member of a combat team, trained like a football squad and with plenty of razzle-dazzle stuff—the Notre Dame stuff and the Army stuff and the Rose Bowl stuff of modern war. But my first job is to take the ground and hold the ground. I may do it forty miles an hour—I may do it two miles a day. I'm going to get cold and wet and hungry and thirsty and tired beyond tiredness. I'm going to see my friends die and hear the wounded cry out like a whispering field. But I'm going ahead and I'm going to win—the ground-gripper—the Private Dogface of the U.S. Army.[41]

Or consider the following excerpt entitled "Smith Against the Axis," from a "This Is War" dramatization written by MacDougall:

NARRATOR: Put another pin in Iceland [in a map], and while you're in the neighborhood, one in Ireland. And then get yourself a whole lot of pins and stick them in wherever fighting's going on . . . by the time you're through you'll have a pin cushion . . . and some idea of what war is these days. From wherever you live . . . in any direction . . . three or four or five or six thousand miles away somebody is fighting somebody else, and it's all the same war . . . the same fight . . . decency versus Hitler . . . honesty versus Yamashito . . . freedom versus slavery . . . Smith against

the Axis. Who's this guy Smith? You're Smith. Whatever your name is—
whatever you do—you're Smith . . . the People. You're everywhere, you
Smiths of the world.[42]

These were words listeners heard on wartime radio—simple, universal, and dramatic—the kinds of words that were intended to uplift a
people to fight and win a war they never sought.

Programming for Children

Not all dramatic programs to spur America's war effort were of a
serious nature. Some were pure escapism and written especially for children. Who can ever forget a few lively bars of the William Tell Overture
and the wild, hypertensive cry of "Hi-Yo Silver! Away!" as the Lone
Ranger ("the masked rider of the plains") and his faithful Indian companion, Tonto, rode each week into America's living rooms fighting for
justice in the old American West. On another radio network rode Red
Ryder ("America's famous fighting cowboy"). Red, who lived in the
western settlement of Painted Valley with his aunt, "the Duchess," his
partner Buckskin, and his Indian ward Little Beaver ("You betchum Red
Ryder"), galloped over the airwaves each week on his horse Thunder to
the music of the "The Dying Cowboy." Children could also listen to
daily dramatic serials such as Dick Tracy, Superman, and of course, Jack
Armstrong, "the All American Boy," an excellent example of how children's programs were used to help the country's war effort. As reported
by *Newsweek*, Jack was the kind of boy who "travelling to the four corners of the globe . . . rubbed elbows with Tibetan lamas, tracked the
arch-villain Lazarro to his Central American hide-out, made a mad bull
elephant in Indo-China say uncle, and escaped from a Philippine cave
tastefully filled with mummies." In addition, "on Speza Island off Casablanca . . . Jack and his friends—Uncle Jim and Billy and Betty Fair-
field—battled Nazis trying to capture the island. The Spanish garrison
had been doped, but Armstrong and Co. somehow held the fort."[43] In
the world of reality, Jack Armstrong made serious contributions to the
war effort. By 1943, the Jack Armstrong Write-A-Fighter Corps had
more than one million members. They pledged to send one letter a
month to a member of the armed forces, collect scrap, plant Victory

Gardens, and sell war bonds and stamps.[44] In this fashion, radio mobilized the children of the nation to contribute to the war effort.

Radio Comedy

Radio also tried to help Americans laugh and momentarily forget their wartime problems and, in this regard, it did more than its share. In fact, the majority of the most popular programs were comedy. Their stars included Bob Hope, Red Skelton, Jack Benny, Fred Allen, George Burns and Gracie Allen, Eddie Cantor, Groucho Marx, Freeman F. Gosden and Charles J. Correll ("Amos 'n' Andy"), Ed Wynn ("the Perfect Fool"), Hal Peary ("The Great Gildersleave"), and Jim and Marion Jordan, also known as "Fibber McGee and Molly."

"Fibber McGee and Molly" integrated a public service message into the show's story line in such a way that the message was enjoyable to hear and, at the same time, gave its listeners a laugh. Entire programs covered serious subjects ranging from the black market to mileage rationing without harming the show's ratings. Set in the fantasy town of Wistful Vista, the show was peopled with such characters as Wallace Wimple, the quintessential wimp who was tyrannized "by my big old wife, Sweetie-face"; the Old Timer; Teeny, the neighborhood child who drove Fibber crazy; and the apoplectic Mayor Latrivia. As the name implies, Fibber began as a tall-tale-spinning windbag from the tradition of Paul Bunyan or Davy Crockett. He evolved into the town bungler and laughing stock as well. His hall closet—one of the all-time great running gags of radio—constantly overloaded with household goods. At one time burglars tied him up and demanded to know where the family valuables were. In the hall closet, of course, which, when opened, buried them until the police arrived. Molly's favorite expressions of "Tain't funny, McGee" and "Heavenly Days" along with Fibber's "Dad-ratted" response to adversity became part of America's wartime language. The following dialogue from a War Production Board program demonstrates how this comedy show, like many others, was used to further the war effort on the home front:

> Fibber McGee: This mileage rationing has got me disgusted.
>
> Molly: You know, he's been raving about it all day, Mr.

Hitler, Hirohito, and Mussolini are pictured as a three-headed snake. In World War II posters, snakes symbolized deceit, danger, and death. *(Courtesy of Library of Congress)*

Lidice was a small Czech mining village that the Nazis destroyed in retaliation for the assassination of Reinhard Heydrich—the Deputy Gestapo Chief and former Reich Protector of Bohemia-Moravia. The destruction of Lidice and the fate of its occupants were a preview of the Nazis' crimes against humanity, which would be discovered at war's end. *(Courtesy of Library of Congress)*

Americans participated in all kinds of scrap drives during the war. The Boy Scouts collected 109 million pounds of rubber, 23 million pounds of tin, and more than 370 million pounds of scrap metal. *(Courtesy of Library of Congress)*

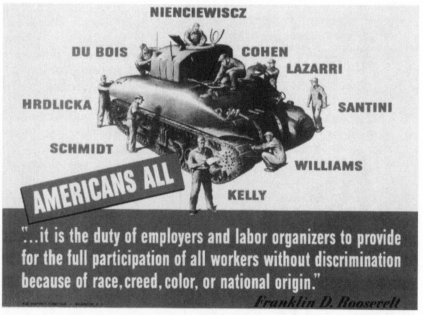

The war opened up new employment opportunities. Persons of all races and ethnicities migrated to cities seeking jobs in defense plants and were confronted with their own prejudices and conflicts. Posters attempted to ameliorate these societal divisions by declaring that we were all Americans working together. *(Courtesy of Library of Congress)*

In 1942, under orders from the U.S. government the automobile industry ceased the production of new automobiles for the duration of the war and converted its assembly lines to the manufacture of tanks, guns, planes, and other weapons. The public was urged to take care of their automobiles as in this Texaco Inc. advertisement. The "A" sticker, meaning general use, on the upper right hand corner of the windshield indicated family's weekly gasoline allowance. Also, notice that prewar cars came with running boards and some had rumble seats in back which not only carried groceries but also passengers. (©1943 Texaco Inc. Reprinted with permission from Texaco Inc.)

During 1942, Hitler's threat to America was real. German submarines landed saboteurs on our shores and sank American vessels off the Gulf and Atlantic Coasts, some within view of our citizens. Hitler controlled the European continent from Scandinavia in the north to North Africa in the south, from France in the west to vast stretches of Russia in the east. America had to be aroused to dangers of Fascism as public polls revealed that Americans did not understand why we were fighting the Germans or what was at stake if the Nazis were to win. *(Courtesy of Library of Congress)*

"We shall soon have our Storm Troopers in America!"
—HITLER

What do YOU say, AMERICA?

The U.S. Army published posters based upon actual events of the war to unify the public against the Axis enemy and to spur home front production. This poster illustrates the Japanese brutality toward American and other prisoners of war during the "March of Death on Bataan." *(Courtesy of Library of Congress)*

What are YOU going to do about it?

5200 Yank Prisoners Killed by Jap Torture In Philippines; Cruel 'March of Death' Described

STAY ON THE JOB UNTIL EVERY MURDERING JAP IS WIPED OUT!

To increase food production on the American home front, both the government and industry encouraged the public to plant victory gardens. This poster stresses several themes: The planting of victory gardens, the role of women in the war effort, and the attractiveness of gardening clothes to encourage gardening. *(Courtesy of Library of Congress)*

"Remember December 7th" was more than just a slogan. The words were translated into a popular song entitled "Remember Pearl Harbor." *(Courtesy of Library of Congress)*

Wartime production and victory depended upon the cooperation of management and labor to produce, in the words of another popular song, "Arms for the Love of America." Here, the American worker through his own production efforts has Hirohito and Hitler, who is leading Mussolini by the nose, on the run. *(Courtesy of Library of Congress)*

Music played an indispensable role in helping America finance the war effort. "Any Bonds Today?" and similar tunes reminded the public to continue purchasing war bonds and war stamps in the 7th War Loan Drive in 1945. *(Courtesy of Library of Congress)*

Wartime music addressed many themes, as expressed by such songs as "Shhh, It's A Military Secret." *(Courtesy of Library of Congress)*

The Minute Man of the American Revolution was a popular symbol on the home front. For example, the image was displayed on war stamps and the war savings flag, which flew over a plant to signify that 10 percent of a company's gross payroll was voluntarily being invested in war bonds. *(Courtesy of Library of Congress)*

Dr. Joseph Goebbels' Ministry of Propaganda and Enlightenment broadcast many kinds of messages to America. This poster summarizes many of the Nazi themes that were intended to sow discord and dissension in American society and weaken America's resolve to carry on the war. *(Courtesy of Library of Congress)*

	Wilcox (program announcer). He thinks the OPA is trying to make an A-P-E out of him.
Fibber:	And they are too. A citizen of my standing, trying to get along on an "A" book. It's a lot of foolishness. I've got business to take care of.
Wilcox:	What business, pal?
Fibber:	Well, in the first place I've got . . . well gee whiz, I've got responsibilities.
Molly:	No, he really has Mr. Wilcox.
Fibber:	Yesss!
Wilcox:	Fibber, you talk like a chump.
Fibber:	Huh?
Wilcox:	Yes! Mileage rationing is the only fair way to cut down nonessential driving. When the rubber this country has got is gone, it's gone. That's all there is. There isn't anymore.
Fibber:	Well, they should have foreseen that and took care of the situation.
Molly:	Well, not everyone can be as farsighted as you, deary.
Wilcox:	Is he pretty farsighted, Molly?
Molly:	Why he's uncanny Mr. Wilcox. He's the one who said we'd lick the Japanese in ten days, remember?
Fibber:	Well, shucks.
Molly:	He's the one who said Germany would fold up from starvation last April.
Fibber:	I know, but circumstances . . .
Molly:	He's the one who said we'd never ship a soldier out of this country. I don't know how he does it. But I will say he made one accurate prediction.
Wilcox:	What was that?
Molly:	Well, last night he said, "well tomorrow is another day" and sure enough it was.[45]

Well, the listeners had their laughs, but between the moments of humor the dialogue also delivered a very serious and important message:

Namely, forget any illusions about easy victories over the enemy. This is going to be a long, hard fought war. Americans must be willing to endure personal sacrifices and hardships and begin putting the country's interests above their own personal desires if they are to achieve victory. This too was how radio united the nation behind the war effort.

However, not all radio comedy was based on fantasy towns like Fibber McGee and Molly's Wistful Vista and the situations its inhabitants encountered. Some were based on the news of the day. As Will Rogers once noted about this kind of comedy, "As long as anything happens, we can make a living." One proponent of this concept was Fred Allen who took a few typical folks like Mr. Rappaport and Falstaff, his poet floreate, and placed them in Allen's Alley (the equivalent of the man-on-the-street interview), putting into their mouths a satire or commentary about current events. One night in 1942 on NBC, Falstaff declaimed the following poem about the U.S. Office of Price Stabilization (OPA): "The OPA Had a Word for It."

> Our language has a new word
> You hear it every day
> It's R-A-T-I-O-N
> It's a word that's here to stay.
> I don't dislike this new word
> I'd rather not denounce it
> I'd prefer not to use the word
> till I know how to pronounce it.
> I hear it on my radio
> The announcer says its ra(h)tion
> He even spells it out for me in true moronic fashion.
> I hear a college man expound
> He insists the word is ra(y)tion
> The college man defines it, says it's simply conservation.
> Is it ra(y)tion, is it ra(h)tion?
> I wish I knew, alas,
> 'Cause they're doing it to sugar and they're doing it to gas.
> How it's pronounced don't matter
> Call it ra(h)tion, call it ra(y)tion
> By either name I'm for it
> If this word will help our nation.[46]

While these nonsophisticates made Americans laugh with their opinions of world events, listeners also could tune in to laugh at real dummies—the creation of ventriloquist Edgar Bergen who with his entourage of Charlie McCarthy, Mortimer Snerd, and Effie Klinker starred on the "Chase and Sanborn [coffee] Hour" each Sunday evening—a night when they could also hear other comedians like Jack Benny and Fred Allen.

Wartime radio comedy cannot be mentioned without noting "Amos 'n' Andy," one of radio's longest running programs and one with the largest following. Originating in 1928, it was radio's first great national program. Each evening for a few moments, the entire nation almost came to a halt as it listened to their adventures. "Amos 'n' Andy" operated Harlem's Fresh-Air-Taxi Company of America, Inc., so-called because its only taxi had no windshield. Andy ran the company and chased the girls while the more stable, married Amos did most of the work. They belonged to the "Mystic Knights of the Sea Lodge," of which George Stevens, a con artist, was "The Kingfish." Amos 'n' Andy were the chief pioneers of getting an audience to develop the habit of listening to a program night after night. Although not black themselves, Charles J. Correll and Freeman F. Gosden were said to have captured the black culture through skillful narration and characterization.

The Washboard Weepers

Wartime radio could also make Americans worry and despair each day when they tuned in on the washboard weepers—known today as "soap operas." These programs were so named because they were largely sponsored by soap manufacturers. As noted in *Newsweek*, "unmitigated tripe . . . drivel . . . As corny as succotash . . . They have scummed the emotional sewers" are examples of the kinds of criticisms these program have received.[47] But, the soap operas, which had been denounced since their beginnings in the 1930s, continued to flourish during the war years and had many names. These included "The Romance of Helen Trent," "Portia Faces Life," "The Guiding Light," "Just Plain Bill," "Ma Perkins," "The Right to Happiness," "The Right to Life," "The Road to Life," "Young Doctor Malone," "Second Husband," "Bachelor's Children," "Stella Dallas," and "Pepper Young's Family."

Not all soap operas were denounced. As *Newsweek* also noted, some such as . . . "Against the Storm . . . won praise, blue ribbons, and [in 1942] the Peabody Award for dramatic presentation. Radio editors talked up its literate quality, its war conscious continuity . . .”[48] The story concerned the life of Dr. Jason McKinley Allen, an American college professor, who tried to alert his students and the world to the Nazi danger. However, the program was canceled in 1942, after airing for only three years.

Wartime soap operas had many common denominators. Their characters were trapped by troubles, struggling with frustration and failure. Along with the suffering heroine, there was usually a benign matron who gave everyone advice on how to resolve their problems, even though she too, on occasion, suffered. Men often were portrayed in unflattering images; designing women could manipulate them; they did not understand the deeper meaning of life, worked six days a week at the office, and always fell for the secretary. Few programs could progress very far without an episode ending up in the courtroom or in a hospital, mental institution, or other medical facility. The characters experienced every kind of medical disease including amnesia, blindness, heart problems, and appendicitis.

An organist was an essential program item, as music bridged the gap from one scene to another. Program announcers tended to be philosophers. They would open an episode with a wise aphorism such as, “No matter what your hope, never can you find happiness so completely as by bringing joy into the lives of others.” Or the announcer might begin a program by stating its central question as in “Our Gal Sunday” where he would proclaim that “the story asks the question: Can this girl from the little mining town of Silver Creek, Colorado find happiness as the wife of a wealthy and titled Englishman?” (Lord Henry Brinthrope whose manor, Black Swann Hall, like the site of the story was located in the state of Virginia.) Again, in “The Romance of Helen Trent” cue announcer Fielden Farrington against a backdrop of a chorus humming “Juanita” proclaimed: “Time now for the ‘Romance of Helen Trent’ who, when life mocks her, breaks her hopes, dashes her against the rocks of despair, fights back bravely, successfully to prove what so many women long to prove in their lives: That because a woman is 35 and more, romance in life need not be over; that the romance of youth can extend into middle age and even beyond” (humming of “Juanita” now reaches a crescendo). Or after the opening chords of the organ and the program aphorism, another announcer in a tense voice against a quivering organ chord would proclaim: “And now the Right to Happiness” (the dramatic story of the Kramers, a family that moved from the slums to a respectable neighborhood, and their attempts to find happiness). A soap opera episode would always conclude with a "teaser or come along," as in the case of the woman who was tricked into believing she was legally married but found herself pregnant by a man other than her supposed husband at which point the announcer would ask: "And what lies ahead for this unwanted baby? Listen to tomorrow's episode and hear the surprising opinion of the doctor."[49]

Surprisingly, into this soap opera setting, which critics described as depressing, salacious and dreadful, came the U.S. government. In April 1942, the War Department began to air its own soap opera called "Chaplain Jim—U.S.A." The purpose of the program was to help loved ones understand the everyday problems of servicemen who were now being parted from their families and friends. The program also tried to reassure listeners that when confronted with personal problems a serviceman could turn to his chaplain for pastoral advice and comfort. The show was "dedicated to mothers, wives, sweethearts and families of men who wear the khaki of the United States Army." Jim was usually there after the show to remind listeners to send that "daily cheerful letter" to a soldier overseas.[50]

Soap operas performed an important function in American society, especially during the stress of wartime life. They dealt with problems with which the ordinary listener (mostly women) could identify and tried to offer solutions within the context of the never-ending story. Soap operas presupposed that the listener's mind—conscious and subconscious—was filled more with memories of loneliness, frustration, and unrealized romantic encounters than with memories of past happiness or current fulfillment. The programs presumed that the great mass of humanity—women being far worse off than men—was poor, troubled and tired; untalented without a future and insecure; or adventuresome and vain. Soap operas took their listeners into their own problems or those of others who were far worse off (which was even better from the viewpoint of morale.) The shows gave listeners two constant and frequently simultaneous choices—participation or escape. Both worked.[51] The radio serial, created during the Depression of the 1930s, was a marvelous success because it furnished just what the nation demanded: the rationalization of national frustration, whether it was during times of war or peace.

Suspense, Thrills, and Chills

Crime and mystery shows also grew in popularity during the war years. In many instances, the program scripts were heavily influenced by the war. "Alias John Freedom" was about a modern Scarlet Pimpernel who aided those suffering from Axis oppression. In "Counterspy," David Harding, a government agent, thwarted the best laid plans of Axis saboteurs. In the world of reality, American counterspies conducted counter-espionage against the German Gestapo, Italy's Zobra, and the Black Dragon Society of Japan. "Mr. District Attorney" aimed at the authentic rather than the macabre in crimes; in June 1942 the program aired an episode in which the radio District Attorney struggled with a group of Nazi agents who had landed on these shores by submarine ten days before the FBI announced the real-life capture of eight Nazi saboteurs who had landed the same way.

Radio's mysteries were solved by many kinds of detectives. Some were married couples like "Mr. and Mrs. North" or Nick and Nora Charles in the "Adventures of the Thin Man," created by Dashiell Hammett, who solved cases with wit and sophistication. Others liked to work alone like "Ellery Queen," "Bulldog Drummond," "Charlie Chan," "Michael Shayne," and "Mr. Keen, Tracer of Lost Persons."

Of course, crime solvers of the war years cannot be noted without mentioning "The Shadow" ("Who knows what evil lurks in the hearts of men? The Shadow knows! Heh! heh! heh! heh!")—an invincible fellow named Lamont Cranston, a wealthy man-about-town, who, while on a trip to the Orient, learned the secret of a hypnotic power to cloud men's minds so as to become invisible. Together with Margo Lane, his girlfriend, and Police Commissioner Weston, the Shadow brought criminals to justice with his secret knowledge. The Shadow then ended each program with the following aphorism: "The weed of crime bears bitter fruit. Crime does not pay. The Shadow knows! Heh! heh! heh! heh!"

Not all radio chillers were detective stories. Some like "Lights Out" portrayed the occult; "The Inner Sanctum," which opened each show with an eerie squeaking door, had program themes of lust, hate, horror, and paranoia; "Suspense," beginning with the revival of crime novels that had passed from the best-seller list, went on to original plays; and "Dark Destiny" was based on the somber premise that some lives were foredoomed.

And the Answer is . . .

One kind of program that contributed to the war effort mostly made its listeners think and, depending upon the show's format, laugh as well. This was the quiz show with such names as "Dr. I.Q.," "Information Please," "Take It or Leave It," "Transatlantic Quiz," and "Truth or Consequences."

"Truth or Consequences" followed a simple formula—if contestants failed to answer a question correctly, they had to pay a consequence, for example, the man who had to diaper a pig as his first lesson in caring for a baby. This program was probably the only audience participation show where a correct quiz answer left the contestant disappointed. Participants considered it more fun to pay a consequence and receive $5 than to tell the "truth" and collect $15. Beginning with only four stations and a few thousand listeners in 1940, "Truth or Consequences" grew to 20 million listeners and was aired over 128 radio stations by 1944.

Perhaps the most startling element of the show's success lay in its adaptability to various government war drives. Regularly, the government requested all radio programs to advertise its current drive, whatever it may have been, and left the method to the producers. For example, listeners heard government appeals like:

The government has asked us to call to your attention a serious situation. We are short nine million pounds a month of the kitchen fats and greases needed to keep fat reserves at a safe level. These reserves must be brought to the safety level at once. And there is only one person who can do the job—the American housewife. Remember, one pound of waste fat makes enough glycerine to fire four 37-millimeter anti-aircraft shells or to make three cellophane gas mask bags. Please start saving waste fats now. Just pour it into a tin can. Store it in a cool place and turn it into your meat dealer the minute the can is full. Start saving fats now. Turn them in promptly.

As *Newsweek* noted, Ralph "Edwards, the creator and master of ceremonies of 'Truth or Consequences,' saw his chance and turned the requests into the consequence of his little parlor game. Net result: everybody got a big laugh and the government got what it was after . . . ."[52] Some examples included:

• Fats: "Truth or Consequences" was playing in Dallas, Texas when Ralph Edwards thought up his answer to the government's need for waste fats. He imprisoned a local man (a genuine 300 pounder) in the local city hall until the people of Dallas could bail him out with his weight in waste fats. Before the night ended, citizens turned in 600 pounds of waste fats and 20 million listeners had a happy reminder of their wartime duty.

• Waste Paper: In 1943, Ralph Edwards announced that he would take his radio show to the grade school or high school that collected the most waste paper on a per capita basis. A month later, he moved the show to Brookfield, Missouri, to a one-room school house with twelve pupils, each of whom had collected an average of 22,833 pounds of waste paper, aided by the townspeople, their hay wagons and mules. The grand countrywide total for the schools was 43,567,715 pounds.[53]

By 1944, Ralph Edwards had taken his radio show on extensive tours to sell war bonds and had succeeded in raising $200 million to finance the war effort.

Another popular quiz program during the war years was "Information Please," more erudite than "Truth or Consequences," but just as entertaining. Listeners would send in questions in an attempt to stump a panel of experts consisting of Franklin P. Adams, the journalist; John Kiernan, the sports columnist; Oscar Levant, the pianist; and a guest panelist; the program was moderated by Clifton Fadiman, literary critic. When Heinz 57 Varieties sponsored the program, a listener was awarded $57 in war bonds and stamps as well as a set of the *Encyclopedia Britannica* for any question the panel could not answer. This program was so popular that people purchased war bonds rather than tickets for admittance to the show. In December 1942, the show raised $3.8 million in war bonds alone in Boston. An orchestra seat sold for a $5,000 bond, while a balcony seat could be purchased for a $50 bond. Because of the program's high educational tenor, the *Saturday Review of Literature* gave the show an award for "distinguished service to literature."

Quiz shows even tried to improve America's foreign relations. In "Transatlantic Quiz," experts from America and England would try to confound each other by testing their knowledge of each other's country. The purpose of the show was to promote Anglo-American understanding with geniality instead of jokes and cash awards. In this instance, radio served another wartime purpose by improving the listeners' understanding of other nations, bolstering their morale through entertainment, serving as an educational medium, and raising funds for the war effort.

Another way radio made its audience think, along with the quiz show format, was through its airing of public service and affairs programs.

Public Service Medium

Public affairs programming came in a variety of formats during the war years. To clarify the events of the day, some came in the style of documentaries like "Report to the Nation," which took its audience in B-17 Flying Fortress bombers, dramatized Lend-Lease, and covered the reaction of farmers in the Tennessee Valley to America's defense program, among many topics. Others were public affairs discussion programs like "America's Town Meeting of the Air" and "For This We Fight," which dealt with national and international issues confronting the nation in the postwar world. Some were aired as book discussions about the issues the publication raised. Each week "Words on War" presented a half-hour dramatization of important war books. In "Radio Reader," a portion of a book was read to its readers; in "Invitation to Learning," guest speakers discussed great books of literature and the relevance of the books to wartime conditions, where appropriate. In airing public affairs programs whether in the form of a documentary, roundtable discussion, or book format, radio confronted the issue of how to present complex intellectual issues to lay listeners of a nonintellectual bent so that they would listen in such numbers as to justify the regular airing of the program. Those who did listen to the variety of public affairs programs were richer for the experience and learned where their country stood in the complex labyrinth of world affairs, how it got there, and where it was headed in the postwar world.

A Changed Medium

The war years brought about many changes in radio. When Franklin D. Roosevelt spoke to the nation after the attack on Pearl Harbor, Americans listened to his broadcast over three radio networks—CBS, the Mutual Broadcasting System (MBS) and NBC. By the time the war had ended, listeners heard the news over four networks—the newest being the Blue Network. During the war, the Federal Communication Commission after studying monopoly charges against CBS and NBC ordered NBC to divest itself and sell either its Red or Blue Network. Today, the Blue Network, which NBC sold, is the American Broadcasting Company. Near the end of World War II, six television stations were in operation throughout the country, and FM (frequency modulation) radio, with forty-six stations in operation, was beginning to compete with the 900 standard AM (amplitude modulation) radio stations then in existence.[54]

Although radio was not sure of its role when America entered World War II, the medium had become a veteran of many different kinds of experiences by the time the war ended. Radio set up shortwave stations to beam propaganda into enemy territories. America sent special broadcasts abroad to improve goodwill and understanding among its allies. Through radio, listeners flew in aircraft, patrolled in submarines beneath the seas, and sailed on aircraft carriers, destroyers, and other naval vessels, and participated in many land battles throughout the world. Radio took its listeners into war plants, shipyards, and other industrial sites where the "Arsenal of Democracy" was being built and showed them individually and collectively how their efforts were contributing to victory. Radio explained to its audience the progress of the war and the implications of the events of the day through its correspondents and commentators whose interpretation represented various perspectives according to their political hues—H. V. Kaltenborn, Fulton Lewis, Drew Pearson, Elmer Davis, Quincy Howe, and Lowell Thomas, to name just a few. Radio broadcast and recorded the nadir of America's wartime experiences when Pearl Harbor was bombed, Corregidor fell, and Franklin D. Roosevelt died. America was there when Arthur Godfrey described with choking emotion the funeral procession on April 14, 1945, in Washington, D.C., two days after the president's death:

> There is the flag draped . . . coffin, resting on this black caisson, the horses with black blankets under their saddles. You'll see this . . . in the pictorial news pictures in the . . . the Movietone newses, I hope. And behind us is the car bearing . . . the successor to the late President Roosevelt . . . God bless him, President Truman. We return you now to the studios.[55]

Radio also proclaimed the zenith of wartime joys when the Allies invaded Europe on D-Day and when V-E and V-J Days finally arrived. America was also listening on August 14, 1945 when Bob Trout announced on CBS the surrender of Japan with the following words:

> 7:00 P.M. Eastern Wartime, Bob Trout reporting. The Japanese have accepted our terms fully. That's the word we've just received from the White House in Washington. This, ladies and gentlemen, is the end of the Second World War. The United Nations on land, on the sea, in the air and to the four corners of the earth are united and are victorious.[56]

Radio was everywhere—at home, at work, and in the automobile. Listeners were only as far away from news, entertainment, laughter, tears, and mystery as the flick of a switch. Wartime radio was all things to all listeners. It had something of interest for each member of its audience whether a home front civilian or a serviceman or woman either at home or abroad. When radio went to war, it could not ignore its responsibility of informing Americans about the reality of battle, but it did try to maintain a nation's morale through its programming efforts. Radio continued to be the country's principal medium of entertainment until the early 1950s when television's ascendancy became dominant. As an unseen world whose words became pictures in the listener's imagination, it is improbable that the likes of wartime radio will ever be heard again.

Notes

1. Norman Corwin, "Radio and Morale," *Saturday Review of Literature*, July 4, 1942, 6.

2. Ibid.

3. David G. Wittels, "Hitler's Short-Wave Rumor Factory," *Saturday Evening Post*, November 21, 1942, 12.

4. S. Wolf, "Berlin-Rome-Tokyo Propaganda," *Contemporary Review Advertiser*, October 1942, 218.

5. Wittels, 12, 118.

6. Ibid., 13.

7. Ibid., 122.

8. Ibid.

9. William L. Shirer, "The American Radio Traitors," *Harper's Magazine*,

October 1943, 347 and John O. Rennie, "Dr. Goebbel's Awkward Squad," *Atlantic Monthly*, September 1943, 107, 109.

10. Mildred Gillars was paroled in 1961, Douglas Chandler was pardoned by President Kennedy in 1963, and Ezra Pound, after spending 13 years in a federal mental hospital, was released in 1958 and returned to Italy where he spent the remaining days of his life. William Joyce was tried and hanged by the British in 1946.

11. "World War 2," Sounds of History: Allied Turncoats Broadcast for Axis Powers, National Archives, Washington, D.C., 1980.

12. Wittels, 122.

13. Ibid.

14. Wolf, 220.

15. Shirer, 403.

16. Wittels, 123.

17. Iva Ikuko Toguri D'Aquino was convicted of treason in the United States on October 6, 1949, sentenced to 10 years in prison, fined $10,000 and pardoned by President Gerald Ford on January 19, 1977.

18. "World War 2", Sounds of History: Allied Turncoats Broadcast for Axis Powers, National Archives, Washington, D.C., 1980.

19. "Stout Truth," *Newsweek*, December 7, 1942, 99.

20. U.S. Bureau of the Budget, "The United States at War," Washington, D.C., June 19, 1946, 207.

21. Ibid., 208.

22. "Air Brakes," *Newsweek*, January 26, 1942, 67.

23. Robert T. Colwell, "Radio Luxembourg," *Life*, March 4, 1945, 17–18.

24. Ibid.

25. WOR-AM, New York.

26. National Broadcasting Company, New York.

27. "Blow-by-Blow War Report," *Newseek*, November 2, 1942, 84.

28. National Broadcasting Company, New York.

29. Ibid.

30. Ibid.

31. Columbia Broadcasting System, New York.

32. WGAR-FM, Cleveland, Ohio.

33. "Mosquito Network," *Time*, July 17, 1944, 89.

34. Larry Wolters, "Command Performance for A.E.F.," *Reader's Digest*, October 1942, 115.

35. Frederick Morton, "Radio Propaganda: New Style," *Theatre Arts*, February 1943, 96–97.

36. Norman Corwin, *On A Note of Triumph*, (New York: Simon and Schuster, 1945), 9, 70–71 and as broadcast by Columbia Broadcasting System, May 8, 1945.

37. John Dunning, "Tune in Yesterday: The Ultimate Encyclopaedia of Old-Time Radio, 1925–1970 (Englewood Cliffs, N.J.: Prentice-Hall, 1976), 603 and Frank Buxton and Bill Owen, "The Big Broadcast 1920–1950 (New York: The Viking Press, 1972), 238.

38. William N. Robson, "Open Letter on Race Hatred," *Theatre Arts*, September 1944, 537, 552.

39. Morton, 96–97.

40. Ibid., 100.

41. Ibid., 100–101.

42. Ibid. 102.

43. "Jack the Nazi Killer," *Newsweek*, August 23, 1943, 80.

44. Ibid.

45. "World War 2," Sounds of History: American Radio Mobilizes for the Homefront, National Archives, Washington, D.C. 1980.

46. Fred Allen program, National Broadcasting Company, 1942.

47. "Scented Soap," *Newsweek*, July 5, 1943, 100.

48. Ibid.

49. Maurice Zolotow, "Washboard Weepers," *Saturday Evening Post*, May 29, 1943, 16, 46, 48, 52.

50. John Dunning, op. cit., 124.

51. Max Wylie, "Washboard Weepers," *Harper's Magazine*, November 1942, 634–635.

52. "War and Consequences," *Newsweek*, April 10, 1944, 82.

53. Ibid.

54. Paul A. Walker, "American Radio After the War," *Vital Speeches of the Day*, December 15, 1944, 151.

55. "World War 2," Sounds of History: American Radio Mobilizes the Homefront, National Archives, Washington, D.C., 1980.

56. Ibid.

Chapter Four

MUSIC
The Songs We Sang

I F MUSIC CAN BE SAID to reflect a nation's spirit, then its lyrics can be said to mirror a nation's soul. The music of a nation demonstrates, as nothing else, the inner feelings of its people—their temperament, hopes, fears, and way of life. In wartime, especially, music can surpass proclamations and oratory in rallying a country to a cause. There has never been a major American war that did not produce at least one major war song. Even Vietnam, the most divisive war in America's history, produced "The Ballad of the Green Berets." Going back in history, the Revolutionary War gave the colonists "Yankee Doodle." The War of 1812 inspired "The Star-Spangled Banner." The Civil War produced many popular songs, including "Just Before the Battle Mother" and "Tenting on the Old Camp Ground." Fifty years later in World War I, the United States and its military forces inspired the world with another song, George M. Cohan's "Over There." General John "Blackjack" Pershing said that "Over There" was one of the potent factors that turned the tide of that war. Its lyrics sent a wave of hope, a will to win through the entire Allied forces.[1] A generation later, World War II was no exception as music influenced America's fighting spirit at home and abroad.

A song of war is often long remembered when other media have been forgotten. It outlives the spoken word. While thousands of speeches may be made during periods of stress and tons of printed material scattered about, most are soon forgotten but the songs invariably carry on. During trying times, music can offer courage and hope because composers usually put courage into their music. Search through the works of great composers; few reflect negative, pessimistic attitudes toward life. Noth-

113

ing is so stirring as martial band music. At the same time, nothing is so soothing to troubled spirits as a fine melody nor so confidence building as a great hymn.

The Earliest War Music

William Allen White, the eminent journalist, once wrote: "The nation that can sing and make joyful noise before the Lord has the spirit of victory in its heart."[2] However, when America officially entered World War II, its voices were silent, and its spirit grim. Six months after Pearl Harbor, there was hardly a musical number, either in America or abroad, that would have been nominated for everlasting fame. America had yet to achieve a stirring victory that might have inspired a dynamic war song, but everyone was trying to write it. Before December 1941, radio networks banned militant songs, and songwriters were limited to such patriotic tunes as Irving Berlin's "God Bless America" or defense songs like his "Any Bonds Today?" When the Japanese bombs fell at Pearl Harbor, America's songwriters, however, went into action. After Pearl Harbor, no holds were barred. Every songwriter, music publisher, and record company rushed to write, publish, and record *the* war song of World War II.

Even before Congress officially declared war on Japan on December 8th, songwriters, in demonstrating America's musical bravado, had already composed "We'll Knock the Japs Right into the Laps of the Nazis" and "You're A Sap, Mr. Jap." At that time the scope of the war and the devastation it was to bring were still unknown. On December 16, 1941, five days after Germany and Italy declared war on the United States, Decca Records released the record, "We Did It Before (And We Can Do It Again)," which pleaded for unity against the Axis powers as memories of the isolationist policies of prewar America lingered in many minds. Eddie Cantor, comedian and singer, used the song in *Banjo Eyes*, a Broadway musical, which opened on Christmas Day 1941; it was performed throughout the war.

Many tunes, especially the "slap-the-Japs" songs died as fast as they were published. None caught the public's mood. Songwriters, and even the government propaganda departments, were becoming restless about the war song situation. With each passing day, America's leaders became more impatient for the arrival of the great hit anthem that would take the Allied world by storm and spread like a tuneful rash.

From the moment America officially entered World War II, Tin Pan Alley (another name for the New York music publishing industry) thought that the conflict would be like World War I. They expected to compose the songs that would stir the nation's spirit and let other accidental war songs become popular by themselves. But Tin Pan Alley was no longer the incubator for developing composers, writing and promoting songs to meet the public's changing mood, promoting new songs through song pluggers and discovering new talent, or finding the right performer to introduce and popularize a song. After 1930 the movie studios had purchased most of the major New York music publishing houses and ordered the songs they needed for movie productions. To compose a new song just for its own sake, or because it dealt with some timely theme, was a luxury few composers and lyricists could afford. The music industry had not yet redesigned its World War I song-writing techniques. It was not prepared for a conflict of global battlefronts, secret war plans, conflicting war announcements, and operations that were hard to understand.

It was a fresh new songwriter who was to give the nation its first major war tune—Frank Loesser, whose later Broadway musicals included *The Most Happy Fella* and *How to Succeed in Business Without Really Trying*. On September 16, 1942, *Variety*—the show business newspaper—announced in a full-page advertisement: "Mr. Bill Lewis [an official under Elmer Davis], Office of War Information, you asked for it; here it is." The Office of War Information (OWI) had been asking for and finally received a song that would arouse the nation—its name, "Praise the Lord and Pass the Ammunition."

The song proved to be so important to the nation's morale that the source of its inspiration, Captain William Maguire, fleet chaplain for the Pacific Fleet, graced the cover of *Life* magazine on November 2, 1942. Stationed at Pearl Harbor at the time of the attack, the chaplain allegedly dropped his Bible and picked up a gun to ward off the Japanese attack. Whether the song was based on fact or fiction, its title told Americans what they would have to do to defeat the enemy. In noting that Captain Maguire didn't remember putting into words the now famous slogan, *Life* quoted the Captain as saying: "If I said it, nobody could have heard me in the din of battle. But, I certainly felt what the statement expresses." *Life* added, "although he definitely did not fire a gun, Captain Maguire helped men who carried ammunition up a narrow ladder which led to the blazing guns. Later, he was in charge of taking the wounded ashore."[3]

The song proved to be so popular that the government asked broadcasters to limit its performance to once every four hours rather once every two so that the public would not become tired of it. Despite its instantaneous record sales, a year later the song was hardly performed in public and the music industry awaited replacements. In 1943, the country's musical situation compelled Colonel William Addleman Ganoe, U.S. Army, to write:

> Mass movements have long since come to America, but where is the mass song? Where is the big tune to urge the Army and Navy of our United States as a whole to brave and noble deeds for the old country? . . .
>
> Our tunes are not yet turned out for tough times. Let us acknowledge we are making facetious gestures and grimaces at ourselves while our music mocks us. Let us recognize that we are lightly covering the surface with the camouflage of swing. Here and there appears a slight pulsation about fighting and dying, but it soon peters out into the weakness of a melodious hypodermic. It's not a shot in the arm we need. It's a shot in the soul . . .
>
> Where is the great march, the compelling melody, the driving harmony, the rhapsody profundo, that by its sheer violence and virility will shock us and shove us into uncomplaining sacrifice and overwhelming victory? Where is the song of songs that will deliver us out of our pleasure-loving bondage . . .
>
> It is only when a nation is great that it produces tragedy. It is only when tragedy is great that it produces the soaring song. It is only when a song is going, is prodding, is lifting, is embracing, is propelling, is transcendent, that we have the inner greatness to exploit well our winning. And there is no victory without exploitation. We have not yet begun to fight. We have not yet begun to suffer. We have not yet begun to sing.[4]

It was believed that no war was complete or respectable without a song or songs to represent it.

Music and the American Spirit

The music performed during World War II was multidimensional. It appealed to America's patriotism ("Buy A Bond"), caricatured and defined our enemies, described the impact of war on the home front ("It's So Nice To Have A Man Around The House"), bolstered the national security, reflected life in the armed services ("What Do You Do In The Infantry?"), and reminded everyone of loved ones ("I'll Be Seeing You"). Music was used to maintain a community's morale, relieve monotony and fatigue on the assembly line, speed up production, and aid recuperation in the hospital. Music was like a portrait upon which all the dimensions and ramifications of war could be observed and understood. Music let people feel emotions they could not verbalize and verbalize emotions they could only feel. Music was an indispensable force that coalesced America's spirit and resolve to "gain the inevitable triumph" that President Roosevelt had pledged before the Congress and the nation on December 8, 1941. Music was the bond that brought and held this nation together in its hours of gravest peril. Music reflected the ordeal known as World War II.

Musical leaders began to urge that music emphasize patriotism. The War Department asked for a singing soldiery; it encouraged parades, community sings, and band music in patriotic programs and pageants. William D. Revelli, a musical leader, encouraged every school and community concert to allow the audience to sing one patriotic song.[5] School bands were also encouraged to march through their city's streets at least once a week and play at the "send-offs" for the men being inducted into the armed services. Government leaders considered musical participation to be very important to the nation's welfare and morale. Marshall Bartholomew, a committee chairman in the Music Division of the Joint Army and Navy Committee on Welfare and Recreation, declared that habitual listening rather than active musical participation weakened the public spirit; that we must fight the "audience habit" because this was the totalitarian rather than the democratic way.[6]

After Pearl Harbor, Americans had no problems in distinguishing between the forces of good and evil in this global conflict. As H. L. Fowler in the musical publication *Etude* noted, in part:

> The present war is a fight between fanatical gangsters and invincible armies of freedom, tolerance, and democracy. On the one side is an international cancer, slowly eating into the vitals of civilization. On the other side is a cool, collected undefeatable army of surgeon-like heroes, determined to destroy this carcinoma of totalitarianism so that freedom, liberty, and righteousness may survive.

> These powerful issues already have been clearly manifested all over the world, so that despite the global battles, there is only one front, and that is the front of righteousness, liberty, and ideals as against one of cruelty, bestiality and slavery . . .[7]

These clearly defined characterizations of the enemies were expressed in American music. For example, during December 1941 in Philadelphia and Washington, D.C., "the Gilbert and Sullivan Opera Co. performed 'The Mikado' as scheduled, but altered the opening lines from 'We are the gentlemen of Japan' to 'We are the gangsters of Japan.' "[8]

Some kinds of music allowed the public to express its personal animosity as well. One such song was "Der Fuehrer's Face." It appeared in 1942 as a novelty song written for one of Walt Disney's propaganda film shorts, a cartoon originally entitled "Donald Duck in Nutzi Land." Because of the song's popularity, the name of the cartoon was changed to "Der Fuehrer's Face." The song allowed Americans to make fun of Hitler, Goering, and Goebbels. After a series of ridiculing heils which mocked the Nazi leaders' grandiose pronouncements of racial superiority, world conquest and other matters, the public could give each of them a vocal raspberry.

"Der Fuehrer's Face" (originally released on the Bluebird label) was recorded in Hollywood on July 28, 1942, by an obscure drummer named Lindley Armstrong "Spike" Jones and his band, the City Slickers, who were accompanied by the Barefooted Pennsylvanians, Horatio G. Birdbath, and the Saliva Sisters. This single recording thrust the musical group up among the top bands at that time.

It was popular to ridicule Hitler and his Axis partners during the early months of war. Charlie Chaplin had done it well in 1940 in his movie, *The Great Dictator.* It was all very humorous until the atrocities and inhumanity of the Nazis became known to the American public at the war's end. When that happened a lot of the humor that such songs as "Der Fuehrer's Face" conveyed was no longer funny. The song is, however, a reminder of how even in the adversity and terror of war, Americans could retain a sense of humor and ridicule their most heinous enemies. Sales reflected the song's popularity. By November 1942, the record had sold 200,000 copies, and in less than a month after its release, the sheet music had risen to the top five on the best seller list. A year after Pearl Harbor, American patriotism remained undaunted and Americans still could laugh and joke.

Americans retained a mature respect for other kinds of music, especially the classics. Unlike Germany, which had banned the music of Allied composers, living or dead, America still performed the works of Wagner, Verdi, and Strauss. The operas of Richard Strauss, Germany's composer laureate, were presented at the Metropolitan Opera more frequently during the war than in previous seasons and were vigorously applauded. At the height of the Sicilian invasion in 1943, Arturo Toscanini, (guardian of liberation in the eyes of the Italian people) conducted and broadcast over the National Broadcasting Company an all-Verdi program. The tolerant attitude Americans displayed toward older classical composers was due in part to their exposure to the works at concerts, on radio and phonograph records. These musical values had become such a part of American society that the compositions were not considered to be those of an enemy culture. Lesser known composers from the same foreign countries were not accorded the same respect; however, composers from countries who were America's allies became more popular, including Benjamin Britton (England) and Darius Milhaud (France). Many Americans could now pronounce the names of Russian composers who only a few years before were known to just symphony audiences. For example, Dmitri Shostakovich was paid the then unheard of fee of $10,000 for the rights to the first American performance of his Eighth Symphony. Roy Harris, the American composer, demonstrated the strength of America's bonds to its Allies by dedicating his Fifth Symphony to the Soviets on the twenty-fifth anniversary of the Red Army; the Office of War Information provided the short-wave broadcast. Morton Gould, another American composer, successfully orchestrated the "Red Cavalry March." Thus, music helped America solidify its identification with its allies to fight a common enemy, while placing above the battle the ageless works of past masters regardless of their national origin.[9]

The music of World War II had many forms and sounds. In addition to the classics, the patriotic, hillbilly, and crooning songs, there was music called sweet and hot (that is, jazz) that included a dance called the boogie-woogie; sultry music also known as torch; swing also called jump, scat, and jive; and the blues. Singing these various styles were such vocalists as Ginny Simms, the Andrew Sisters, Frank Sinatra, Perry Como, and Dinah Shore. Playing this music were such dance bands as Tommy Dorsey, Gene Krupa, Harry James, Benny Goodman, Sammy Kaye, Guy Lombardo, Freddy Martin, Hal McIntyre, Shep Fields, and

Jack Teagarden. Other band leaders such as Glenn Miller, Wayne King, Artie Shaw, Ted Weems, and Phil Harris also entertained the public before they joined the armed services or Merchant Marines. Americans also listened to the melodies of Phil Spitalny and his all-girl orchestra.

Music and the War Effort

Music was so important in the war effort that the U.S. Treasury Department and the United Service Organization (USO) sent choral evangelists from coast to coast to raise the nation's spirit through music. The U.S. Army offered a prize for new songs and distributed millions of song pamphlets to the soldiers in camp. The country established a Music War Council to seek out and judge the "morale" of tunes.[10]

When Johnny Jones, America's and George M. Cohan's "Yankee Doodle Dandy," marched off to war in 1941, one song reminded him:

> Let's remember Pearl Harbor as we go to meet the foe.
> Let's remember Pearl Harbor as we did the Alamo.
> We will always remember how they died for liberty.
> Let's remember Pearl Harbor and go on to victory.[11]

Although few Americans may have understood the meaning of total war immediately after Pearl Harbor, the country was ready to exert every effort and sacrifice to achieve victory. President Roosevelt exemplified this spirit when he addressed the nation on radio, October 12, 1942, and stated, in part:

This whole nation of 130,000,000 free men and women and children is becoming one great fighting force. Some of us are soldiers or sailors, some of us are civilians. Some of us are fighting the war in airplanes five miles above the continent of Europe or the islands of the Pacific, and some of us are fighting it in the mines deep down in the earth of Pennsylvania or Montana. A few of us are decorated with medals for heroic achievement, but all of us can have that deep and permanent inner satisfaction that comes from doing the best we know how—each of us playing an honorable part in the great struggle to save our democratic civilization.

Whatever our individual circumstances or opportunities, we are all in it, and our spirit is good; and we Americans and our allies are going to win—and do not let anyone tell you anything different.[12]

War production was one of the keys to victory. President Roosevelt's call for 60,000 planes, 45,000 tanks, 20,000 anti-aircraft guns, and 8,000,000 tons of shipping in 1942 almost took away the breath of many military and industrial leaders. Hanson W. Baldwin, military expert of the *New York Times,* said, "He set the sights so high indeed that it will be an industrial miracle if we achieve these goals."[13] But, the United States possessed a secret weapon to make that industrial miracle an everyday reality—the American workers who stood behind the man behind the gun. They forged the arms, rolled the steel, refined the oil, machined the parts, made powder and aluminum, and expressed their support of every Mr. Jones with the following lyrics:

> *Arms for the love of America*
> *And for the love of ev'ry mother's son . . .*[14]

During World War II, the composition of the American labor force changed dramatically. In greater numbers than ever before, women began to fill the positions that men were vacating as they went off to war. Women worked in such diverse jobs as riveters, ambulance drivers, metal stampers, and welders. A new term emerged to describe the wartime working woman, a term of affection. She was "Rosie the Riveter" and was saluted in song.

> *All day long*
> *Whether rain or shine*
> *She's part of the assembly line*
> *She's making history*
> *Working for victory*
> *Rosie, the Riveter.*[15]

The achievements of the American labor force during World War II were truly outstanding. In 1944, its highest year of production, the United States turned out more than 50 percent more munitions than its enemies and, in fact, produced 45 percent of the total output of all enemy nations. In 1944, America built about 96,000 military planes, including 16,000 bombers, compared with 86,000 in 1943; 48,000 in 1942; and only 2,100 in 1939.[16] During the war, the United States also built 5,200 vessels of nearly 53 million dead-weight tonnage. Before the war ended, a Liberty ship, the standard wartime freighter, could be built in 42 days, compared with the 244 days it took to construct the first vessel. In all of these cases, music helped the workers establish these production records. When the 35,000-ton battleship U.S.S. *Alabama* slid off the ways at the Norfolk, Virginia, Navy Yard on February 16, 1942, the vessel was known as the "rhythm ship" because recorded music, ranging from symphonies to boogie-woogies, had spurred on her welders, riveters, and fitters. "Ballads and Battleships" was even suggested as a new defense slogan.

Music was such an essential part of war production that the *New York Times* stated in an editorial:

> The best things that men do, including both work and worship, demand music. Folk songs would be poor if it weren't for sowing, harvesting, hauling, loading and unloading, blacksmithing, carrying burdens, raising anchors, making sail and so forth. The best artisans whistle.
>
> It would be better if the music came out of the builders of the *Alabama* instead of having to be put into them by loudspeakers. But, perhaps, if enough music is put into them, some music will come out. Perhaps, they will get to whistling, humming and singing that sweet, swing, classic and corny music they are hearing. The effect on the *Alabama* herself may be something that couldn't be expressed in blueprints. A battleship whose beams and plates are vibrating not only with the usual strains and tensions of the sea but with the eloquent remembered saxophone, the loud cornet, the boastful trumpet and the arrogant echo of drums, might be formidable indeed.[17]

The Psychology of Music

Music was used to relieve boredom and fatigue in war plants and shipyards, especially among the workers who were performing light, repetitive, and monotonous duties. It also reduced strife and arguments among employees by reducing personal tension and improving worker morale, all of which helped the country achieve its war production goals. As an editorial in one music periodical noted, in part:

> A nervous, jittery, hysterical, rumor-mongering personality is a menace to the civil and military forces at this time. The nation needs calm, unfrightened, industrious persistent workers in all fields. The stimulation of music, the inspiration, the refreshment, the stabilizing effect of the permanence of an art which will go steadily on, centuries after all of the armies of the

world have vanished, can do more to provide a practical antidote for the deadly poisons of fear, worry and the apprehensions of calamity, than almost any other thing . . .[18]

The kind of music war production facilities played even had a psychology behind it. Military music was considered very masculine and not advised for women workers who could be reminded of their loved ones in the armed services. Victor Herbert's music was a good relaxer for the rest periods but not good at specific time intervals between 11 A.M. and 4 P.M., such as 2:30 P.M., when fatigue in factory workers began to peak.[19] During this time period, stimulating music was played. Vocals and unfamiliar music were to be avoided because they distracted workers from their jobs, thus slowing down production and causing accidents. Desk-bound workers required unobtrusive music that would not interfere with their thought processes. Music was even chosen according to sex, age level, and nationality. A facility with a high percentage of Polish workers might include some polkas, whereas Italian workers might hear excerpts from operas.

Day-to-Day Reality

The home front was more than just a huge production effort of turning the country into President Roosevelt's "Arsenal of Democracy." It was also a place of hardships and sacrifice. Americans were encouraged to save coal, electricity, gasoline, and fuel oil. Housewives were urged to save their waste kitchen fats because fats and greases would be used in the manufacture of munitions. The government banned the use of metal for beer mugs, cocktail shakers, hair curlers, and other so-called necessities of life. Old toothpaste tubes had to be turned in for new tubes. The government sponsored salvage drives to collect waste paper, rags, pots and pans, worn out rubber tires, and junked automobiles, which could be converted into useful items for the war effort. Cosmetics, hairpins, and tinfoil began to disappear. Coffee vanished from the grocery shelves, while the era of whipped cream ended as the sale of heavy cream stopped. Cigarettes, apartments, taxicabs, and liquor were also in short supply.

Priority clothes were created for men and women. In 1942 economy suits for men saved cloth by eliminating such tailoring as trouser cuffs.

At the same time, feminine fashions stressed short skirts, fabric shoes, string knit jackets, and acetate plastic jewelry. The government asked women to turn in their nylon and silk stockings and replace them with cotton.

Troop-crowded trains, canceled cruises, shortages of new tires and gasoline rationing prevented many people from traveling. The public was asked to reconsider train travel and other modes of transportation if it meant that a soldier would not be able to get home on his last furlough or if the arrival of a casualty would be delayed.

The public now purchased meats, sugar and cheese with ration books as grocers, butchers, and the purchasers struggled in learning how to use them. The labor shortage hurt such services as laundries, hotels, plumbers, and electricians. People tried to overcome a vegetable shortage by raising their own in millions of Victory Gardens throughout the country.

During the war years the standard of living plunged and once again one song expressed everyone's feelings:

> *Who's complaining?*
> *I'm not complaining.*
> *You'll see we'll see this thing through.*
> *Because of Axis trickery*
> *My coffee now is chickery and I can rarely purloin a surloin.*
> *No complaining through the campaigning*
> *Who cares if carrots are few,*
> *I'll feed myself on artichokes*
> *Until that Nazi Party chokes*
> *So long as they don't ration*
> *My passion for you.*
> *Who's complaining?*
> *I'm not complaining*
> *The sacrifices are few.*
> *My shoes may not be leathery*
> *My pillow not feathery*
> *My legs may be forgotten in cotton. . . .*[20]

The Girls I Left Behind

While her legs may have been forgotten in cotton, she certainly wasn't. As in all wars, sweethearts were always left behind. One of the most popular songs of 1942, "Don't Sit Under the Apple Tree," reflected the sentiments of all the Mr. Joneses and their sweethearts.

> *Don't sit under the apple tree with anyone else but me,*
> *Anyone else but me,*
> *Anyone else but me,*
> *No, no, no,*
> *Don't sit under the apple tree with anyone else but me*
> *Till I come marching home.*[21]

Songwriters popularized the names of many girls who were left behind and also met abroad during World War II. They had names like Mandy, Dolores, Margie, Dinah, San Antonio Rose, Candy, and Sweet Sue. Of all the names with which Americans became familiar, one of the most famous and most popular was Eileen. Millions of servicemen met their Eileens at local community social centers called Canteens operated by churches, civic clubs, and welfare organizations. Here the servicemen and women could find free food and beer, parties, theater tickets, and even invitations for dinner or a weekend with a family. Celebrities, local or national, were often an additional attraction. As they marched off to war, many Mr. Joneses left their hearts at the Canteen too. As the song recalls:

> *I left my heart at the Stage Door Canteen . . .*
> *I left it there with a girl named Eileen . . .*[22]

One of the most famous Canteens in America was located in Hollywood, California; only here, movie stars were the local citizens who hosted the men and women. Founded by actress Bette Davis and actor John Garfield, the Canteen offered a place to meet, dance, and be entertained by such show business luminaries as Lana Turner, Marlene Dietrich, and Red Skelton. The Canteen represented a welcome and morale-building respite to many members of the armed services who were going to and returning from battlefields around the world.

As the years passed and 1942 became 1943 and 1943 turned into 1944 and 1944 melded into 1945, the length and strain of the war on those left behind became telling. "They're Either Too Young or Too Old," a popular song of 1943, probably best expressed the emotional emptiness that unfulfilling relationships and lonesomeness can bring.

Music Sells Bonds

The war was not just costly in terms of human emotions but in money as well. The financing of World War II staggered everyone's imagination. America's participation in World War I, which lasted less than two years, cost the country about $35 billion. By mid-1943 World War II was costing $8 billion a month.[23] Between July 1, 1940, and June 30, 1946, the U.S. government raised $389 billion, $360 billion of which was allocated for defense and the war. In 1945 alone, the United States spent $100 billion or more than ten times its prewar annual expenditures.[24] To raise this money the government imposed taxes that raised about 46 percent of the war costs; the remainder came from public borrowing.

Music played an indispensable part in helping America finance the war effort. "Any Bonds Today?," a 1941 tune by Irving Berlin, contributed significantly in helping America secure its wartime financial goals by stimulating the public's purchase of government war bonds and war stamps, in part, with the following words:

> *Any stamps today?*
> *We'll be blest if we all invest in the U.S.A. . . .*

Indeed, the public did invest. People bought war bonds and war stamps everywhere—at the movies, in public schools, at the work place through payroll deductions, and at bond rallies. As a reflection of America's changing military posture, early in 1942 the government changed the name from defense bonds and defense stamps to war bonds and war stamps and conducted seven war loans and one victory loan drive for the public—some of the largest endeavors to raise money in history. One measure of the success of these drives was that 85 million investors purchased $156.9 billion in war bonds. By selling various kinds of bonds, 40 percent of the funds that people had available for investment went to the government as the country's gross national product (the total value of all the goods and services the country produces) rose from $43 billion on June 30, 1940 to $269.4 billion on June 30, 1945.[25]

Various techniques were used to sell war bonds. According to *Newsweek* magazine, Ralph Edwards, host of "Truth or Consequences," a radio program,

> piped in a sailor contestant from St. Albans Naval Hospital on Long Island, whose consequence was to sing "Wait for Me, Mary" to his girl.

With the stage set, Edwards then announced that if listeners would buy bonds, send the serial numbers to him, and if the amount was $1,000,000 he would buy the sailor a $1,000 bond. This simple request turned almost $5,000,000 into the Treasury coffers.[26]

By 1944, Edwards had taken his show on extensive tours twice in his role as war bond salesman. Altogether, he sold about $200 million worth of war bonds for the U.S. government.[27]

National Security

The purchase of war bonds and war stamps was not the only way the home front demonstrated its patriotism. Many families displayed in a window the government "V" for Victory symbol, which they received if they met special criteria—buying war bonds and war stamps regularly; squelching rumors; salvaging essential materials that were quickly convertible for war use; conserving food, clothing, transportation, goods, and help; knowing first aid; and being prepared for air raid emergencies. Window stickers were not the only reminders that people had a responsibility to preserve their national security. Once again music assumed an important role in telling the public how important loose talk was to the enemy and how dangerous it was for the country's survival.

As the song, "Shhh, It's A Military Secret," noted:

> *Take a tip,*
> *Button your lip,*
> *Don't get yourself unstrung,*
> *Harm may come*
> *Just from the slip of a tongue.*
> *Don't talk about the weather,*
> *Shhh IT'S A MILITARY SECRET,*
> *Just keep your wits together,*
> *Shhh that's the safest way to keep it.*
> *These are critical times,*
> *Be careful of espionage,*
> *In such critical times you've gotta watch out for sabotage.*
> *If you must talk to someone,*
> *Shhh don't give any information,*
> *It's smart to be a dumb one,*
> *Shhh simply change the conversation.*

Let's just talk about love,
'Cause that's what I'm thinking of
And it's no MILITARY SECRET that I love you.

According to Walter Bishop, the composer of these lyrics, this song was played continuously at the Pentagon during the war.[28] At America's central military command, music assumed an important role in helping to ensure our nation's safety. The necessity to keep the nation secure against foreign spies was brought to the public's attention rather pointedly in June 1942, when the Federal Bureau of Investigation (FBI) announced the capture of eight Nazi spies and saboteurs who landed at Amagansett, Long Island, and Jacksonville, Florida. Subsequently, all were brought to trial and found guilty. Six subsequently died in the electric chair, while two others received prison terms—one for life and the other for thirty years. By 1945, the FBI had reported that the agency had rounded up about 1,500 Axis spies in North and South America during the war.[29]

This is the Army, Mr. Jones

Knowing he was being backed up by such patriotic fervor, Mr. Jones could march off to war confidently, his mission defined, in part, by the words of another popular song:

I'm bringing a song of freedom to all people wherever they may be . . .[30]

As Mr. Jones left home and embarked upon a new way of life in the armed services, our music reflected the many pieces of that life—the memories of loved ones left behind, the sneak attack on Pearl Harbor and other U.S. territories, the hardships and sacrifices of those remaining behind, America's susceptibility to sabotage and invasion, and that once again following his father's example in 1917 he had to take up arms to win the war that wasn't won. Perhaps, Irving Berlin summarized the feelings of all the Mr. Joneses when he wrote for *This Is The Army*, a 1943 movie musical, "This time we will all make certain that this time is the last time." It seems that each generation must take up the arms the previous generation thought it had laid down forever. The cycle never seems to end as much as everyone hopes and prays that it will.

While millions of men and women passed through the portals of military training camps throughout the United States during the war, many more millions did not. For those who did not, songwriters went to work and gave America a portrait of life in the armed services. In addition, music gave servicemen and women an emotional release from the rigors of military training while raising their morale and fighting spirit in battle. In the words of British Field Marshal Lord G. J. Wolseley (1833–1913):

> Troops that sing as they march will not only reach thier destination more quickly and in better fighting condition than those who march in silence, but, inspired by the music and words of national songs, will feel that self-confidence which is the mother of victory.[31]

Colonel William Addleman Ganoe even more pointedly described the importance of music, especially band music, to the soldiers:

> In the long, tedious evening after the hike, the maneuver, the choking day, when the last chow is eaten and the last rattling mess tin is washed, when the last bit of activity is over and there's nothing to look forward to but grime and darkness, it is then that he is surprised into warmth and wholesomeness by the waves of harmony of the band suddenly breaking all over him—restoring him, reviving him, wrapping him around with welcome and cheer. It's no little tinkle. It is he-man's music—big bursts and blasts of crescendo and fortissimo—the only strains in the open that can grab and hold with arresting power. There's the surge of "The Dashing White Sergeant," "Directorate" and "Down the Street." The soldier is holding hands with his sweetheart again. He's waving at pop and mom and they are waving back at him. He's home after all. The darkening clouds have disappeared. The trumpets and trombones are blowing him up again and out of his sordid, rough surroundings. He's singing, he's humming, he's whistling, following the strains of the striding marches. He hasn't slumped. He's going forward again. He doesn't have to try to escape into rotten thoughts . . . the band has done its service as shepherd and comforter. It has assuaged.[32]

The first official notification the prospective GI (an affectionate acronym applied to American soldiers in World War II meaning government issue) received from Uncle Sam was a telegram beginning with the word, "Greetings," and requesting that he report to his local draft board to determine his qualifications for induction into the armed services. Perhaps the first musical greeting he received of his prospective service life came from Irving Berlin, who wrote

> *This is the Army, Mister Jones*
> *No private rooms or telephones . . .*

Before long, the new recruit may have been thinking of the sentiments Irving Berlin expressed in another song, written during World War I but applicable to the armed services at any time whether in war or peace:

> *Oh! how I hate to get up in the morning*
> *Oh! how I'd love to remain in bed . . .*

When the GI did get out of bed, he returned to the army routine. One parody, sung to the melody of "Sleepy Lagoon," described his first morning's encounter:

> *A sleepy latrine, a pastoral scene*
> *And two at the basin*
> *The job isn't fun, the mirror is one*
> *You can't see your face in.*
> *The lighting is bad, it's driving you mad*
> *That's half of it brother—*
> *The farther you go, the first thing you know*
> *You're shaving each other.*

Once the GI had dressed and breakfasted, his next appointment may have been with the camp's barber. In the words of an old World War I song which were just as relevant in World War II:

> *Good morning, Mister Zip-Zip-Zip,*
> *With your hair cut just as short as mine,*
> *Good morning, Mister Zip-Zip-Zip,*
> *You're surely looking fine! . . .*

Of course, not all of the day's activities prepared him for combat duty. Some were of a more domestic nature such as KP (kitchen police). This parody of John Philip Sousa's "U.S. Field Artillery March" of 1918, perhaps, expressed many of his own thoughts:

> *Hi, hi, hee, in the kitchen scullery,*
> *Sixteen long hours of the day*
> *And where we go, by our smell you'll know—*
> *That the KPs are scrubbing away*
> *That the KPs are scrubbing away.*

These parodies of well-known verses and songs were another important variation of the tunes American servicemen sang during World War

II. Generally, servicemen liked bawdy parodies, old favorites, and songs with a barbershop quartet flavor. Some songs were so popular that GIs named their weapons of war with song titles. For example, flying over enemy territory were the "Paper Doll," "Star Dust," "Stormy Weather," "Sunrise Serenade," and "In the Mood"—all bombers of the American Eighth Air Force.[33]

Each month, as already noted, the Army's Special Services Division distributed millions of musical "Hit Kits" to encourage soldiers to sing at home and abroad. These little brochures contained the words and music to the Army's latest selection of popular tunes such as "Dinah," "Margie," "For Me and My Gal," and "Sweet Sue." Tin Pan Alley also worked in a frenzy to produce a song that would strike the soldiers' fancy. They brought forth "Goodbye Mama, I'm Off to Yokohama," "We'll Be Singing Hallelujah Marching Thru Berlin," and "Let's Put the Axe to the Axis," to cite but a few.

The soldiers, however, did not sing these songs very much; they sang for their own amusement. Once they learned a song, they generally parodied the tune to fit service life. The service morale officers also taught their men every new song they could pick up. The parodies served as a safety valve to ease the tensions of war rather than as a sign of low morale. Regardless of the theater of war or the rank of the commanding officers, there were parodies to fit the situation. As *Life* magazine observed, "Marine Corps fliers in the Pacific seem to like parodies. They [took] the 'Road to Mandalay' and put these words to it":[34]

> *Take me somewhere east of Ewa*
> *Where the best ain't like the worst*
> *Where there ain't no Doug MacArthur*
> *And a man can drown his thirst.*
> *Where the Army takes the medals*
> *And the Navy takes the Queens*
> *But the boys that take the rooking*
> *Are the United States Marines.*
>
> *Hit the road to Gizo Bay*
> *Where the Jap fleet spends the day.*
> *You can hear the duds-a chunkin'*
> *From Rabaul to Lunga Quay.*
> *Pack a load to Gizo Bay*

Where the float-plane Zeros play
And the bombs come down like thunder
On the natives 'cross the way.

Life went on to say "whenever airmen gather in the Southwest Pacific, sooner or later they get around to "I Want to Go Home," a sad waltz-time plant revived from World War I," and from which they created the following parody:[35]

These B-26s they rattle and roar,
I don't want to fly over Munda no more.
Take me back to Brisbane,
Where the brass hats clamor in vain.
Oh, ma, I'm too young to die.
I want to go home.

The lyrics and the sentiments expressed in the original song are identifiable with any conflict whether it be World War I or those that followed generations later. The song, composed by Lieutenant Gitz Rice, 1st Canadian Contingent, at the battle of Ypres in 1915, says, in part:

. . . I've been in France just sixteen months
and fighting now as yet,
I haven't seen a German
all I have seen is mud and wet . . .

I want to go home,
I want to go home;
The "Whizz-Bangs" and Shrapnel around me do roar,
I don't want this old war anymore . . .

War with all its terror, bloodshed, and tragedy—be it World War II or other conflicts—is the same for the civilian soldier in the field. Its geographical location, enemy, weaponry, and scope may change, but for the soldier waging the battle, as these songs and their parodies reveal, war has one constant—the immediate and most personal drive to survive, get out, and go home. Considering some of the places where American forces found themselves stationed, it is not difficult to understand why. One song popular with GIs and Australians alike in 1943 was simply called "Darwin" and seemed to say it all. The song described a town and all its amenities—from its environment to its sanitation—with a simple Australian expression. The town was just bloody—bloody, bloody, bloody—as noted, in part, by the following lyrics:

> *All bloody clouds, no bloody rains.*
> *All bloody stones and no bloody drains.*
> *The dust gets in your bloody brains.*

War has another constant—the need for human relationships. The effect of war on the relationships between those going off to battle or being left behind is reflected in the lyrics of such songs as "Don't Sit Under the Apple Tree" or "They're Either Too Young or Too Old." But the longing for such attachments was poignantly clear in the songs American servicemen sang after joining the armed forces, especially when they were sent overseas.

Musically, our servicemen met many women overseas. One girl came from Germany and was popularized in song by the German Afrika Korps before the British and American troops increased her musical fame. Her name was "Lilli Marlene." In 1943, the *New York Herald Tribune* quoted John Steinbeck as saying about this song: "War songs need not be about the war at all. Indeed they rarely are. . . . Politics may be dominated and nationalized, but songs have a way of leaping boundaries. And it would be amusing if, after all the fuss and heiling, all the marching and indoctrination, the only contribution to the world by the Nazis were— 'Lilli Marlene.' " Another girl our servicemen met overseas was Tunesian, and her name in song was "Dirtie Gertie from Bizerte." Still another in Sicily was called "Filthy Annie from Trapani." But, regardless of her name or social status, these and other women symbolized in song the GIs' need for companionship, however fleeting it might be. Perhaps another song sums up all these feelings. When American soldiers got together over a beer or so, they sang and adopted "Bless 'em All," an English tune from World War I, as one of their favorites, or perhaps the "Beer Barrel Polka." No matter the locale—an American bar, an English pub, a ship's mess—servicemen used songs to raise morale, have a barrel of fun, or chase away the blues.

However, the songs our GIs sang reflected more than the emotional desolation that war can bring. Our servicemen also sang tunes that reflected their inner longing to return to those they left behind. The titles of some of these songs can relate a story all by themselves—"When the Lights Go On Again (All Over the World)," "I'll Be With You in Apple

Blossom Time," (because) "You'd Be So Nice to Come Home To," (and) "I Don't Want to Walk Without You." Regardless of the theater of war, loved ones were never far away from the thoughts and memories of millions of servicemen and women.

Finale

Well, apple blossom time finally did come for millions of GIs. It began May 8, 1945—V-E Day, Victory in Europe—a day of untold and immeasurable joy for all freedom-loving people around the world.

Not long after V-E Day, the risin' sun also finally set and as quickly and unexpectedly as it had risen nearly four years before at Pearl Harbor. Just as America's war began with a surprise attack, it ended abruptly with another attack that surprised the whole world—an attack that ushered in mankind's newest era: the atomic age. On August 6 and then on August 9, American bombers dropped atomic bombs first on Hiroshima and then on Nagasaki. On August 14, Japan sued for peace and on September 2, 1945 (Tokyo time), the representatives of the Empire of Japan signed the instruments of unconditional surrender on the deck of the U.S.S. *Missouri* in Tokyo Bay. Ten days later on September 12, the remaining Japanese forces in Southeast Asia surrendered in Singapore. The war was over. At last, there was peace in the world. Our GIs were finally coming home. Only good times lay ahead. As another tune noted,

> Long ago and far away,
> I dreamed a dream one day
> And now that dream is here beside me.
> Long the skies were overcast,
> But now the clouds have passed.
> You're here at last.[36]

Once again, music brought Americans home from another conflict—in this instance, the music of World War II. Even before Pearl Harbor, President Roosevelt recognized the importance of music to a country's way of life. In a letter dated April 24, 1941 to Mrs. Vincent Ober, a former President of the National Federation of Music Clubs, President Roosevelt wrote:

The inspiration of great music can help to inspire a fervor in our way of life; and thus to strengthen democracy against those forces which would subjugate and enthrall mankind.

Because music knows no barriers of language; because it recognizes no impediments to free intercommunications; because it speaks a universal tongue music can make us all more vividly aware of that common humanity which is ours and which shall one day unite the nations of the world in one great brotherhood.[37]

The compositions noted herein were not, of course, all the music composed and sung during this extraordinary time. Some of the mentioned songs might not even have been the most significant music of the period. However, these songs and music reflected life during time of war—the hopes, fears, joys, and loneliness. Songs, perhaps more than any other medium, reflect the times in which people live. They sustained the spirit of the country in its darkest hours and those who went off to defend its liberties. In their own way, the songs Americans sang and the music they played brought peace to the nation and the world and contributed greatly toward ending the international cataclysm known as World War II.

Notes

1. Doron K. Antrim, "Dynamite in Songs," *Etude*, February 1942, 192.

2. "Forward March With Music," *Etute*, February 1942, 81.

3. "New U.S. War Songs," *Life*, November 2, 1942, 43.

4. William Addleman Ganoe, "Tunes for Tough Times," *Etude*, May 1943, 342, 344, 354.

5. William D. Revelli, "How Music Can Help Win the War," *Etude*, November 1942, 741.

6. George L. Lindsay, "Music Unites the Americas," *Etude*, July 1942, 458.

7. H. L. Fowler, "The World's War Call for Music," *Etude*, December 1942, 810.

8. "Wartime Trends in Music: German Opera Still Performed; 1917–1918 Bans Held Unlikely," *Newsweek*, January 5, 1942, 53.

9. Arthur Berger, "Music in Wartime," *New Republic*, February 7, 1944, 176–77.

10. Minna Lederman, "Songs for Soldiers," *American Mercury*, September 1943, 296–97.

11. Sammy Kaye and Don Reid, *Remember Pearl Harbor* (New York: Music Sales Corporation and Davadon Music, 1941).

12. Franklin D. Roosevelt, "Manpower and the Second Front," *Vital Speeches of the Day*, October 15, 1942, 2.

13. U.S. Bureau of the Budget, "The United States at War," Washington, D.C., 1946, 103.

14. Irving Berlin, *Arms for the Love of America*, (New York: Irving Berlin Music Company, 1942).

15. Redd Evans and John Jacob Loeb, *Rosie the Riveter*, (New York and San Francisco: Music Sales Corporation and Fred Ahlert Music Corporation, 1942).

16. Donald M. Nelson, *Arsenal of Democracy: The Story of American War Production* (New York: Harcourt Brace, 1946), 245–46.

17. As quoted in "Forward March With Music," *Etude*, March 1942, 149.

18. Ibid.

19. O. H. Caldwell, "More Music, More Defense," *Etude*, June 1942, 371.

20. Jerome Kern and Ira Gershwin, *Who's Complaining*, (Los Angeles: Polygram International Publishing Company, 1943).

21. Lew Brown, Charlie Tobias, Sam H. Stept, *Don't Sit Under the Apple Tree (With Anyone Else But Me)*, (Miami: EMI Robbins Catalog Inc. and Ched Music Corporation, 1942).

22. Irving Berlin, *I Left My Heart at the Stage Door Canteen*, (New York: Irving Berlin Music Company, 1942).

23. Julius Mattfield, *Variety Music Calvacade 1620–1961*, (Englewood Cliffs, N.J.: Prentice Hall, 1962), 547.

24. A. Russell Buchanan, *The United States and World War II*, (New York: Harper & Row, 1964), (Volume 2), 316–17.

25. Ibid.

26. "War and Consequences," *Newsweek*, December 7, 1942, 99.

27. Ibid.

28. Personal correspondence with author.

29. Mattfield, 556.

30. Irving Berlin, *Song of Freedom*, (New York: Irving Berlin Music Company, 1942).

31. Alvin C. White, "Let's Have More Music on All Fronts," *Etude*, January 1943, 11.

32. Ganoe, 310.

33. Paul Fussell, *Wartime*, (New York and London: Oxford University Press, 1989), 188.

34. Lilian Rixey, "Soldiers Still Sing," *Life*, September 27, 1943, 54.

35. Ibid., 52.

36. Jerome Kern and Ira Gershwin, *Long Ago and Far Away*, (Los Angeles: Polygram International Publishing Company, 1944).

37. "Music, The Homefront . . . And You," *Etude*, July 1942, 364.

Chapter Five

MOVIES
The Films We Saw

DURING WORLD WAR II, most Americans did not personally experience the realities of war. Our shores had not been invaded. Our existence as a nation had not been as physically threatened as that of other countries. These home front circumstances presented another element of the media—the film industry—with unique opportunities. In addition to entertaining the troops and weary home front workers, the movies could further the war effort by providing information about the conflict, instructing Americans about the principles for which they were fighting, and helping to maintain their morale.

When the United States officially entered World War II after Pearl Harbor, the movie industry already had a model for developing its wartime role. When the country entered the Great War in 1917, the youthful film industry proved to be a very powerful instrument for propaganda. Hollywood stirred up the patriotism of the American people, celebrated the gallantry of the English and the French, ridiculed the Kaiser, and depicted the Germans as heinously as possible. The titles of the films produced in 1917 and 1918 reflect these sentiments: *The Kaiser, The Beast of Berlin, Crashing Through to Berlin*, and the *Geezer of Berlin*. The U.S. government through the Committee on Public Information—its official propaganda and censorship agency during the war—also produced several patriotic dramas, including *America's Answer* and *Pershing's Crusaders*. The latter film compared World War I with the purposefulness of the Crusades. Well-known movie stars like Mary Pickford and Charlie Chaplin went out among their fans to help raise money for the Liberty Loan Drives.

137

Following World War I with its atrocities, Hollywood made a series of films which increased Americans' hatred of war and everything military. Movie audiences became familiar with the mud and filth of the trenches, with the sight of men and animals being blown to pieces and the nervous tension of "zero" hour. *The Big Parade*, for example, was the distressing story of doughboys returning from France only to find their jobs gone and nothing but despair awaiting them at home.

For the most part, however, in the years between the two world wars, the movie industry maintained that the American public, above all else, wanted to be entertained. As a result, Hollywood produced about 600–700 movies a year in a variety of categories, including musicals, westerns, comedies, mysteries, and romances.[1]

At the same time, as the Nazi party began its rise to power in Germany, it realized the power and impact of movies on the national life. The Nazi government built and subsidized movie theaters throughout the Reich—even in the smallest towns—to form a network over which the German Propaganda Ministry could distribute what it believed to be the most powerful medium in existence. The Nazis found that the effect of visual propaganda was instantaneous and lasted much longer than any other kind. The films *Baptism of Fire* and *War in the East*—showing the annihilation of Poland and distributed in Belgium, Holland and the Balkans before the blitz of 1940—were very important elements in softening those countries. The Nazis considered movies so important to their cause that a cinematographer was assigned to every German regiment in the field. In the opinion of foreign observers, their newsreels, carefully edited to include only the most favorable commentary on the German soldier's life, were among the most stimulating morale builders the Germans had.[2]

As soon as Hitler had plunged Europe into war, Hollywood began to promote democracy and condemn fascism without any urging from the government. However, Hollywood did not abandon its principal purpose of making movies that would entertain the public and increase industry profits; propaganda had to be incidental to entertainment. With the prewar films *Mortal Storm* (1940) and *Escape* (1940), both bitter indictments of Nazi brutality and oppression, Hollywood did poorly at the box office.

However, by combining propaganda and entertainment, Hollywood soon discovered that the stereotyped mystery thriller was easily adaptable to Nazi fifth-column films. The criminal could be changed into a "bad" Nazi, and the patriotic Americans could be like Tyrone Power who had volunteered to fight with the British Royal Air Force in *A Yank in the R.A.F* (1941), or Robert Stack who, with other American fliers in the *Eagle Squadron* (1942), also volunteered to fight alongside the British before America entered the war and, on a commando raid in France, brings back a captured enemy airplane of advanced design. Without anyone's help, these heroes could foil scores of Nazis and prevent the Nazi agents from stealing a secret bombsight, like Wallace Ford did in *The Marines Come Though* (1943). One anti-Nazi film, *Confessions of a Nazi Spy* (1939), demonstrated the danger of a fifth column operating within the United States; this film drew the anger of the America First Committee, a very powerful isolationist group, which attacked Hollywood for including antifascist propaganda in its films.[3] In another movie produced before Pearl Harbor, Charlie Chaplin made fun of Adolph Hitler by portraying Adenoid Heynkel in *The Great Dictator* (1940) and made money for the studio. Despite these and other movies and World War I experience, when the United States officially entered World War II in December 1941, the film industry still had to rethink its role and responsibility for the time that lay ahead.

One of the first major steps Hollywood took to involve itself in the war effort occurred immediately after Pearl Harbor. The motion picture industry established a War Activities Committee. This committee recommended that President Roosevelt appoint a single agency or individual to coordinate the film production of the government and the industry. In May 1942, the Office of the Coordinator of Films was established with headquarters in Hollywood. This Office later became the Motion Picture Bureau of the U.S. Office of War Information (OWI). From its beginning, the office interpreted the needs and policies of the government to motion picture producers, supplied the producers with special information to help them make certain war films, and at the request of the movie studios analyzed short subjects and feature film scripts for their potential effect on the war effort. The function of this Office was purely advisory. The motion picture industry had final responsibility for the films produced during the war.

A Variety of Movies

Hollywood made various kinds of motion pictures during World War II: propaganda shorts appealed to the audiences' patriotic zeal; newsreels portrayed the events of the day, including battles around the world; documentaries or information films provided military and civilian audiences with lessons on the history in the making; educational films (short and full-length features) covered all kinds of subjects, from military bridge-building to home front civil defense; and of course, the fictional or semi-fictional dramatizations with which Hollywood is most associated.

Propaganda Shorts

The brief propaganda films appealed directly to the audiences' patriotism by reminding moviegoers that they should be as willing to make as much sacrifice for the war effort as the movie star who was making the appeal. The pitch might sound like this:

> Mr. Star: See that, 5:30 in the morning. I've been here since 5:00 getting ready for today's work that may last till 10 tonight. So I'm not asking anything of you that the rest of us in Hollywood aren't willing to do ourselves. Let's all stay on the job.

Or—

> Movie Announcer: This theater has a magnificent record in the war loan campaigns. They [the theaters] have a quota in this victory loan. It's part of the state's [your city's] quota.

> Mr. Star: This theater and movie theaters throughout the country are making it possible for you to shorten this war . . . For your convenience bonds and stamps are on sale at the box office of this theater . . . So stop on your way out and buy some . . . Do it today at this theater as you leave . . . Can you say you can't afford to buy victory bonds? Let's all back the attack!

> Movie Announcer: It's up to you!

These patriotic appeals were quite successful. Moviegoers purchased 11 percent of the government E bonds sold during the war years, worth billions of dollars. Theaters were an excellent source of raising funds for the war effort. The diversity and cost of their entertainment annually attracted huge numbers of patrons. For example, on a Saturday afternoon for a 10 cents admission at Boston's Morton theater children could see, in addition to the previous appeal, two feature films, the latest installment of the weekly adventure serial, some cartoons, a newsreel, a preview of coming attractions, and, possibly, a stage show.

Theaters were also used to collect funds for other wartime causes. During the intermission between double features, for example, the audience might be asked to give to the March of Dimes fight against infantile paralysis (polio), the Army-Navy Relief, or the Red Cross. Ushers would pass collection cans from one row to another to collect the donations. The local movie theaters played a significant role in soliciting the public's help for the war effort.

The Newsreels

Often moviegoers were motivated to contribute to various causes by the newsreels, government-produced documentaries (domestic and foreign), and commercially produced "think films."

The weekly newsreels (two new programs a week) had names like "News of the Day" and were produced by such companies as Paramount, Hearst, Fox-Movietone, RKO-Pathé, and Universal. Through the newsreels, the public followed the course of the war; they witnessed the aftereffects of the attack on Pearl Harbor, of Nazi tyranny when our armed forces entered and liberated concentration camps, and of the atomic bomb dropped on Hiroshima. From the war's beginning to the war's end, newsreels took movie audiences to battlefields around the world—from the deserts of North Africa and the lush tropical islands of the South Pacific to the world's capitals, Manila, Paris, and Rome. Moviegoers were there as the Allies captured an endless number of towns in what seemed like an endless number of countries; they watched scenes of the Allies arriving and being celebrated, hugged, and kissed by the local townspeople. Often these scenes of liberation were followed by pictures of last-ditch fighting by remnants of the enemy forces. Movie audiences saw the Allies feeding and cheering the local citizens, and they saw the townspeople dealing with the traitors who had lived among them.

Initially the newsreels were very sanitized in reporting the horrors of war that the Allied forces were encountering, and the government began to fear that the American public would become complacent about this international conflict. In 1943 a presidential directive gave OWI authority over the War, Navy, and State Departments in deciding when, how, and where all war news would be released. Not long after this directive was issued, the horrific side of the war confronted those on the home front as the pictures of the U.S. paratroopers who were killed in the invasion of Sicily and other scenes were added to the newsreels. Throughout the war, however, the newsreels continued to highlight the lighter side of the news as well—sporting events, fashion shows, beauty contests, and national politics.

Documentary Films

The documentary or informational film assumed an important role during the war. Former Hollywood director Lieutenant Colonel Frank Capra produced *Why We Fight* for the U.S. government. Before being sent abroad, every U.S. soldier was required to view this series in order to understand how the war came about and why he had to fight. The first, *Prelude to War* (1942), described the rise of Fascism, Nazism, and Japanese militarism between 1931 and 1938. *The Nazis Strike* (1943) covered the events in Central Europe from the time of the Austrian Anschluss to the invasion of Poland. Then came *Divide and Conquer* (1943), which told the story of the German invasion of Scandinavia, the Low Countries, and France. *The Battle of Britain* (1943) showed that country's brave defense by the Royal Air Force. With the remaining films of the series, *The Battle of Russia* (1943), *The Battle of China* (1944), and *War Comes to America* (1944), the American soldier received a complete picture of the origins of the war and its progress. The British people also had an opportunity to view the series.

The prose of these films could be quite elaborate. *Prelude to War*, a series of newsreel clips that contrasted the freedoms in America with their demise in Germany, Italy, and Japan, concluded with the following statement:

This is what we are fighting. Freedom's oldest enemy—the passion of the few to rule the many. This isn't just a war. This is a common man's life and death struggle against those who would put him back in slavery. We lose it, and we lose everything—our homes, the jobs we want to go back to, the books we read, the very food we eat, the hopes we have for our kids, the kids themselves—they won't be ours anymore. That's what's at stake. It's us against them. The chips are down. Two worlds stand against each other. One must live. One must die. One hundred and seventy years of freedom decrees our answer.[4]

The home front moviegoers were transported to the war's front lines by combat films, which the armed services had photographed. War consists of many more moments than those of its greatest action. War is the time between battles before the fighting begins; it is bugs, sand, and mud. It is being shot at and killed by snipers while on night patrol. It is the lonely moments of holidays passed in hostile surroundings, with longing, warm memories of home. War is also the anticlimax of the degrading spectacle of an apparently invulnerable enemy in captivity being reduced abruptly to a ragged mass of defeated men. The combat photographers also showed this side of war. In some instances, Hollywood movie directors who were in the military put the footage together to create films that have stood the test of time with their perspective of what war is really all about from the view of the men who fight it.

Fresh from the war front, these films were rushed to the screen before they became too old for news and yet too young for history. Two such films were *Memphis Belle* (1943) and *The Battle of San Pietro* (1945).

Former Hollywood director Lieutenant Colonel William Wyler produced the *Memphis Belle*, the story of the twenty-fifth bombing mission of the famous Flying Fortress. Assembled from some 16,000 feet of film shot over Europe and England, *Memphis Belle* is skillfully put together to appear as the record of a single bomber flight to Wilhelmshaven, Germany. This film begins with scenes of the English countryside and the commentary, "This is a battlefront, a battlefront like no other in the long history of mankind's wars. This is the airfront." It ends when, after its successful bombing of Wilhelmshaven, the Memphis Belle returns to America "to train new crews and to tell the people what we are doing."

Moviegoers watched the beautiful patterns created in the stratosphere as the planes' exhaust condensed into vapor trails, the ground crews sweating out the mission on the field, the youthful, yet old, faces of the fliers over the target, the incongruously harmless look of flak as it burst in silent smudges about the plane, the Memphis Belle dropping its bombs and hitting its target. They listened to the anxious conversation of the airmen as the German fighters attacked again and again and heard the shattering concussions of the explosions. Moviegoers saw the face of war when some of the planes returned and others did not, as the film's narrator said: "Our losses were heavy, but the enemy's were far heavier. We destroyed a German aircraft factory, a rail junction, submarine pens, docks, and a harbor installation." Over Germany, a flying fortress, a seemingly impregnable graceful giant, was hit, its power gone, and the plane abandoned by its crew. As it lumbered clumsily down the sky, the camera caught it and held it for a moment, a machine-age symbol of the eternal tragic theme: how the mighty have fallen.[5]

Another outstanding combat documentary, *The Battle of San Pietro*, was made for the Army Signal Corps by then Major John Huston, another Hollywood director. This film brought the moviegoer to the side of the foot soldier and displayed his bravery as well as his despair, as he shot and was shot at by the enemy while trying to capture the Italian town of San Pietro Infine in December 1943. Though at first repulsed, the American soldiers eventually captured San Pietro and part of Huston's narration seemed to sum up their plight:

> . . . Many among these you see alive here have since joined the ranks of their brothers-in-arms who fell at San Pietro for ahead lay San Vittori and the Rapido River and Cassino and beyond Cassino more rivers and more mountains and more towns, more San Pietros, greater or lesser—a thousand more.

Houston's movie "about the battle gave such a stark picture of the terrible reality of war that it had to be cut from five reels to three."[6]

The home front moviegoer could also witness the plight of foreign comrades-in-arms in battlefields throughout the world in similar films produced by and about other countries and their armed forces; for example, *Moscow Strikes Back* (1942)—the story of the Russian repulsion of the German Army at the gates of Moscow. *Desert Victory* (1943) celebrated the British Eighth Army's victory at El Alamein and its triumphal march to Tripoli against Field Marshal Erwin Rommel's Afrika Korps.

One of its most stirring scenes was filmed on October 23, 1942, at El Alamein when the British started their counter-offensive against the German Army. The British opening night barrage flashed on the movie screen for four and one-half minutes with such amplified staggering noise that many moviegoers could not sit through it. The scene was meant to be unbearable and was intended for American and other audiences who had never experienced and were never destined to witness the physical devastation of war on their homeland.

Occasionally local movie theaters would show commercially produced "think" films, which were released periodically by the "March of Time," "The World in Action," (the Canadian National Film Board) and Pathé's "This is America" series. These informational films directed much of their attention to international affairs. The National Film Board of Canada was established in 1939 and became internationally recognized in the field of propaganda during the Second World War. Its two series, "World in Action" (1942–1945) and "Canada Carries On" were exhibited theatrically throughout Canada and in many parts of the world. The purpose of "The World in Action" was to inform the public on the progress of the war as a supplement to "Canada Carries On," which dealt with domestic topics.[7] "This is America" produced such films as *Private Smith of the U.S.A.* which told how civilian draftees were transformed into soldiers, despite their gripings of having to leave civilian life, and that they were going to do the job that had to be done. Finally, the "March of Time" was a series of documentaries released monthly from 1935 to 1954. The short films, about 15 minutes in length, covered domestic and international affairs. Critics state that the films were influenced by the editorial policies of *Time, Life,* and *Fortune* magazines and had a distinct editorial viewpoint. Originally intended to inform audiences about current events in an entertaining format, the series during the early years of the war also sought to influence American opinion in favor of the British against Nazi Germany and its allies and may have influenced American public opinion against isolationism with such films as *Inside Nazi Germany* (1938), *The Ramparts We Watch* (1940) and *America Speaks Her Mind* (1941).[8] During the war the series touched upon almost every aspect of the conflict, emphasizing the brutality of the Axis powers and the necessity of the Allies to remain united.

A "March of Time" report entitled "One Day of War—Russia 1943," filmed by Soviet Army and Navy photographers, showed what the Russians were doing along their vast stretches of battlefield, which extended from the Arctic to the Caucasus and from the Western front to the Bering Sea. Edited in America with such scenes as the Russian Navy in action in the Black Sea and the siege of Leningrad, the film emphasized that "all of Russia is a battleground, all its cities and fortresses, all its people combatants." Omitting any discussion of Communism, the film's commentator went on to note: "They will keep fighting because this is their homeland—because they love Russia; they love it as the English love England, as the American people love and believe in America."[9] Irrespective of the nonaggression pact Russia had signed with Germany in 1939 and the division of Poland, these were still inspiring words for those on the home front to hear as the Allies engaged in a life-and-death struggle with the Axis powers. Other films in the series took audiences to the war in India, China, Norway, Australia, North Africa, and China, to name but a few locales. The films were an important addition to movie theater programs during the war years.[10]

Educational films

During the war, films were produced as morale boosters for industrial workers on the home front and as teaching tools for the American and allied military forces. The Army and Navy established Industrial Services Divisions, which produced and released films to factories and industrial workers throughout the country. These movies were intended to stimulate and make home front workers aware that they were an integral part of the war effort. *The Case of the Tremendous Trifle* told how the bombings of the Schweinfurt ball bearing works in Germany were important to the production of small parts at home. An Army Signal Corps short, entitled *How to Build a Trestle Bridge*, provided a group of thirty-six inexperienced men with sufficient information to build a forty-five-foot bridge in three and one-half hours. Another feature, *Resisting Enemy Interrogation*, taught airmen how to conduct themselves if captured. Many of the service-oriented films were re-recorded in Chinese, Russian, Spanish, and Portuguese and sent to our Allies so they would understand American military methods and be able to coordinate their strategies with U.S. forces, learn how to repair and maintain the American equipment they were being sent, or help them train their own armed forces.[11]

A great deal of the information Americans received about the war was dispensed at the movie house. When the government wanted Americans to maintain self-discipline in view of wartime shortages, the film unit of OWI produced a movie called *Salvage*. This film explained the government's need for rubber, iron, tin, and other materials and told how all Americans could help by saving and collecting such scrap. Until Congress abolished the domestic filmmaking function of OWI in 1943 on the grounds that the government should not be making any films at all, the agency distributed free films to the country's 16,000 movie theaters. Interestingly, after Congress eliminated the film production funds of OWI, fifty-seven other federal agencies continued to make motion pictures. Meanwhile, the War Activities Committee took over OWI's domestic filmmaking functions.[12]

A Serious Industry?

Before Pearl Harbor, critics held two views of Hollywood and the impending war. The first held that because Hollywood had yet to produce a single film that showed the American public the gravity of the situation it now faced, Hollywood's version of the war would be light matter interspersed with a few attractive spies, some uniformed, singing sisters who encourage the soldiers to do their duty and a few Nazis who run away at the sight of a bayonet. Critics believed that if Hollywood could not treat the impending war with seriousness, then the movie studios should confine themselves to entertainment films. The other view held that Hollywood could "bring its tremendous power to bear in awakening the nation to an appreciation of its heritage, its traditions and its might" and at the same time "acquaint the country with the actual nature of war—before showing Clark Gable defeating the German panzer divisions single handedly."[13]

This dichotomy of opinion raised many questions. Aside from propaganda shorts, newsreels, documentaries, and educational training films, how did Hollywood treat World War II in its traditional fictional or semifictional films? What did these films tell the moviegoer about the war, the Allies, the enemies, and the times they were living in? What were their message and impact? Were the movies realistic portrayals of the war, or did they show the international conflict in an unreal or misleading light? Did the films help Americans cope with wartime conditions on the home front? Did they bolster America's morale and will to win? The answers to these and other questions illustrate the movies' role in wartime and their ability to shape a society's values, will or purpose to achieve a common goal whether it be victory in war or any other objective which is necessary for its ultimate survival.

Hollywood Dramas

In general, the film industry produced four kinds of dramatizations during the war years. These included the in-praise-of-the-average-GI Joe films, the half-fiction, half-historical accounts of actual battles and the resistance of native populations to the conquerors, and stories of the home front. Before the war ended in 1945, Hollywood had produced more than 300 films about this global conflict, about one-third of all the films made during the war years. The films dealt with most of the theaters of war, including North Africa, Japan, China, England, Russia, Germany, France, the South Pacific, and Southeast Asia.

The themes of the servicemen films were very similar. The movie's principal character could be the leader of an Army Air Force squadron or an officer of a submarine landing a reconnaissance team on Japanese soil. By the end of the film, he had become a hero, regardless of how he may have begun, whether as a misfit, or a rebel, or the boy next door. Given a democratic mix of names like Canelli, Greenbaum, Skvosznik and Ross (*The Purple Heart*) to represent a cross section of American society and gratify audiences who are anxious for some evidence that the American experiment is a success, these heroes were given one personality. They were men with average looks, but on the handsome side; they were very sociable and capable of exchanging wisecracks, but they were not very adept at expressing thoughts and emotions. Early in the film, the hero finds that he is fighting an honorable war because he sees the enemy taking blood from children to use for the soldiers (*The North Star*), firing on the survivors of ships it has torpedoed (*Action in the North Atlantic*), or behaving ruthlessly in some country it has invaded (*Behind the Rising Sun*).

The only conflicts in the film begin when someone in the service unit is not happy with his life in the service—he should never have been flunked out of a service training school, or he is too arrogant to be liked or he is asked to go out on reconnaissance patrol too many times in a row. All of these circumstances play havoc with the morale of his comrades. But the first battle ends these conflicts when the malcontent realizes how barbaric the Germans or the Japanese are, that he would rather be fighting them than leave the service, or that the Captain is not as bad as he had thought because of a kindness the Captain has shown him. The compassion of this American soldier is demonstrated by the way he looks after a dog that he either finds or is given by another group and which he names Tojo or Hirohito.

To show the realities of war, there usually is a father who lost one or more sons in battle (*The Fighting Sullivans*) or a serviceman who had to have a limb amputated (*Thirty Seconds Over Tokyo*), as well as a mother, girlfriend, or wife at home as in *God is My Co-Pilot* (1945) to read a letter from a loved one in the service to show the importance of family relationships and remind the audience that the home front is behind its fighting men. The movie employs various techniques to diminish death and destruction. The death of one of the group is hardly noticed; individual dying is glossed over in a mass killing as in *Gung-Ho!* (1943) so that the audience does not see individual men dying but rather many men running wildly and falling down. Death is diminished further as the scene quickly turns to more heroic acts, a great deal of activity, or even humor.[14] This was the standard war film and hero.

In a 1943 article, the *Atlantic Monthly* described two films from Hollywood's make-believe war:

- In *Crash Dive* (1943), Tyrone Power represents the latest generation of a traditional Navy family which lives in an old southern-type mansion in Massachusetts. His youth had been wild and romantic. His family even had to use its personal connections to prevent his expulsion from the Naval Academy during his freshman year. Yet, Mr. Power becomes sufficiently mature as an adult to join a petty officer and a black cook from his submarine, at the big moment, to destroy an entire secret Nazi base. To be sure, Mr. Power does most of the demolishing but the American spirit does prevail.

- In *China* (1943), Alan Ladd [a civilian] is a man of very questionable character. In fact, he is an opportunist who transacts business with anyone who conducts it with him. His principal occupation is selling oil to the Japanese until the illuminating selflessness of Loretta Young sinks into his business mind. The sight of Japanese atrocities in addition to Miss Young guarding a group of small Chinese school girls alters his entire viewpoint. Coolly, he steals some dynamite and blows up a Japanese Division. As a paean of praise to the Chinese people, the movie wanted to say that the Chinese were doing a good job of holding and harassing the Japanese who were murderous and rapacious villains.[15]

Whether the film concerned the problems of men in combat or the morale of loved ones left behind on the home front, there was always the movie message. In *Stage Door Canteen* (1943), movie audiences listened to the following conversation between Katharine Hepburn and Eileen, a Stage Door Canteen hostess who became despondent when she learned her boyfriend, Ed "Dakota" Smith, was sent overseas before they could marry:

Ms. Hepburn:	Why did you volunteer for this work?
Eileen:	Because I wanted to help.
Ms. Hepburn:	Help what?
Eileen:	I wanted to help my country.
Ms. Hepburn:	Why do you think your country needs your help?
Eileen:	We're in a war and we've got to win.
Ms. Hepburn:	Yes, that's right. We're in a war and we've got to win and we're going to win. And that is why the boy you love is going overseas . . . He knows what he's fighting for. He's fighting for the kind of world in which you and he can live together in happiness, in peace, in love. Don't ever think about quitting. Don't ever stop for a minute working, fighting, praying until we got that kind of world—for you, for him, for your children, for the whole human race—days without end. Amen.[16]

Hepburn was not just speaking to Eileen; she was addressing every moviegoer whose loved ones were being sent to fight a war for which they never asked and reminding them of their duty and the principles for which the war was being fought. She was also telling servicemen that they were not forgotten "over there" by those they left behind "over here."

Battle Movies

Hollywood also transported movie audiences away from the home front to battlefields around the world. In *Thirty Seconds Over Tokyo* (1944), they flew with Lieutenant Colonel James H. Doolittle's bombing raid over Japan, which lifted the morale of a nation whose spirit was devastated by Pearl Harbor. The audiences could identify emotionally with the war aims of one of the pilots when he said, "If we could only fix it so that this would be the last one."[17] Not only could the public fly over Tokyo with Doolittle, in *Destination Tokyo* (1943), they could cruise beneath its harbor in the American submarine, U.S.S. *Copperfin*. After eluding a series of mine fields and submarine nets, the submarine discharged three men who went ashore to make readings that were radioed to the aircraft carrier *Hornet* from which the Doolittle raid over Japan originated. Another film that dealt with the Pacific theater was *Winged Victory* (1944), which presented an excellent view of the training and preparation of those who made up the Army Air Force. It is the story of how American youths from diverse parts of the country are turned into pilots, navigators, and bombardiers to bring about victory—a winged victory. Or as one airman noted at the film's end, they were making every possible effort like no one had attempted before.

One of the destinations of the Air Force was Southeast Asia where in *Objective, Burma!* (1945), Hollywood saluted the U.S. paratrooper. The film was a straightforward account of a raid by American paratroops on a Japanese radio station inside Burma and of their attempt to walk out of a dense jungle to safety after an earlier endeavor to evacuate them by plane had failed. From Burma, Hollywood traveled to the Philippines where in *Bataan* (1943) it paid tribute to the American and Philippine forces who gallantly held out against the Japanese until the enemy's superior strength defeated them. In *So Proudly We Hail* (1943), the movie saluted the nurses who remained behind on Bataan to treat the wounded.

From the Philippines, Hollywood went to one of the Pacific islands that American forces had lost but eventually recaptured on their way to victory in the Pacific. In *Wake Island* (1942), Hollywood attempted its first documentary approach to the war—a battle in which 478 Marines and 1,100 construction workers of the American Federation of Labor held against the Japanese attacks from December 8, 1941, to December

22, 1941, allegedly wiring the U.S. War Department to "send us more Japs." For the first time, Hollywood showed the folks at home that the war and the enemy were very real indeed.

If the audiences wearied of lush tropical Pacific settings, other battle-fields around the world were available for viewing at the local movie house. They could watch the desert warfare in North Africa; in *Sahara* (1943) a small group of men—separated from their American and Brit-ish units—cross the Libyan deserts with their captured German and Italian prisoners, fight sandstorms and thirst, and eventually capture a German battalion. Moviegoers could brave perils of the Atlantic Ocean; in the film *Action in the North Atlantic* (1943), they could observe the bravery and tenacity of the U.S. Merchant Marines as they fought the terrors and fell victim to German submarines, only to return once again to ferry supplies to the Allies at such ports as Murmansk, Russia.

Portrayal of the Enemy

Most of the movies seemed to concentrate on either the Germans or the Japanese. For whatever reasons, films about the Italians were not as numerous; perhaps because Benito Mussolini and his Italian forces were perceived as Germany's puppets and not equal partners. Perhaps Italians did not have the public image of being as cruel or as bestial as the Germans and Japanese. Perhaps, after suing for peace in 1943 and be-coming an Ally only to be subsequently occupied by German forces, Italy was viewed as just another country that had to be liberated. Perhaps Benito Mussolini did not seem as menacing as Hitler or Premier Tojo but rather as a leader who had a comical image. Perhaps the Italian military machine seemed so ineffectual in battle whether in Greece or elsewhere. Whatever the reasons may have been, Hollywood did not give as much attention to the menace of the Italians as it did to the villainy of the Germans and Japanese.

The Japanese

Hollywood's portrayal of the Japanese mirrored what Americans heard, saw, or read about the wartime behavior of their Far Eastern adversary. This included their inhumane treatment of the Chinese as witnessed in the rape of Nanking during the 1930s and their treatment of other peoples whose lands they invaded, their brutal treatment of American and other prisoners during the "March of Death on Bataan," their Emperor worship, their fanaticism in battle as well as their preferences for death rather than surrender, and the relatively cheap value the Japanese seemed to place on human life whether it be their own or others. Rarely did the fictional or semifictional movie attempt to objectively explain or give insight into the intricacies of the Japanese character, mind, or culture that contributed to such behavior, though some documentaries did make an effort to educate the American public about this enemy.

Various movies reinforced the stereotypes Americans held of the Japanese during the war. In *Betrayal from the East* (1945), a title perhaps chosen to remind moviegoers of the Japanese attack at Pearl Harbor, the Japanese with slanted eyes, vicious voices and hideous tortures of their enemies, are thwarted by American government agents in their efforts to learn America's defense plans for the Panama Canal.

The Purple Heart (1944) only reinforced the inhumane image of the Japanese character, especially regarding the torture of prisoners of war. This movie told the semifictional story of the eight American flyers who had been captured after Doolittle's raid over Tokyo and other Japanese cities in April 1942. The men were captured, tortured, and subsequently placed on trial in violation of international law for supposedly bombing nonmilitary targets; three of them were executed. The real reason for their trial was to get them to reveal the base from which the Doolittle mission began. While acknowledging that some Japanese acted inhumanely toward American prisoners of war, critics of the film noted that the actions of a few Japanese at the trial could be falsely translated into being characteristic of every Japanese citizen. In addition, critics believed the movie did nothing to help the American moviegoer understand the Japanese character (for example, why cruelty seemed to be so much a part of it) and, thus, understand the kind of enemy America was fighting.

Perhaps, to counter such stereotypes, Hollywood, on occasion, attempted to show that some Japanese did have second thoughts about their country's war aims and that not all Japanese supported their government goals. *Behind the Rising Sun* (1943) told the story of how a Japanese youth who was educated in America, returns to Japan and is influenced by its culture, by his father who believes that Japanese world domination is all that matters, and by the army that drafts him and sends him to China where he acquires a taste for torture. This movie also reinforced the stereotype of the Japanese occupier who sells girls into slavery, abuses the Chinese, gives the Chinese children opium, and perhaps even kills children for sport. When the father realizes how his country has changed his American-educated son and this kind of Japan might actually win the war, he tries to atone for his sins by committing hara-kiri (Japanese suicide). This film gave the moviegoer two important messages. A nation in which the buying and selling of human beings, drug addiction, torture, and other heinous qualities are part of its character cannot be allowed to rule the world. The other message was that Japan was not a monolith with the complete support of its people; dissidents existed within its population who eventually could distinguish right from wrong. This too was an encouraging message at a time when Japanese military forces dominated the western Pacific.

The Germans

When Hollywood movies focused on the Germans, they slightly altered the stereotypes attributed to the Japanese. Whereas the Japanese were portrayed as cruel or bestial, the Germans were either all bad or all good, which in reality was not necessarily true. The common soldiers were unmitigated thugs and killers, while the officers often were brave, independent, civilized men. Just as Hollywood found it difficult to explain in its fictional films why the Japanese were so cruel and bestial, it was also vague in explaining what a Nazi actually was or how German society could bring out and maintain the irrational behavior that Americans perceived to be the dominant characteristics of the Nazi personality. The films, especially those about the Gestapo (an acronym for the State Secret Police—*Geheime Staatzpolizei*), focused on torture, relentless questioning ("Vee haff vays to make you talk"), the beheading of prisoners, jackboots, monocles, facial scars from duels at Heidelberg, sneering comments about the enemy's softness, spying, concentration camps, and many "Heil Hitlers."

A movie called *The Hitler Gang* (1944) was presented in semidocumentary style without blatant editorializing and attempted to show the nature of the Nazi leaders, their careers between World War I and World War II, and the manner in which they had gained power. Critics noted, however, that this film represented too simple a history, making it appear that the rise of Nazism was very easy and suggesting that Hitler was a dangerous fanatic with no mind of his own and whose only talent was oratory.

Some films tried to point out that not all Germans were pro-Nazi, that some still opposed and worked against the Nazi regime. *Nazi Agent* (1942) told the story of German twin brothers, one a German consul in America and the other a nice quiet philatelist who wanted to make America his home. When the German consul forced his brother to let him use his store as a front for passing on secret messages to German spies, the philatelist kills him and takes his place as German consul. The philatelist-turned-consul then effectively exposes German spies, one of whom says: "I hope you do not think that you have put an end to our work," to which the philatelist replies, "No, but I am only one of 130 million Americans who would do all they can for their country."[18]

Hollywood also attempted to tell the moviegoer that the Nazis were neither fools nor a master race, that they were people with an insidious ideology which threatened to bring the world back to the Dark Ages. In *Hangmen Also Die* (1943), Hollywood told the story of the murder of Reinhard Heydrich, the Reich-protector of Czechoslovakia, because of whose assassination the Nazis razed the town of Lidice and murdered its citizens. The film portrayed Heydrich, not as a stereotype or stupid Nazi villain, but as a wily human being who was to be feared.

How to play the villain?

The labor shortage of the war extended to the question as to who would be portraying the movie villain. Until Pearl Harbor, filmmakers did not consider foreign villains because foreign film-buying countries threatened to boycott the industry. However, once America officially entered the war, the Nazis became the heavy heavies, the Italians the light heavies, and the Japanese the cruelest heavies of all. It was relatively easy to turn a Chinese or Philippine actor into a Japanese character. According to Frederick C. Othman, "all the makeup personnel had to do was just straighten the [actor's] hairline across his forehead, comb his hair straight back, accent and turn down his eyebrows, build out his mouth and the transformation was complete."[19] The arduous part was persuading actors to play the roles of Japanese—most of whom were interned in camps in the United States during war.

Resistance Films

Hollywood did not forget that subjugated countries had not abandoned their efforts to throw off the yoke of their Axis oppressors. Toward this end, Hollywood made a number of films about their resistance and the methods and problems they used and encountered in their quest for freedom. *This Land is Mine* (1943) portrayed the difficulty in rising up against the Nazi conquerors whether in Czechoslovakia or other subjugated nations. The film pointed out certain conditions of occupation that war movies often omitted. The locale of the story is never mentioned except that the action takes place "somewhere in Europe." The film showed the confusion of the middle class when the Nazis overrun the country, the difficulty in being a hero when starvation is the order of the day, the inherent dignity of human beings, the immutability of truth no matter how many people are killed, the fascist hatred of labor unions, the character of education under a fascist regime, the importance of sabotage in time of sacrifice, and the danger of people who are safe in free countries and are smug about collaborationists. The movie attempted to make an honest statement about conditions in the occupied countries of Europe.[20] Another film, *Commandos Strike at Dawn* (1942), showed how a people can be transformed by their conquerors. As a result of Nazi brutality, peaceful Norwegian villagers are urged by their leader to learn the tactics of their oppressors and the use of the weapons of war, including clubs, dynamite, and knives. In other words, the Norwegians are urged to fight the Nazis on their own terms. After the village leader kills the Nazi commander, he escapes to England only to return to his country in charge of a commando expedition.

At Rick's Café Americain in *Casablanca* (1942), refugees, especially from France, gathered as they sought transit papers to freedom and out of the country, then controlled by collaborationist Vichy France. Two such refugees were Ilsa, Rick's former lover, and Victor Laszlo, her husband and head of the Czechoslovakian resistance movement, whom the Nazis wanted to arrest. The film portrayed the active resistance found in every country occupied by the Nazis.

The Allies in Film

While the movies portrayed the Axis enemies as cruel and fiendish, the members of the United Nations were always depicted as courageous and good. Films were made about the Russians, the Canadians, the French, the English, and other Allies. *The North Star* (1943) depicted life in a Russian village during the two peaceful days preceding Hitler's attack on Russia on June 22, 1941, and the immediate consequences of that attack. It is a tale of an ordinary group of people who defend their homes, fighting and dying for Russia. At the movie's end when the Russians retake their village from the Germans, Hollywood notes why fascism can take root and grow in a country. The Nazi military surgeon—the proud liberal who has tolerated Nazism—confronts the Russian village surgeon with the statement, "I do not like much what I have done for the past nine years." The Russian answers, "I have heard about men like you. The civilized men who are sorry. Men who do the work of the fascists and pretend to themselves they are better than those for whom they work. It is men like you who have sold your people to men like . . . [Hitler]."[21] The Russian then shoots the Nazi. By presenting the Nazi physician as a civilized man with a conscience, the movie demonstrates that fascism can arise anywhere—even among civilized people as long as they do nothing but acquiesce to it with their conscience—a principle applicable to any ideology that deprives a people of its freedom.

Movies About Home

Hollywood also portrayed what the war was like on the home front. The movies presented many portraits of the American home front. One such film, William Saroyan's *The Human Comedy* (1943), took the moviegoer to Ithaca, California, where the MacCauley family lived. It was the tale of a good family living in a good town during wartime, but also it was a story about love and loneliness, singing, praying, music, home, family, death, and life. The film represented an affirmation of what Americans were fighting for rather than being just another movie depicting the brutalizing character of their enemies and skillful heroics of their armed forces. Here moviegoers met Mrs. MacCauley, Bess, her college-aged daughter, Marcus, her idealistic son who was in the Army, and

Homer, the son who worked as a postal telegrapher and the family's breadwinner, while serving as a father figure to Ulysses, the youngest member of the family. Many of the messages Homer delivered said much about the war on the home front: "I am coming home," "Happy Birthday," "The Department of War regrets to inform you that your son _____," "Meet me at the Southern Depot," "Here is a kiss," "I am all right, don't worry," "God bless you!" These messages that Mr. Grogan, the telegrapher, tapped out and Homer delivered to Ithaca's families were as meaningful to moviegoers as some of the greatest battles being waged abroad.

From Ithaca, California, the movies traveled to Waterloo, Iowa, one of the saddest towns in America during World War II. Through *The Fighting Sullivans* (1944), movie audiences lived the true heartbreaking story of how one American family lost all five of its sons when the cruiser, the U.S.S. *Juneau*, on which they were serving, was sunk on November 15, 1942, in a naval battle off Guadacanal in the Solomon Islands. Not since a mother in Boston lost five sons in the Civil War had any single American family suffered so many dead in service to its country. As a result of this tragedy, the Navy changed its policy of having members of the same family serve in the same military unit. As the film begins, the father and mother are seen watching proudly as each of their children are baptized and toward the movie's end the remaining family—father, mother, daughter, and daughter-in-law—are present at the launching of a new destroyer, the U.S.S. *The Sullivans* (September 30, 1943). By portraying this brave family, Hollywood paid tribute to all the courageous families in the country who lost their loved ones during the war. Because of the tragic theme of this film, many theaters refused to show *The Fighting Sullivans* in their home towns while the war was on.

While movies spoke of brave Americans who sacrificed their lives to preserve their country's freedoms, they also warned the American public to be vigilant for other Americans who might be willing to betray the country to the Axis cause. *Pilot Number 5* (1943) warned Americans that fascism could legally take over their government as it told the story of a fascist-leaning politician who occupied one of the highest political offices in the country, namely, a state governorship. Alfred Hitchcock's *Saboteur* (1942) illustrated America's determination to defeat the fascists. The film's hero, pursued by the police across the country after being falsely accused of incendiary sabotage at a California aircraft plant, finally finds out who the true culprits are. When the accused meets the real saboteur, he tells the Axis agent that Americans will keep fighting for as long as it takes to defeat his kind of people who care for no one at all. Well, in *Hail the Conquering Hero* (1944), it didn't take long for a phony hero to return from the war, and to the exasperation of the town's mayor, campaign for the mayoral position himself. Even after admitting he was a phony, the so-called hero still retained the support of the townspeople because, as one of them noted, politics doesn't require any reasons.[22] This was a movie whose message is timeless.

Changes during the War

Movies tried to illustrate how World War II began, who the enemies were and what their ideologies and character were. The films also tried to show that while the United Nations were waging war on one side, those living in conquered lands had not yet submitted to Nazi domination and were also attempting to throw off the Nazi yoke themselves nor were all Germans pro-Nazi. In bolstering the hopes of the moviegoer, Hollywood sent the message that the United Nations were not alone in their fight against the Axis powers and people should not despair about the struggle in which they were engaged.

The movies Hollywood produced during the war years revealed changing patterns of subject matter as the war progressed. In 1942, America saw the Japanese conquer the Philippines, threaten Australia, lose the Battle of Midway and the Coral Sea, and engage American troops in a long drawn-out battle for Guadacanal. Meanwhile, American forces landed in North Africa. Through all this uncertainty, the American public was unprepared for war materially and psychologically and sought some way to deal with the crisis effectively. During this time, the feature films Hollywood produced did little to help mobilize the public for an all-out war effort. Home front activities such as Red Cross work, the role of air raid wardens and civil defense activities were treated comically in the movies which made volunteer recruitment more difficult. Films about the enemy were also inappropriate. At a time when the public needed a serious evaluation of the enemy's strength which was then far greater than America's, spy pictures were the order of the day. Some films even ridiculed the enemy. Sixty-five percent of the war films and more than 15 percent of all films (Hollywood produced 486 feature films in 1942) were spy films, comedies or musicals about military camp life, thus giving audiences a poor understanding of the war effort.[23] Examples of such films include *Air Raid Wardens* (1943) in which Laurel and Hardy, rejected by the draft board, manage to stumble upon and capture a group of Nazi agents. In *Cairo* (1942), a spy spoof, Metro-Goldwyn-Mayer's singing star Jeanette MacDonald and Robert Young travel to the Middle East where MacDonald opens a secret pyramid by reaching the note of high C. In *The Yanks Are Coming* (1942) a band enlists in the Army as an act of rebellion against their bandleader who disparages the common soldier.

During 1943 the proportion of movies devoted to the war increased, and the character of the war films changed. Compared with 1942, twice as many films attempted to tell why America was fighting the war. In addition, thirty productions—three times as many as in 1942—were made about the Allies. Meanwhile, the enemy was less characterized as slant-eyed Japanese or guttural-sounding Germans and more clearly as fascists.[24]

By 1944, the war film began its decline. Although movies about the American armed forces were numerous, those about the enemy continued to decrease, and spy melodramas became almost extinct. Fearful of being caught with a backlog of war films on the day of victory, Hollywood went back to known prewar formulas and began to produce many light musicals, murder mysteries and other escapist films unrelated to the war effort. From December 1, 1941, to December 4, 1944, the movie industry released 1,321 feature films. In three out of ten of these films the main story concerned the war.[25] While critics may debate the significance or the contribution of movies as an appropriate vehicle for providing information about the war—film is a fantasy form of communication. But the movies did fulfill one basic function: in a world at war, they provided entertainment to those who were fighting abroad and those who remained at home. In doing so, they also provided many kinds of images and messages about our enemies, our allies, and ourselves.

These films represent a sample of war-related movies Hollywood produced during World War II. They do not include the many comedies, mysteries, musicals, dramas, and other kinds of films that did not directly reflect the war. These movies were not necessarily the most important films of the war or those of the most artistic award-winning merit.

But they do illustrate the messages films were sending Americans and the rest of the world to bolster their morale, namely, despite the early setbacks in the war Americans were tough and were willing to make the necessary personal sacrifices to see the war through to its victorious conclusion. The fictional film may not have always portrayed the real nature or true character of the enemy or what war was really like for those who actually participated in battle or lived through its aftereffects (though documentaries related many of these experiences). Some of the fictional or semifictional stories may have been contrived. Maybe Americans appeared to be supermen on many occasions when reality would reject such a notion. Maybe movie battles were won under the strangest of circumstances and against immense odds. However, the possibility of winning the war in its earliest stages was also against great odds. If one of the purposes of propaganda is to bolster a nation's spirit and not just demoralize the enemy's, then the fictional or semifictional films Hollywood produced during the war years accomplished their purpose. If winning against all odds on the silver screen while being defeated in real battles at the war's beginning enabled a nation to enjoy some self-esteem, the movies achieved their purpose. If the films gave a nation hope that victories on the screen could be translated into victories in the real conflict, the movies achieved their purpose. If the fictional or semifictional film showed that the enemy was not as invincible as his own propaganda or military victories suggested, especially at the war's beginning, and thus bolstered and kept up the morale of the armed forces and those on the home front, then the movies achieved their goal. Along with documentaries and other kinds of films Hollywood produced, Americans learned a lot about themselves both as individuals and as a nation. The movies tried to make the public understand what was at stake in the conflict and helped maintain its unflagging support to bring the war to a successful conclusion. The films Hollywood produced helped Americans and others understand what the United States stood for—a message which was an indispensable element for achieving final victory in the greatest conflict the world had ever known.

Hollywood and Wartime Shortages

Whether absorbing the defunct activities of a federal agency, producing films for other government agencies, or continuing the entertainment business, Hollywood had to deal with wartime shortages, human and material; and Hollywood found itself making some unique improvisations. Movie technicians had to develop the first synthetic wig when the European and Chinese sources for real hair were cut off. Extras in a western were told to grow their own beards because there was no hair to make false ones; leading ladies at Universal Studios were told to let their hair grow long. Rubber was not available to make such props as spider webs or knife blades. Beer bottles, chairs, and vases with which villains were hit became expendable because the supplies of resin from the German-occupied Balkans and balsa wood for chairs from the Japanese-occupied Philippines were cut off. Even the breakaway windows through which actors were thrown or jumped fell victim to the war; the windows were made of candy sugar and, in view of the sugar shortage, the government did not consider the windows essential and did not issue sugar rations to the studios. At Republic and other studios, Army officials requisitioned all the firearms that were used in westerns and other films and gave them to civilian authorities for civilian defense. The cowboys at Republic, a specialist in the singing-cowboy western, were given wooden guns. Because blank cartridges were not available, villains began to meet their fate, not with gunfire but lassoes or the hero's fists. Whatever gunfire was heard in the film was usually dubbed in by the studio sound department. Even snow scenes began to disappear because the snow was made from untoasted corn flakes and gypsum; corn flakes were reserved exclusively for eating and gypsum went into a variety of war products.[1]

On May 6, 1942, the War Production Board ordered that no more than $5,000 worth of new materials could be used for film sets in any picture. Accustomed to spending $50,000 or more on movie sets, filmmakers devised various schemes to conform to the government's order and meet their own needs. Canvas sets were painted to resemble wood. Electromagnets were used to recover nails from discarded sets, and other machines straightened bent nails. Miniature sets were built whereby a small pool became the setting of a naval battle or via the camera, a doll town assumed the appearance of a metropolis.

Even the rate of film production suffered during the war years. In 1943, the War Production Board asked the movie industry to reduce its use of film to three-quarters the rate of its film footage in 1941 because films used about one-half of the peacetime production of basic nitrocellulose, a prime ingredient for gun powder.[2] As a result, all rehearsals that required film were eliminated; stills were used for wardrobe and sets; and reprinting of approved takes was eliminated as was the use of single takes for rushes (studio review of filmed scenes). To save money, producers began to shorten the listing of screen credits (the listing on the final screen print of everyone connected with the picture) and reduced the number of films in distribution. The use of millions of promotional signed, movie star photographs was curtailed because of the squeeze in printing paper and chemicals.[3] One of the results of these various shortages and conservation measures at the Warner Brothers studio was that Jack Benny filmed *George Washington Slept Here* (1942) before a background designed for the movie *Arsenic and Old Lace*.

The war created manpower problems. Many leading actors including James Stewart, Clark Gable, Tyrone Power, Robert Montgomery, Burgess Meredith, Douglas Fairbanks, Jr., Victor Mature, Wayne Morris, and Ronald Reagan entered the armed services; as a result, children and older actors were in demand. One film director had his female chorus dress in men's clothing to replace choristers who had been drafted. These are just a few examples of how World War II affected Hollywood film production.

1. Frederick C. Othman, "War in the World of Make-Believe," *Saturday Evening Post*, October 17, 1942, 29, 110–11.
2. "Big Movie Year," *Business Week*, February 13, 1943, 40.
3. "Retake for War," *Business Week*, July 25, 1942 38, 40.

Notes

1. Dorothy B. Jones, "Tomorrow the Movies: Hollywood Goes to War," *Nation*, January 27, 1945, 95.

2. Frederic Sondern and C. Nelson Schrader, "Hollywood Handles Dynamite," *Commonweal*, December 12, 1941, 195–96.

3. Anthony Rhodes, *Propaganda The Art of Persuasion: World War II*, (Secaucus, N.J.: The Wellfleet Press, 1987), 151.

4. *Prelude to War* (1942), War Activities Committee.

5. Hermine Rich Isaacs, "War Fronts and Film Fronts," *Theatre Arts*, June 1944, 345–46 and Philip T. Hartung, "The Memphis Belle," *Commonweal*, April 14, 1944, 652–53.

6. Martin Gilbert, *The Second World War*, (New York: Henry Holt and Company, 1989), 481.

7. Liz-Anne Bawden, ed., *The Oxford Companion to Film*, (New York and London: Oxford University Press, 1976), 448.

8. Ibid.

9. Philip T. Hartung, "The Stage and Screen," *Commonweal*, March 5, 1943, 495–96.

10. Larry Langman and Ed Borg, *Encyclopedia of American War Films*, (New York and London: Garland Publishing, Inc., 1989) 360–61.

11. Robert Furman, "They Fight with Film," *Reader's Digest*, February 1943, 133.

12. Arthur L. Mayer, "Post War Preambles," *Theatre Arts*, November 1944, 645.

13. Sondern and Schrader, 197.

14. Manny Farber, "Movies in Wartime," *New Republic*, January 3, 1944, 18.

15. "Make Believe War," *Atlantic Monthly*, July 1943, 117–18.

16. *Stage Door Canteen* (United Artists/Sol Lesser, 1943).

17. Philip T. Hartung, "Hollywood's Reply to December 7," *Commonweal*, December 22, 1944, 255–56.

18. "To Be or Not To Be Laughed At," *Commonweal*, March 13, 1942, 514.

19. Frederick C. Othman, "War in the World of Make-Believe," *Saturday Evening Post*, October 17, 1942, 28.

20. Philip T. Hartung, "This Land is Mine," *Commonweal*, June 4, 1943, 170.

21. Manny Farber, "The Cardboard Star," *New Republic*, November 8, 1943, 653.

22. Philip T. Hartung, "Hail the Conquering Hero," *Commonweal*, August 25, 1944, 87–88 and Manny Farber, "To Be and Not to Be," *New Republic*, August 21, 1944, 220.

23. Jones, 93.

24. Ibid., 93–94

25. Ibid., 94–95.

Chapter Six

THEATER
What the Playwrights Said

I N A COUNTRY WEARY of war, Americans sought many forms of recreation to alleviate the stresses of the day. They attended movies, concerts, and sporting events, and they participated in a whole host of other activities. One source of available entertainment was the stage. Theater could be found everywhere in America—on college campuses, military bases, and in communities, large and small. Performed by amateurs and professionals, plays were presented in many forms—as musicals, comedies, and dramas. But whatever the format, the theater brought some measure of emotional relief to a country enveloped by war.

The use of theater to present ideologic messages was not new. As far back as the Middle Ages, the Christian church recognized that the stage could be more impressive than the pulpit, and began to present its sermons in dramatic form, first as dialogues, then as mystery, miracle, and morality plays. Following World War I, drama in Europe concentrated largely on political propaganda. Germany spread its totalitarian principles through the Nationalist Socialist Theater; Italy used theater sponsored by the Ministry of Propaganda; and the Soviet Union organized theatrical troops of "flying brigades" to help spread its new communist ideology throughout the country.

At the beginning of World War II, theater critics argued that the American stage was not being used as a powerful weapon in the ideologic struggle between the Axis powers and the United Nations. They cited as examples the activities of other countries. In China, politically educative theater companies were performing behind the front lines, and in Russia mobile theater units followed the Russian Army as playwrights turned out many antifascist dramas. Nearly a year after Pearl Harbor, American theater critics were still clamoring for a war drama. Both the professional and amateur theaters were being prodded to produce plays that would express the ideas for which the war was being fought. Perhaps, the power of the democratic ideals for which the United Nations were fighting (and which theater critics thought the stage could convey into the everyday consciousness of all citizens) was observed on Broadway when World War II arrived for one theatergoer with the following thoughts:

> . . . The picture was of Britain at war—casual, unperturbed, minimizing the heroic, holding the "Enemy of Mankind" at bay with steely determination.
>
> As the curtain went up after the second act of "Golden Wings," a new voice not of any actor in the play came from a loud speaker. "My fellow Americans: The sudden criminal attacks perpetrated by the Japanese in the Pacific . . ."—President Roosevelt addressing the people of the United States, the people of England, the free people of the world! Time and space were obliterated. We in the theater in New York sat with our brothers-in-arms in England and listened to words that hammered out a bloody indictment: "In 1931 Japan invaded Manchukuo—without warning. In 1938 Hitler occupied Austria—without warning. In 1939 Czechoslovakia, Poland. 1940, Norway, Denmark, The Netherlands, Belgium, Luxembourg, France, Greece. 1941, Yugoslavia, the United States! Without warning . . . Without warning!" The Theater of War had engulfed us. Engulfed us and made us one with English men and women on the stage, with "the vast majority of the human race whose cause we share," whose hope is our hope, for "liberty under God."
>
> And so war came to Broadway—no longer as something to be looked upon from an orchestra seat, something removed by distance, objective, deeply moving, perhaps, but not truly shared. Now we are all actors in the same world-wide drama . . .[1]

Such was the enormous potential of theater during the war. Free of radio censorship and the taboos of film, theater could deal with the issues of the day. Critics argued that the theater had done so during the Depression years of the 1930s, why not again?

During World War II, theater in America was everywhere. Although most people tend to think of the New York theater district, also known as Broadway, when the stage is mentioned, in terms of actual playhouses,

Broadway was and remains a very small part of the legitimate stage in America. One of the most numerous forms was the community or tributary theater, nonprofessional groups who performed outside the territory covered by professional theatrical road companies. These community theaters were found in converted barns, community playhouses, college campuses, and other locations. They not only entertained civilians, but also brought their productions to military camps as well.

Plays were used for many purposes during the war years—to sell bonds, recruit Red Cross volunteers, collect scrap iron and paper, and dramatize messages the government wanted to convey to the public, to name but a few. For example, students at Smith College in Massachusetts wrote the words and music for a production called *Make with the Maximum*. Taking this play to industrial plants, cast members joined with plant workers in singing such lyrics as

> *Switch on the contact*
> *Turn on the juice*
> *Double the output or*
> *There's no excuse—*
> *Life can be pretty when you're being of use*
> *Hey, fellas, we gotta produce—so*
> *Make with the Maximum!*[2]

Theater and the Military

Although the tributary theater entertained civilian and military camp audiences, the armed services also promoted another kind of theater, the "soldier theatricals." Military theater had two purposes: To entertain and maintain the morale of troops as they trained for battle and to teach soldiers the art of self-entertainment after they were sent overseas and stationed in some inaccessible spot where mental hardship and nervous tension accompanied their military duty.

The U.S. Army, for example had a Special Services Division (previously called the Morale Branch), which was constantly distributing to its military personnel original songs, skits, and other material written by soldiers. One such theatrical was *Hi, Yank!*, a musical extravaganza produced by members of the Special Services Division at Fort Dix, New Jersey. Based on *Yank*, the Army Weekly, the revue featured the universal figure of the Sad Sack who has been described as "the perfect personification of the Army's little man, the hopeless underdog who has no stripes, no glory, no friends in the orderly room, no escape from the dreaded terrors of red tape and higher ranks. Since he is the Army's little man, none of his troubles are ever of his own making. No matter what he does or leaves undone, trouble will come to him from outside forces. The only thing he can ever be sure of is the perversity of his fate."[3] His military instructions were simple: If it moves, salute it. If it doesn't move, pick it up. If you can't pick it up, paint it.

The armed services had a third form of theater available for their entertainment, the United Service Organization (USO) Camp Shows, the Hollywood Caravans, and similar organizations. These shows were fully professional, recruited from a talent pool organized by the entertainment industry, including theater, radio, and movies. Entertainers like Bob Hope, Bing Crosby, Martha Raye, and Al Jolson were just a few of the big name stars who entertained the armed forces at home and abroad under the auspices of these professional camp shows. But they were not the only show business personalities who dedicated their lives to the war effort. Most were just ordinary show people to whom *Yank*, the Army Weekly, paid tribute:

> Most of the troop entertainment in this war has come from the rank and file of ordinary men and women whose stage names are not famous but who have been working on the stages of camps and overseas bases without a break since Pearl Harbor. They don't rush home to fulfill radio obligations because they haven't got any radio obligations. And they are not planning to cash in on their Army tour publicity because newspapers never mention them. We have never seen headlines, for instance, about Maxine Marsh, a tap dancer; Christine Street, an accordionist and singer; and Adelaide Joy, a comedienne. Those three girls, typical troop entertainers, were killed in an RCAF plane crash March 27, 1943, while touring our North Atlantic bases. It's about time that the hundreds of unpublicized, self-sacrificing show people on overseas duty shared the burden they have been carrying so quietly with more of the higher-paid glamour personalities of Hollywood and Broadway.[4]

Three years before these comments were written (1941), an Englishman remarked that "it is possible that this war will be won by the side whose troops are least bored."[5] Well, the entertainers *Yank* saluted may not have achieved the publicity, fame, or income of their Broadway or Hollywood counterparts, but who is to say that their efforts as well as those who appeared in soldier, civilian professional, and community theatricals were not among the most important factors that contributed to our eventual victory.

During the war, theatricals served many purposes. They were functional, instructional, and entertaining, but they also raised serious and profound questions about these times. Functionally, the theater was used to advance war drives such as bond sales, scrap collection, or volunteer recruitments. Instructionally, plays informed civilians what to expect during air raids or how the draft board functioned, and the military used the theater to indoctrinate recruits into its way of life by having inductees witness and act in such plays as *Manners in the Military* or *Stack Arms, Mr. Murphy*.

For entertainment, one show that delighted the civilians and military was *This Is The Army*, a soldier theatrical written by Irving Berlin. After a start on Broadway, the musical played at military camps both at home and overseas. Written for and produced by the U.S. government, the show raised at least $10 million for the Army Emergency Relief Fund. Featuring such Berlin tunes as "I Left My Heart at the Stage Door Canteen" and "Oh! How I Hate to Get Up in the Morning," the show was cast entirely with soldiers, most of whom were experienced theater people who were now in the armed services. In this swift-paced show, the performers sang and danced, impersonated chorus girls and celebrities like Gypsy Rose Lee, and presented minstrel, vaudeville, and other production numbers. Overseas, the show was received with wild enthusiasm and toured such battle zones as North Africa, Sicily, and Italy. In England, a writer remarked that the show "increased a hundred-fold the growing understanding and friendship of our two peoples."[6]

The Literary Theater

Theater had yet another purpose during the war. Playwrights sought to illuminate the understanding of these times, as well as the issues and problems that mankind had to resolve if it was to live in a world of peace and freedom. Some playwrights were successful in their effort; others were not.

The Moon Is Down

"The people are confused and so am I." So speaks the mayor of a small snow-sheltered mining town on a northern sea, which had suddenly and inexplicably been conquered by a murderous military power. John Steinbeck, the playwright, was not. Although confused at first, the townspeople learn little by little and in their bitter, silent, and devious ways become unconquerable. In *The Moon Is Down* (1942), Steinbeck relates the almost silent struggle of humankind to be free of oppression. Here, the struggle of the forces that were tearing the world apart in war was played out on a miniature scale, but with no less intensity than was occurring on major battlefields throughout the world.[7]

In the interest of universality, Steinbeck did not identify any nationalities, but the play clearly suggests that the invaders are Nazis and the conquered people are Norwegian. The invaders hope to consolidate their victory and through collaboration avoid bloodshed; the mayor bides his time, waiting to learn the wishes of the people. Those desires gradually emerge in the underground resistance to increasing violence. The invaders learn that "herd men" may control momentarily, but they cannot conquer free people. The conquerors kill, brutalize, and starve the inhabitants, but as the winter progresses, the underground war continues and becomes more bitter and murderous.

"We have taken on a bad job," says the leader (colonel) of the enemy forces.

"Yes," the mayor answers in a gentle, deprecating but unswerving manner, "the one impossible thing in the world. The one thing that can't be done . . . !"

"And that is?"

"To break man's spirit permanently."

The colonel agrees although his profession forces him to use methods he has seen are futile. For Steinbeck has not fashioned his Germans of wood or steel: "Free men cannot start a war," the mayor points out to the colonel, "but once it is started they can fight on in defeat. Herd men, followers of the leader, cannot do that, and so it is always the herd men who win the battles and the free men who win the wars."[8]

Steinbeck endowed each of the invaders with an individuality. One young lieutenant is driven to the verge of insanity by the tension and horrors that slowly invade the snowbound village, crying out hysterically that he had a dream or a thought—that the leader was insane—that the communiqués might well read "the flies have conquered the fly-paper." That Steinbeck portrayed the invaders as human made more devastating the shooting of hostages, the hate and fear consuming both sides, and the starving of children to force their fathers to work. Although the colonel may have been a humanist haunted by memories of World War I, he orders the execution of the mayor just the same.

The power and poignancy of Steinbeck's play lay in its relevancy; its ability to express world issues and at the same time affirm the dignity and nobility of man. The setting of the play could have been in any country or community—wherever the war was being waged or might be fought. Some critics believed that Steinbeck expressed an eloquent plea for democracy, a stirring call-to-arms to all free fighting spirits.[9] Other critics believed that Steinbeck's view of democracy caused complacency and blinded democracy to the need for immediate decisive action, and that the play gave an unreal and highly sentimental picture of the Nazi soldier. Hitler's followers—the argument continued—were too tough to break down under cold, loneliness, and fear. Then, in December 1942, the Associated Press reported from London, on very good authority, a serious increase of mutinies, desertions, and suicides as well as a general lowering of morale among the 200,000 German troops who were occupying Norway. The story added "Norwegian circles here attribute the slackening Nazi morale to the severe climate, particularly in the far north; to virtually no home leaves, fears of being sent to the Russian front and the cold shoulder attitude of 98 percent of the Norwegian people."[10] It was *The Moon Is Down* almost word for word.

Watch on the Rhine

Playwrights also noted that not all Germans were Nazis. Even those who were, if reached in time and at a young enough age, could have their minds and opinions altered from the influence of their upbringing. When Americans heard and read each day about the horrors that the fascist powers were perpetrating upon the world, they could understand the anguish of Kurt Mueller, the antifascist underground hero of Lillian Hellman's play *Watch on the Rhine* (1941), when he decried: "Shame on us! Thousands of years and we cannot yet make a world."[11] The play pointed out that an entire nation cannot be indicted when it falls from grace because within it may be men and women who oppose the evil it is carrying out.

The setting of the play is in a country home, not far from Washington, D.C., where a friendly widow lives in comfort and security, not greatly disturbed by the troubles of the world. Along with a Rumanian Count and his wife who are house guests, she is awaiting the imminent arrival of her daughter, Sara, who is returning home with her German husband and three children, after having been away for 20 years. But Sara's husband, Kurt Mueller, is no ordinary refugee but a member of a German underground organization that has fought Hitler in his own land. The Rumanian Count, a fascist by nature and a blackmailer, gambler, and spy by necessity, recognizes and attempts to blackmail Mueller and his family to keep his silence. Mueller realizes the Count must die to save his own life, those of his friends, and his cause. For the ultimate good of mankind, Mueller kills the Count, but with repugnance, deep-seated disgust, and without any illusions. As Mueller tells his children, men will steal and lie and kill, even kill for a good cause "but don't forget—it is bad—it is still bad."[12] So the violence of the war comes to a peaceful home near Washington, D.C. Before Mueller leaves on his undoubtedly fatal mission to continue his fight against the fascist enemies, another American family is shaken out of its wartime complacency.

In the character of Kurt Mueller, Hellman shows a man who is heroic, thoughtful, peace loving, gentle, compassionate, human, brave and fearful—a man who has been called upon to stand up for his ideals by taking direct action against his enemies. In Maxwell Anderson's *Valley Forge* (1934) George Washington speaks a thoughtful phrase: "This liberty will look easy by and by when nobody dies to get it."[13] Hellman stated this thought another way. When Sara's mother says "We are all antifascist," Sara with anguish points out the difference, "Kurt works at it." "Working at it in and near Germany during Hitler's reign meant persecution, torture, flight, misery, and the constant threat of death and worse."[14] When Kurt Mueller departed from America, he was not just leaving to fight fascism for that moment, he was returning home in an attempt to save the world's future generations—its children—from being enslaved and corrupted by this perverse ideology.

Tomorrow the World!

Another play, *Tomorrow the World!* (1943) ("Today we rule Germany, Tomorrow the world!"—so ran the Nazi Horst Wessel song), posed the question of what could the world do with the millions of children raised under Nazism once peace came. To conquer the world, the fascist youth were trained since impressionable infancy to idealize force, blind obedience, and prejudice. James Gow and Arnaud d'Usseau, the play's coauthors, conceived the problem in simple yet dramatic terms. A twelve-year-old German youth is sent to live with his uncle,—a midwesterner, a widower, and a professor—whose household consists of his sister, daughter, and fiancée. The boy Emil is by birth half-American and half-German. His deceased mother was the professor's sister, and his father, a liberal, a philosopher, a distinguished citizen of the world, was killed in a German concentration camp for refusing to bow down to the German state. Emil, on the other hand, subject since his earliest childhood to a thorough Nazi education turns out, to the professor's surprise, to be the exact opposite of his father. The youth is a convinced Nazi who is positive that his father had traitorously betrayed the Third Reich. Appearing in his Nazi uniform, complete with swastika and knife, he espouses his belief in the New Order and like a recording recites speeches on decadent democracy, anti-Semitism as well as the sins and cowardice of his own father—ideas that had been driven into his impressionable mind until he could not forget them. Or, nearly so.

The drama's action concerns Emil's one-boy battle against America in the guise of his uncle's family. A liar, bully, and a spy, he creates trouble between his aunt and his uncle's fiancée who is Jewish and head of the progressive school to which he is sent. He is soon thoroughly disliked by everyone, except his cousin, a little girl whose friendliness he rewards by striking her when she discovers Emil stealing the key to her father's laboratory. The idea of a world filled with Emils was terrifying. Americans had already seen what his elders had done and were doing. Eventually this generation would die off, but the Emils of the world had another 50 years of active life. How was this youth and those like him to be cured of their fascist mind and spirit? The authors offered hope. In the play, Emil eventually succumbs to the little girl's candid reasonableness, supplemented by his uncle's disciplinary action, and a great deal of tact on the part of all. It is at least a civilized formula for treating the conquered of the world.[15]

A Bell for Adano

Americans demonstrated the civilized way they would treat the conquered of the world in the theatrical production of *A Bell for Adano*

(1944), Paul Osborn's dramatization of John Hersey's novel of how Major Victor Joppolo, U.S. Army, revives a Sicilian town and its people after they have been devastated by war. "I beg you to know the man Joppolo well," John Hersey wrote, "we have need of him. He is our future [in the world]. Neither the eloquence of Churchill nor the humaneness of Roosevelt, no Charter, no Four Freedoms or Fourteen Points, no dreamer's diagram so symmetrical and so faultless on paper, no plan, no hope, no treaty—none of these things can guarantee anything. Only men can guarantee, only the behavior of men under pressure, only our Joppolos."[16]

In attempting to restore the town, with its streets filled with debris from bombardment, its unburied dead, its people starving or fled to the hills and to reeducate its heterogenous townsfolk, Major Joppolo, Civil Affairs Officer of the Allied Military Government, tries to teach the liberators and liberated alike the basic principles of democracy and fair play. Joppolo, the practical idealist, reminds the townspeople of certain American principles. He lives them continuously and explains them to the town's officials whom he was trying to wean from the fascist formula:

"Your" Adano has been a Fascist town, but as I told you when we appointed you to your positions it is no longer being run that way. It is now being run as a Democracy. I am afraid some of you are forgetting that or perhaps you do not know what a Democracy is. I will tell you. (*He starts to tell them, leaning forward, but finds it difficult.*) One of the main things about a Democracy is that the men of the government are no longer masters of the people. They are the servants of the people, elected by the people, paid by the people with their taxes. Therefore, you are now the servants of the people of Adano. I too am their servant. When I go to buy bread, I'll take my place at the end of the line and wait my turn. Now, if I find any of you not willing to act in this way, I shall remove you from Office. Just remember that you are now the servants—not the rulers—of the people of Adano. And watch—you may find that this thing will make you happier than you have ever been in your lives.[17]

But the town is looking for something more than a political ideal or even food in the midst of its starvation. "The town needs its bell back. You can always eat!" argue two of its inhabitants. The town's great bell is missing. This is the most serious problem of all. "The bell is more important than the stomach," shouts an inhabitant. "The bell was our spirit!"[18]

Eventually the people of Adano happily return to life under Major Joppolo's understanding leadership. Even when he is replaced and relieved of his mission, there is some victory at that final moment when the bell is actually restored to Adano. As Major Joppolo, dejected and alone, leaves the scene of his victories and his final defeat of having to leave Adano, the tremendous stroke of the bell rings overhead—a bell whose restoration was as necessary to the townspeople's spiritual rebirth as food and water was for their physical rebirth. Looking up to where the loud notes shatter the air, he touches the solid, grey wall of the old building housing the bell and exclaims: "Listen! It shakes the whole damn building."[19] It is a good bell. It has a fine sound, and the message it bore might be said to have shaken the whole damn world—namely, that human reclamation whether it involves a whole town like Adano or just a single German youth like Emil must precede political reclamation if freedom is to survive in this world.

The Wookey

Major Joppolo and the military were not alone in trying to rid the world of its fascist presence. Many civilians in many countries were also trying. Mr. Wookey, a Cockney tugboat captain, represents in his person all the qualities that enabled England to withstand Hitler's bombings. His story was told in a play by Fredrick H. Brennen entitled *The Wookey* which appeared in 1941. "He is 'rough and gruff and nasty and tough,' a typical four-square sea dog though he sails only a barge. To his family, however, he is God-in-person—the dispenser of justice, the provider of all good, the center of the universe."[20] Rising from a garbage collector to a scrap-iron junk dealer to a voyager on the seas in search of cargo, Mr. Wookey has made his way in the world. As a property owner and family man—for he has a small house and garden, a wife, a son and daughter-in-law,—he has thought much about public affairs, observing the terrible course of events in Europe.

Believing that his government's foreign policy was leading to trouble, he had now and then offered it his advice. But the government did not listen and as a result, came the war. Thoroughly disgusted, Mr. Wookey determinedly overlooks the mess in which Hitler and Prime Minister

Neville Chamberlain had involved the world. But the war does not disregard Mr. Wookey; his sister-in-law arrives one day and begs him to go to France to try and save her husband. This war is now his business. It has touched the Wookey family. Government or no government, her husband must be rescued. "Where did you say I should find him?" he asks the shivering weeping woman who herself barely escaped death in an open boat while crossing the waters. "Dunkirk," she answers. "Dunkirk!"[21]

Then tragedy strikes the Wookey clan. Even though Mr. Wookey's boat has saved a British vessel, it is seized upon his return to England because he owes an oil bill. Then London suffers another blitz from German aircraft—bombs fall, buildings crash, planes roar, and antiaircraft guns deafen. As a result of the air raid, Mr. Wookey's home is destroyed, and his wife is killed. Finally, Mr. Wookey makes peace "with the powers that be, recognizing that Mr. Churchill and the Army have a vision of the whole battlefield that even he in his great wisdom may lack."[22] Leaving the basement shelter of his destroyed home with a machine gun and ammunition, Mr. Wookey becomes a leader of the civilian wardens in his section of the London docks and is determined in his outrage, defiance, and individualism to fight the oncoming German planes singlehanded.[23] Mr. Wookey was not only master of his home and family, he and his compatriots were the masters of the fate of England. Identifying with the Wookeys of England and what they had to endure, Americans found it easy to believe in him and give him cheers and tears.

The Russian People

England was not the only Ally Americans cheered. Another was Russia in the East, and Americans were transported there in Konstantin Siminov's drama, *The Russian People* (1942). His play presented a portrait of the Russian people as they resisted and drove back the Nazi troops. The drama is set in a town beyond the Russian front in a section of the country that the German Army has already encircled. On one side of a river are the Germans who have taken over the town; its leading citizen, a doctor, in fear of his life, betrays his people and becomes the German's puppet mayor. Across the river are the Russian fighters, men and women—awaiting relief, but more probably death—and a no-longer gentleman's army. Rather, theatergoers see a people's army composed of professional soldiers and ordinary citizens like farmers and laborers. It is an army that despite its dire predicament can still sing, love, yearn for loved ones now far behind the front lines, and remember its country way of life before the arrival of the Germans. Meanwhile, the Russian people in the occupied part of the town do not accept their circumstances with proverbial Russian patience. Rather they plot, conspire, and perform the most dangerous of duties such as maintaining underground contact with Russian fighters across the river without hesitation. But, most of all the civilians and soldiers make the supreme sacrifice—they die for Mother Russia in defense of their homeland.

This play appeared as the war was reaching a turning point in late 1942 and early 1943, and the struggle between the Axis powers and the United Nations could go either way. It was intended to appeal to the hearts and minds of the American people as they witnessed their Russian Ally engaged in a heroic struggle against the German invader. But, most importantly, the play encouraged the Russian people as it was presented in more than 100 theaters throughout the Soviet Union and for the Red Army at the front. The drama reminded American and Russian audiences that the Allies had the determination to resist the Axis aggressors and turn the tide of the battle against the enemy.[24]

Jacobowsky and the Colonel

Although the United Nation liberators and those they liberated in lands throughout the world brought many moments of cheer, the war also brought many tears, especially among the refugees who, dispossessed of their belongings, wandered from country to country trying to save their lives. Franz Werfel's *Jacobowsky and the Colonel* (1944), a play adapted by S. N. Behrman, dealt with such a theme. Set in France at the time of its surrender to Germany in June 1940, the play tells the story of Jacobowsky, a gentle and endearing Polish Jew who, having been driven out of Warsaw, Berlin, Vienna, and Prague, now must also flee Paris ahead of the invading German Armies. Purchasing an automobile he cannot drive, he charms a haughty, aristocratic Polish colonel—a man who, in Jacobowsky's opinion, has "one of the finest minds of the fifteenth century"—into driving the car, thus saving each other.[25] Thanks to Jacobowsky's ingenuity, the colonel, all elegance and dash, his orderly, and a lady friend are able to escape the Germans and, with one close escape after another, finally reach the French coast. However, only two can cross to England and carry on the war to free France. "The Colonel must go; he is the man of the hour, a leader, a fighter, a man of action, and the bearer of secret orders for his Government in exile. He is also a far wiser person than at the beginning of the journey."[26] He actually sees in Jacobowsky for whom he initially had such crushing contempt an ally beyond value. Having to choose between his friend and Jacobowsky, he selects Jacobowsky who is equally dedicated to the colonel's cause. Leaving his friend behind, the colonel and Jacobowsky climb down into a waiting boat as dawn breaks over the green-gray sea. Their newly discovered alliance, mutual respect, and understanding seem like a portent of better things and the dawn of a new tomorrow in a world torn apart by war.

The Eve of St. Mark

Fighting for that tomorrow, Quizz West died at his gun, as he engaged in a futile rear-guard action on a lonely island in the Philippines. He was the hero of the first American play to be produced about America at war, Maxwell Anderson's *The Eve of St. Mark* (1942). Quizz is the typical warm-hearted, honest, self-sacrificing person in whom all mothers and lovers believe—a loving son, a faithful lover, a gallant comrade-in-arms. The play exhibits many pieces of his life: learning to roll dice in the barracks, going out on the town where the soldiers outnumber the girls, trying to break through barriers of reticence to reach the girl he loves at home, and waiting at the embarkation point with his comrades as they listen to the top sergeant's tale of the greatest crap game ever played. But, behind these various glimpses Anderson revealed some of the problems troubling the minds of the new draftees.[27] The play noted the soldier's eternal question when he sees his comrades get killed yet he survives—how much injury, if any, he must sustain to be so deserving, a question that may haunt a soldier's mind long after the battles are over and the guns fall silent. In the barracks, Quizz and his Southern comrade-in-arms, Francis Marion, briefly speak of this:

> Marion: There's going to be a hell of a war; some of us are going to
> die young, and others are going to benefit by it. Which are
> the lucky ones? Which would I rather be?

Quizz: You'd rather be the one that almost got killed and didn't.

Marion: Yes, but then another question arises. How close do I have to come to being horizontal before I earn the right to be perpendicular?

Quizz: I don't know.

Marion: I guess nobody knows or we'd have God-damn well been told by this time!

Quizz: I know this much. I read the entire Manual of Arms coming down on the train and it's not there.

Marion: No, I looked for it there. I shall look for it tonight at the bottom of a coke with rum—That's the bus now.[28]

Millions of men asked the same questions—men, who until the war began, perhaps never left their own home towns, never mind having traveled to foreign shores. Anderson illustrated this experience by a brief vignette in the play's embarkation scene:

"What's that noise?" one of the boys asks, as he rests on his gun, his duffle at his feet, under the shadow of the ship that is to take him and his comrades to their destiny.

"That long withdrawing roar?" another answers. "That's the Pacific Ocean beating at the Golden Gate . . . You mean you don't know the ocean when you hear it?" "How would I know?" answers the first speaker—quietly, quietly as they all have spoken under that ominous hull. "Closest I ever came to an ocean was Lake Michigan."[29]

In this fashion, one serviceman like millions of others who were to be his comrades gained a new experience he might never have received if it had not been for the war.

The soldiers were not alone in having personal concerns. Those whom they left behind also had theirs as well. As Quizz's mother stated, "It doesn't matter about the other things! Only come home!" How trivial and unimportant everyday concerns become when a person is confronted with the possible loss of a loved one. As in peace, these too are the sentiments of war and Anderson took America there in *The Eve of St. Mark*.

A Stage for Wisdom

The previous productions were not all the plays nor necessarily the best plays, from the critics' viewpoint, that were staged during the war years. Although the contributions of the theater toward winning the war might not be as discernible as the manufacture of weaponry or the public's financing of the war effort, the creative ways in which theater was used during this period were vital to final victory. As did all the other media, plays attempted to inform the American people about the meaning of the war and the principles for which they were fighting. Some productions attempted to raise morale; others attempted to deliver practical messages; still others attempted to explore the deeper philosophical questions of World War II. The theater was a source of instruction for military and civilian wartime activities; provided entertainment and relief to a war-weary populace and military; and helped bring about a closer affinity and understanding between America and its Allies. Theater addressed the public's questions about the war effort, the answers to which contributed to the public's maximizing its activities to secure victory, and helped Americans understand the tumultuous times and the social, economic, and political problems that confronted them individually and collectively as a nation.

There may not have been as many plays about the war during this period because great war plays, like great war books, are written after the conflict by those who have experienced war's reality and after the heat generated by the bitter destruction has cooled and people can recall their emotions in tranquility. Playwrights were not only competing against the reality of war which could be witnessed in movie newsreels, documentaries, and other media forms, but also they had to satisfy audiences with a fictional version of the war while the real version was everywhere to be seen and heard.

The plays that were produced demonstrated the horrors and suffering war needlessly brings to so many innocent people. As Aeschylus, the Greek playwright, wrote more than 2,300 years ago

> *Drop, drop, in our sleep, upon our hearts,*
> *sorrow falls, memory's pain,*
> *and to us, though against our very will,*
> *even in our own despite comes wisdom,*
> *by the awful grace of God.*[30]

Perhaps, one day nations will have gained sufficient wisdom through the sorrows of war to be able to live in peace with each other. The theater has been and will continue to be one of the forums through which such wisdom is dispensed—a goal playwrights sought to achieve during the Second World War in trying through their writings to contribute to the building of a better world for tomorrow.

Notes

1. Rosamond Gilder, "A Job to Be Done," *Theatre Arts*, July 1943, 396, 401.

2. Hallie Flanagan, "Theater in Wartime: College, Camp, Community," *Theatre Arts*, July 1943, 423.

3. Walter Bernstein, "Report on Hi Yank!" *Theatre Arts*, November 1944, 657.

4. "Honor to the Rank and File," *Theatre Arts*, January 1944, 4.

5. "Theater for the Army Camps," *Theatre Arts*, October 1941, 699.

6. "American Theater Around the Globe," *Theatre Arts*, April 1944, 195–96.

7. Rosamond Gilder, "Moon Down, Theater Rises," review of *The Moon Is Down*, by John Steinbeck, *Theatre Arts*, May 1942, 287.

8. Ibid., 288.

9. Ibid., 289.

10. "The Radio, The Poet and The News—The Moon is Down Once Again," *Theatre Arts*, December 1942, 734.

11. Flanagan, 423.

12. Rosamond Gilder, "The Kingdom of War," review of *Watch on the Rhine*, by Lillian Hellman, *Theatre Arts*, November 1941, 792.

13. Rosamond Gilder, "Prizes That Bloom in the Spring," *Theatre Arts*, June 1941, 410–11.

14. "The Kingdom of War," 791.

15. "Broadway in Review," review of *Tomorrow the World!* by James Gow and Arnaud d'Usseau, *Theatre Arts*, June 1943, 331–33.

16. Rosamond Gilder, "A Bell for Broadway," review of *A Bell for Adano*, by Paul Osborn, *Theatre Arts*, January 1945, 70.

17. Ibid., 71.

18. Ibid., 69.

19. Ibid., 72.

20. Rosamond Gilder, "The Kingdom of War," review of *The Wookey*, by Frederick H. Brennan, *Theatre Arts*, November 1941, 782.

21. Ibid., 783.

22. Ibid.

23. Ibid., 784.

24. John Gassner, "The Russians on Broadway," review of *The Russian People*, by Konstantin Siminov, *Current History*, February 1943, 549–50.

25. Rosamond Gilder, "The Gay and the Grim," review of *Jacobowsky and the Colonel*, by Franz Werfel and adapted by S. N. Berman, *Theatre Arts*, May 1944, 261–62.

26. Ibid.

27. Rosamond Gilder, "Matter for Thanksgiving," review of the *Eve of St. Mark*, by Maxwell Anderson, *Theatre Arts*, December 1942, 735–36.

28. Ibid., 736.

29. Ibid., 737.

30. "The World and the Theater," *Theatre Arts*, June 1945, 324.

Chapter Seven

PUBLICATIONS
The Books We Read

O NE OF THE MOST important weapons America used during the Second World War to fight the Axis powers was books. World War II was not just a war of guns, ships, airplanes, tanks, and other weapons of battle; it was also a war of ideas and, for the most part, books were their purveyor—thoughts so powerful that the Nazis tried to eradicate them by burning books. Our enemies waged war on books as surely as they waged war on other nations. However, as they were to learn, flames alone cannot eradicate written ideas.

A book is a depository. It contains the thoughts, feelings, passions, prejudices, memories, hopes, facts, and perhaps, the life philosophy of the writer. The Nazi philosophy that Adolph Hitler was trying to impose upon the world was not new; its concepts can be traced back through the decades and centuries in books. Nazi Pan-Germanism, with its theory of a master race and a Europe dominated by a greater Germany, has a great library behind it. The writings by and about Frederick the Great (1712–1786) reveal the ideas about the German military state and war. Frederick II, for example, wrote *Frederick the Great on the Art of War*, while Charles W. Ingrao published *The Hessian Mercenary State: Ideas, Institutions, and Reform under Frederick II, 1760–1785*. The German moral concept of World War II—whatever benefited Germany was right—can be read in the German philosophers of the eighteenth century. To learn about a particular set of prejudices, passions, propaganda, future hopes, and proper attitudes of the Germans toward their neighbors and the duty of these neighbors to serve the Greater Germany, the

public could read Hitler's *Mein Kampf* (*My Struggle*)—the most powerful and most dangerous book of its time.

In the United States, books also served a very important purpose.
They helped to mold public opinion about the role America should adopt
in World War II and in the postwar world. They informed Americans and
people in other nations what the Democracies were fighting for and the
principles for which America stood. They explained what a fascist victory
might mean for the future of mankind and, in doing so, helped thwart
the Axis menace to civilization.

Council of Books in Wartime

When the Japanese attacked Pearl Harbor, the United States was
caught by surprise on many fronts, military and civilian, but the nation's
lack of preparedness did not last long. One group that immediately reori-
ented its activities toward the war effort was the publishing industry. By
the spring of 1942, this group had organized the Council of Books in
Wartime. The council's guiding principle was "Books are Weapons in the
War of Ideas."[1]

The council was established for several reasons; it wanted to provide
servicemen and women who were overseas with worthwhile reading material and increase the home front's understanding of why the war was
being fought and why it had to be won. To achieve its goals, the council
created many committees. Their activities included publishing booklists
about various phases of the war; selecting outstanding books as reading
"Imperatives"; sponsoring radio programs; furnishing speakers for book
fairs, club programs, schools, and other organizations; promoting suitable children's books; producing movie newsreels; working intensely
with bookstores and libraries to promote war books; carrying out publicity campaigns through the nation's press; and cooperating with the Office of War Information.

The publication of pocket-sized books, which were designed to be
expendable and easily carried by servicemen and women—the "Armed
Forces Services Editions"—was extremely important to the council. The
books were both nonfiction and fiction, with topics and genres ranging
from history, science, and biography to modern novels, westerns, and
collections of short stories. In addition to the overseas distribution, the

books were sent to military staging areas, hospitals, and isolated posts with no libraries. Through the cooperation of the International YMCA, some copies even reached American servicemen who were interned in German and Japanese prisoner-of-war camps.

The publishing industry also sponsored the Book and Author War Bond Committee, which was established in 1943 in cooperation with the U.S. Treasury Department. Between 1943 and 1945, the committee sponsored 53 rallies throughout the United States, bringing some 78 authors and about 126,000 people to these meetings, and sold $143,536,000 in war bonds. The Writers War Board, a private organization, helped secure the authors for these rallies. One popular feature of the meetings was auctioning off an author's autographed book. War bonds were always the currency. At one rally for 3,000 air cadets and civilians at an Army airfield, Kathleen Winsor's *Forever Amber* was auctioned off for $1,750,000 in war bonds. An insurance company made the winning bid and then turned the book over to a serviceman who bought it for $5,000 in war bonds.[2]

Books and the Home Front

Books helped Americans adjust to wartime living. They helped people make their own clothes, repair their own homes, and maintain their health in spite of labor shortages. Books helped increase industrial production by providing information on welding, machine use, and other technical subjects. Books on foreign languages and world geography became popular as people sought to understand the nature of this global conflict. As the war also brought families closer together, books on family or group activities were in demand, as were song books for community sings.

Books went to war in many different ways because the knowledge they had to dispense was unlimited, broad, and diverse. Books became so popular and essential during the war years that *Time* magazine called 1943—the year in which the war was at its height—"the most remarkable in the 150-year-old history of U.S. publishing . . . for 1943 seemed to mark the second year in an epoch that all sober, responsible publishers and all carriers and custodians of U.S. culture had hoped for all their lives: a time when book reading and book buying reached outside the narrow quarters of intellectuals and became the business of the whole vast literate population of the U.S."[3] The article stated that in 1943 Americans "bought 80 million novels, biographies and books about war and politics, 70 million textbooks, 40 million children's books, 45 million technical books, 15 million Bibles and religious books—a total estimated at between 250 and 350 million, and from 20 to 30 percent more than in 1942."[4]

Books were an indispensable tool for teaching the public how to cope with wartime shortages, human and material. Some books helped divert the readers' minds from wartime difficulties, while others explained what was happening and why. Whether they were a source of education, pleasure, or escapism, books provided an essential underpinning to the war effort.

Writers and the War

What caused World War II anyway? Given the power and influence of books, were writers responsible for Germany, Italy, and Japan going to war with the United States? Did writers through their books convey false impressions about the resolve and strength of the United States to defend itself against the Axis powers? Did books give America's enemies the incentive to engage the nation in war? As far-fetched as these questions may seem today, they were raised very seriously during the war years. Bernard A. DeVoto, teacher, editor, and author, stated the issue quite directly when discussing American literature of the 1920s:

> Clearly, the master race accepted in good faith the description of America which American writers had provided, and made their plans in accordance with it. I am not obliged to determine whether a decade of our literature thus invited our enemies to aggressions which they might not otherwise have dared or hoaxed them to their doom. But . . .[5]

However, those American authors who were most widely discussed in Germany after 1925 hardly portrayed a picture of a weak, degenerate, and soft America. Upton Sinclair's books, for example, portrayed America as a powerful, not decadent, nation. Although his people may have been prejudiced and unenlightened, they were well intentioned and good at heart. His audiences consisted primarily of socialists and communists. Margaret Mitchell's *Gone With the Wind* was popular in Germany for the same reasons it was in the United States; in addition, its portrait of a defeated South helped create a romantic atmosphere about Germany's defeat in World War I. Another American author with huge sales in Germany was Sinclair Lewis and his book, *Babbitt*. Its audience may have chuckled at George Babbitt's failings, but they did not regard him as a decadent American. Germany did attempt to use John Steinbeck's *Grapes of Wrath* for anti-American propaganda to demonstrate how miserable life was for "the peasants of a pluto-democracy." By hailing some American works, the Germans, inadvertently, also exhibited how American writers had the ability to produce meaningful works and the freedom of thought that German writers lacked in depicting their own world.[6]

There is no evidence that Hitler's views of the United States were based upon the previous books or that he ever read them. On the contrary, according to Konrad Heiden, author of *Der Führer: Hitler's Rise to Power*, "America is for Hitler an object for terror. America, to his mind, mustered every hostile power against Europe; in America, space and race joined forces against the Old World."[7] Hitler did not believe America was a decadent or degenerate nation. When Hitler decided to declare war on America, his hopes for victory were not based on national decadence but rather national disunity—a condition he tried to exploit in his shortwave radio broadcasts to the United States. Hitler was depending on help from America's anti-interventionists, its "I-hate-the-Russians," "American Firsters," and those who were afraid of the labor unions more than they feared the triumph of his Nazi ideals. American literature had nothing to do with Hitler's decision to wage war on the United States, but literature always seems to be blamed when literary critics try to explain the reasons for political movements.

Because the writer has the ability to think through and express in words many thoughts the average person would not consider, questions did arise as to their responsibilities in the war. On several occasions, William Rose Benét expressed the following thoughts:

> And yet a greater responsibility rests upon him which is to delineate and define that Democracy for which we fight; to define the limits of "free enterprise" and techniques and controls that must—or we go under!—

assure us *actual* Liberty; to delineate line by line the humane and universal doctrine that is going to serve us for *the future*, not only as it was and as it served us in *the past* . . . Never before has the world needed sane, clear honest thought. The tidal wave of perverse "ideologies" has wellnigh overwhelmed us. The Lie and the End-That-Justifies-The-Means were never so rampant or so shameless in writing . . . It is up to them [the writers] to keep clearly before us the highest aspiration of the human spirit, and to damn the merely expedient. It is up to them to lead their country, to keep it from profound pitfalls, both on the right and on the left. They abdicate their duties when they address their talents to any lesser duties.[8]

On another occasion, Benét wrote:

. . . writers should, as never before, be trying to the utmost to exercise their best intelligence and keep brave, humane, noble ideas burning. If *they* don't, who will? . . . We can leave to our fighting men the job of killing, till the Killers cry "Uncle." We writers have a job to do; and, fundamentally, that consists merely in doing the best writing that is in us, in this cataclysmic time. The men fighting for civilization certainly wish civilization to *be* there when they get back.[9]

On still another occasion, Benét stated:

His duty then is to speak the truth as clearly to his countrymen as, if he is an honest man, he speaks it to himself. Not in mere contentiousness, not in malice, but with a deep and abiding concern for what our American notion of liberty really means, must he speak on any and all occasions that demand it. As never before is the obligation laid upon him not only to speak the truth but the *whole* truth. As never before does the future of the whole world tremble in the balance. Those who have imagination must use it to see as truly as possible *beyond* this war, into some lasting condition of equity for Mankind.[10]

What was the meaning of this war for which the writers' talents were needed so desperately? Wallace Deuel, a foreign correspondent, seemed to summarize the purpose of World War II when he stated:

This is not a "back to normalcy" war. People are not fighting to get back to 1938 or 1928 or 1918 or 1908. They are fighting for a brave *new*

world, a world where ordinary, decent human beings have a greater freedom and greater opportunities, a world where people *believe* that they
must have greater freedom and greater opportunities, a world where people do things that have never been done before to secure this greater
freedom and these greater opportunities. This is what this war means.[11]

In adding his own thoughts, Norman Cousins, editor of the *Saturday
Review of Literature*, urged writers to think of the next generation when
telling their story:

Write now; get the story down in its full colors while it is fresh before you;
don't be afraid of honest emotion or honest sentiment; don't be afraid to
talk about the obvious things—the things that seem obvious now but
won't be obvious a few years from now. Pass up the usual sidelights, the
shining out-of-the-way episodes that may make good story material today
but which are no more representative of the larger drama than a single
book is of a library. For it is only too likely that these out-of-the-way
episodes will be taken up later as a valid full view. Give the next generation such a sharp, intimate picture of the real problems of the present that
it won't slide so easily into the usual glib misunderstanding of how war
happens and what war is.[12]

Thus, writers were being urged to develop their fullest potential for the
war effort—to disseminate as widely as possible their knowledge of the
war, its causes and the actual problems confronting the world at that
time. Through their works, the writers had the potential to help make
people truly free.

Even before World War II began, writers were warning of the impending event. John Gunther's *Inside Europe* told Americans of the explosive
forces that finally blew Europe apart in 1939 and 1940. Ernst Henri's
Hitler Over Europe and *Hitler Over Russia? The Coming Fight Between
the Fascist and Socialist Armies* foresaw the events that occurred between 1939 and 1941. Although sympathetic to the Communist cause,
Edgar Snow's *Red Star Over China* and *Battle for Asia* spoke of events
in that part of the world.

The War Correspondents

As of 1941 and before Pearl Harbor, publishers already had divided
their books into three basic categories: the "I-seen-it-happen," the "Hit-

ler-can't-win," and "Wake up America." These books were more successful than the "Let's-stay-out-of-it" books that were mildly popular
in 1939. Even though the isolationists were still very vocal publicly, they
had already lost the war on the literary front by the time the United
States officially entered the war. Between 1939 and 1941, Americans
had watched the Nazi panzer divisions vanquish one European country
after another and had witnessed the destruction of many cities and the
deaths of innumerable men, women, and children. American writers and
correspondents were already telling of the Finns who were dying in the
sub-Arctic as they defended their homeland; English men, women, and
children huddled in the bomb shelters of London, Coventry, and Plym-
outh as death fell from the sky in the blitz; heroic Greek troops who,
with their British allies, were being killed on the slopes of Mount Olym-
pus; soldiers dying on the desert sands of North Africa, or in the freezing
waters of the North Atlantic. During this period, books convinced the
American public of two facts: War had become more destructive and
more terrible than at any time in history, and the nations that had broken the delicate peace following World War I had to be defeated.[13]

Most books published about the war, both in numbers and popularity,
were written by news correspondents. Their various perspectives included "I-told-you-so" evaluations of the enemy and eyewitness accounts. In many instances, these books were considered journalism
rather than war literature. The literature of war was expected to be
written after the surrender by those who had participated in it—who
could reflect upon their experience and develop a viewpoint which time
did not allow while they served as active combatants.

Factual writing concerns itself with the planning of victory or the use
of the implements of war to achieve that strategy, but fiction demonstrates what moves the hearts of the men who use those instruments—
men who sweat and die, live with boredom and fatigue, are fearful and
brave, joke and curse, scratch their mosquito bites, and eat C rations on
distant battlefields. From both perspectives, nonfiction and fiction, readers at home could begin to understand what war was like because of
those who lived through it.

During World War II, many books were published about the Axis powers to give Americans a better insight into their enemies. One of the first
publications to present a penetrating examination of Germany in wartime was William L. Shirer's *Berlin Diary: The Journal of a Foreign*

Correspondent, 1934–1941, published in 1941. Shirer was CBS radio's correspondent in Berlin from 1937 until after the fall of France in 1940. His greeting, "William L. Shirer speaking from Berlin," was well known to radio listeners on the home front.

Shirer's book included many observations that the Nazis had censored from his broadcasts. He told the story of the mother of a German aviator who was notified that her son was missing and presumed dead. A few days later, the British Broadcasting Corporation (BBC), which read off a weekly list of German prisoners, announced that her son had been captured. Eight of her friends wrote her the good news. She, in turn, gave the letters to the police, and the eight friends were subsequently arrested for listening to an English radio broadcast. Shirer was able to gather evidence of the "mercy killings" of mental defectives by finding the death notices of many victims published in German provincial news-papers. The notices always described the victims as having died suddenly or unexpectedly and as having been cremated at one of the three places—Grafeneck at Württemberg, Pirna in Saxony, or Hartheim, near Linz on the Danube. The form letter that the families received read, in part, "Considering the nature of his serious incurable ailment, his death, which saved him from lifelong confinement in an institution, is to be regarded merely as a release."[14] Shirer believed that Nazi extremists sug-gested these killings to Hitler, as a logical step in their program to purify the race. As a correspondent, Shirer noted that the Germans painted the Red Cross on top of their gasoline trucks and many of their staff cars.[15]

From the facts he gathered and his own observations, Shirer believed that Germany as a whole shared the guilt of war that was often attrib-uted to Hitler alone. Although the Germans did not want war, they did want to be masters of Europe and, having achieved that goal by the spring of 1941, they were terrified of what would happen to their coun-try if they lost. They were fighting for nationalism rather than the ideal of totalitarianism. Based on what he saw around him, Shirer concluded that there would be a war between the United States and Germany unless America was willing to accept not only the totalitarian system but also a place in that system subordinate to Germany. If Britain was de-feated, Shirer did not know how or where the attack would come, but he believed for a long time that Hitler would begin with Russia and then turn west. Many Germans told Shirer that Hitler's road would go through Africa to Brazil. As they said, "Once established in South America, the battle is won."[16]

In 1942, Howard K. Smith, another CBS radio broadcaster and the last American correspondent to leave Germany before Pearl Harbor, published *Last Train from Berlin*. In describing how life in Germany had begun to deteriorate after the invasion of Russia, Smith spoke about meat rationing; shortages of living quarters, clothing, and cigarettes; a decline in public morale; disruptions in public transportation; the absence of consumer goods; sabotage and declines in war production in German-occupied countries; the evolving chaos of the German government as experienced administrators went into the military; and Hitler's preoccupation with the battlefronts. Smith noted that the German people were like men holding a lion by the tail and were afraid to let go: "They are not convinced Nazis, not five percent of them; they are people frightened stiff at what fate will befall them if they do not win the mess the Nazis got them into."[17] Smith added, "Unless the British, the Russians and the Americans offer, with deep sincerity, to the German people another way out besides life or death with Nazism, this war is going to last for an unnecessarily long time, and the Germans, to avoid their horrible fate, are going to fight with the reckless spirit of men who have absolutely nothing to lose but their lives."[18]

After this book was published, the war lasted another three years, and when the Allies thought that the Germans had been beaten in December 1944, the German Army launched its last great offensive through the Ardennes Forest, the Battle of the Bulge. Thus, Smith seemed to predict this sequence of events when he warned that the Germans would continue to fight with spirit to avoid defeat, even though they were suffering losses on the home front.

The GIs' Favorite Correspondent

The one person who was best able to describe the war to those at home was Ernie Pyle—the GIs' favorite war correspondent. On April 18, 1945 a Japanese sniper on the Pacific island of Ie off Okinawa ended Ernie Pyle's life. Through his reporting for *Scripps Howard* newspapers Pyle united millions of loved ones separated by war. Unlike most war correspondents, Pyle did not write about armies but about the men who made up those armies; the soldiers who fought with fear and courage, sleep and without sleep, with full stomachs and empty stomachs, with humor and sadness, in the rain, snow and sunshine, amidst life and death. Of the war's soldiery Ernie Pyle once wrote:

> We will go from one battleground to another until it's over, leaving some of us behind on every beach, in every field. We are just beginning with the ones who lie back of us here. I don't know whether it was their good fortune or misfortune to get out of it so early in the game. I guess it doesn't make a difference, once a man is gone . . . They died and thereby the rest of us can go on.

One of Pyles' last published commentaries from Okinawa in April 1945 describes another aspect of the environment of war:

> That was one of the most miserable damn nights I have spent in this war . . . Right after dark the mosquitos started buzzing around our heads. The Okinawa mosquitos sound like flame throwers. They can't be driven off or brushed away. . . . Along about 4:30 we did get some sleep from sheer exhaustion (of the battles and mosquitos). That gave the mosquitos a clear field. When we woke up at dawn (from the sacks) and crawled stiffly out into the daylight, my right eye was swollen shut as usual (from the mosquito attacks). All of which isn't very warlike to describe, but I tell you this so you'll know there are lots of things besides bullets that make war hell.

Pyle didn't write as much about his own experiences as he did about American servicemen and women. What they could not express from their hearts in letters home, he said for them. He spoke about all elements of the Army—the infantry, the artillery, the engineers, the tank corps, the bomber pilots, the ordnance soldiers, and the quartermaster corps.

Americans could read about their Army in Ernie Pyle's *Brave Men*. One book reviewer wrote that "when future generations of Americans seek to know what kind of Army fought for them in this war, they will be thankful for Ernie Pyle."[19] One wartime advertisement stated that "our soldiers overseas do not know yet why they are fighting; that they understand few implications of the struggle between democracy and fascism, and they look on the war only as a job they must do and get done quickly."[20] Pyle understood these feelings and captured them in *Brave Men* when he wrote about the American assault ships that were nearing Sicily:

> Then darkness enveloped the whole American armada. Not a pinpoint of light showed from those hundreds of ships as they surged on through the night toward their destiny, carrying across the ageless and indifferent sea tens of thousands of young men, fighting for . . . for . . . well, at least for each other.[21]

Brave Men spoke about the war on many fronts—the war in Italy, the vicious fighting on the Normandy beaches, and the liberation of Paris. In "describing the job of an officer who had to spend every day in a landing craft checking cargoes in Anzio harbor with 'shells speckling the whole area,' Pyle wrote 'I wouldn't have his job for a million dollars.' " But in the next paragraph Ernie [said], 'I rode around with him one day . . .'"[22]

Perhaps, that comment provides a clue to Ernie Pyle's popularity and why he was the American GIs' favorite war correspondent. Perhaps, two of those GIs were Willie and Joe, the cartoon subjects of Bill Mauldin's book, *Up Front*. Through his cartoons, Mauldin gave those on the home front a different perspective of Army life. In his Pulitzer Prize-winning cartoon, a weary Joe walks head down through the rain and some equally tired Germans walk with him in the same spirit as the cartoon caption quotes a news item: "Fresh, spirited American troops, flushed with victory, are bringing in thousands of hungry, ragged, battle-weary prisoners . . ." Willie and Joe also brought the home front to battlefields across the sea in ways, perhaps, news reports never could.[23]

Contemporary Books About the Enemy

Germany

Other books noted the internal problems in Germany during 1942. Paul Hagen, a prominent organizer of New Beginning, a German underground group that was organized after Hitler came to power, published *Will Germany Crack?* in 1942. He argued that "the strength of German militarism is undermined by antagonistic masses within the Reich who

Hollywood found it difficult to portray and explain the Nazi character. Here an apparently aristocratic German officer looks on his barbarous act without emotion, his lips almost snarled in seeming contempt for the victim. *(Courtesy of Library of Congress)*

This is the Enemy

During the war, the Army and Navy produced and released films to factories and industrial workers throughout the country to boost their morale and remind home front workers that they were an integral part of the war effort. *(Courtesy of Library of Congress)*

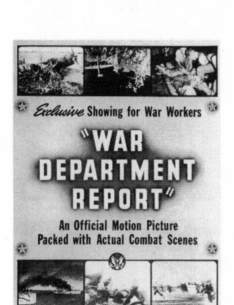

Exclusive Showing for War Workers

"WAR DEPARTMENT REPORT"

An Official Motion Picture Packed with Actual Combat Scenes

Based on Lieutenant Colonel James H. Doolittle's raid over Tokyo and other Japanese cities in April 1942 and the capture, trial, and execution of one of his air crews, Hollywood produced three motion pictures depicting various aspects of these events: "Destination Tokyo," "Thirty Seconds Over Tokyo," and "The Purple Heart." *(Courtesy of Library of Congress)*

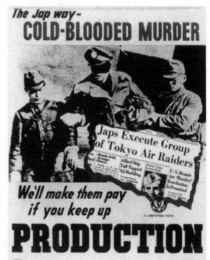

The Jap way—
COLD-BLOODED MURDER

Japs Execute Group of Tokyo Air Raiders

We'll make them pay if you keep up

PRODUCTION

In "The Fighting Sullivans," Hollywood paid tribute to the first American family since the Civil War to lose five of its members in battle. The five Sullivan brothers died when their cruiser, the U.S.S. Juneau, was sunk in a naval battle off Guadalcanal in the Solomon Islands on November 15, 1942. As a result of this tragedy, the Navy changed its policy of having members of the same family serve in the same military unit. *(Courtesy of Library of Congress)*

the five Sullivan brothers
'missing in action' off the Solomons

THEY DID THEIR PART

"Books are Weapons in the War of Ideas" was the guiding principle of the Council of Books in Wartime, a group organized by the American publishing industry shortly after Pearl Harbor. *(Courtesy of Library of Congress)*

Books cannot be killed by fire.

People die, but books never die. No man and no force can put thought in a concentration camp forever. No man and no force can take from the world the books that embody man's eternal fight against tyranny. In this war, we know, books are weapons. *Franklin D. Roosevelt*

BOOKS ARE WEAPONS IN THE WAR OF IDEAS

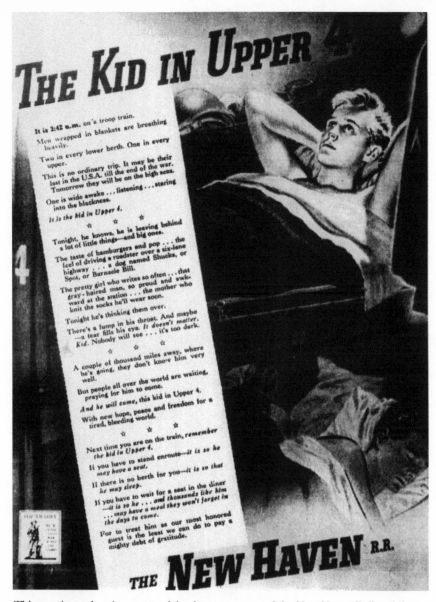

This wartime advertisement explained to passengers of the New Haven Railroad that the inconvenient delays they were experiencing were necessary because of the wartime priority to move troops. Although a regional advertisement, it was later published in newspapers throughout the country and has become one of the most anthologized Ad Council advertisements of all time. *(Reprint permission granted by the Advertising Council.)*

Pulitzer Prize-winning cartoonist of World War II, Bill Mauldin, made his two GIs, Willie and Joe, symbols of the misery of war. His caption for this cartoon reads: *"Fresh spirited American troops, flushed with victory, are bringing in thousands of hungry, ragged battle-weary prisoners . . ." (News Item) From UP FRONT. (Reprinted by permission of author and the Watkins/Loomis Agency.)*

On December 18, 1941, President Franklin D. Roosevelt established by Executive Order 8989 the Office of Defense Transportation. This agency directed and coordinated all domestic transportation systems, including railroads. Its motto, "Is Your Trip Necessary?," reminded the public that the movement of military personnel and matériel had first priority over personal pleasure trips. *(Courtesy of Library of Congress)*

Millions of troops are on the move...

Is **YOUR** trip necessary?

OFFICE OF DEFENSE TRANSPORTATION

"Keep It Under Your Stetson" became one of the most popular slogans of the war and synonymous with national security as it reminded the public that "Loose Talk can cost Lives." *(Reprinted by permission of the John B. Stetson Company.)*

To boost the morale of a war-weary country, advertisements told the public what kind of products would be available once the war was over. *(Courtesy of Library of Congress)*

This Texaco Inc. advertisement speaks about the scope of the war, the conditions under which American servicemen were fighting, and what the American home front had to do to help win the war. (©1943 Texaco Inc. Reprinted with permission from Texaco Inc.)

Military posters stimulated recruitment by promising adventure and excitement to prospective enlistees.
(Courtesy of Library of Congress)

This Texaco Inc. advertisement depicted life aboard a U.S. naval vessel. *(©1941 Texaco Inc. Reprinted with permission from Texaco Inc.)*

Until the United Nations opened a second front in Europe, all that stood between Hitler's domination of Europe and, perhaps, the rest of the world was the Russian Army which, in the words of Winston Churchill, performed a unique mission in the war by "ripping the guts out of the German Army." *(Courtesy of Library of Congress)*

"...THE HOPES OF CIVILIZATION REST ON THE WORTHY BANNERS OF THE COURAGEOUS RUSSIAN ARMY."—Gen. Douglas MacArthur

HELP RUSSIAN WAR RELIEF!

Created by artists at the Douglas Aircraft Company in California, "The Tokio Kid" was used by hundreds of American companies to improve their production efficiency and by the U.S. government to sell war bonds and stamps. The racism of the cartoon was as obvious as the Japanese victories in the Pacific and Asia in 1942 when "The Kid" was created and America, engaged in a two-front war, found the threat to its freedom very real. The swastika on "The Kid's" armband, before becoming inextricably linked to the brutality of the Nazi regime, is an ancient symbol used variously to represent the sun, fertility, and good luck. The word *swastika* is derived from the Sanskrit word for wellbeing. The rays from the Rising Sun on "The Kid's" hat were the ensign of the Japanese Imperial Navy. *(Courtesy of Larry Merritt)*

TOKIO KID SAY·

BROKE UP TOOLS WASTE FOR SCRAP JUST LIKE BULLETS MAKE FOR JAP! THANK YOU

today are unorganized but will act at a moment of serious military set-backs."[24] He noted that the Nazi regime had suppressed the majority of the German people and could not avoid the internal dissensions that increasingly disrupted the "national unity."[25] By the end of 1942 German citizens and newspaper correspondents were telling the American people that Germany was not a united monolith despite its conquest of Europe; Germany was beginning to experience the effects and disruptions of war; and many Germans were not loyal to the State but with encouragement from outside sources might at the appropriate moment rebel against the Nazi regime and help bring about its downfall. These books brought a great deal of hope to Americans, who, at the time, saw the Nazi grip on Europe extending from the English Channel in the west to the gates of Moscow in the east and from the Scandinavian countries in the north to the deserts of North Africa in the south.

While some books described Germany's changing social and economic conditions, others told how Germany reached the point where it decided to go to war; how the Nazi Party rose within the German political system to obtain power; the kind of men who surrounded Hitler; and what Hitler himself was like, as revealed for example, through his speeches and by others who were purported to have known or knew him. As examples the American public could read *The Speeches of Adolph Hitler, April 1922—August 1939* (1942) by Norman H. Baynes and *Inside Hitler, from the German of Kurt Krueger, M.D.* (1941) by Kurt Krueger. According to Konrad Heiden, in *Der Führer*, Hitler was not the creator, not even the guide to Nazism; the Nazi Party officers found him in the lowest mass of their subordinates and commanded him to command. Hitler did not conquer the masses but rather portrayed and represented them.

In addition to discussing the rise of Nazism and the kind of leaders who fostered the movement, books also spoke about the German military machine and the reasons for its effectiveness. Lieutenant Colonel Paul W. Thompson's *Modern Battle: Units in Action in the Second World War* (1941) reviewed the tactical methods of the German Army, beginning with its attack on Poland to its conquest of Crete. An expert on German war tactics, Thompson analyzed how the blitzkrieg (lightning war) was waged by detailing its technical and tactical parts. The public could learn about the countries against which Germany directed its military machine whether it be in Robert Goffin's *White Brigade* (1944)—an autobiographical, semi-fictional, semi-factual report of Belgium's organized underground—or Louis de Jong and Joseph W. F. Stoppelman's *The Lion Rampant* (1944), which told about the suffering of the Netherlands under the Nazi yoke.

In terms of sales, the books about Germany and Nazism were not necessarily the most popular books of the war, but reading matter was available to the American people that spoke about Hitler, his armed forces, the effects of his subjugation of other countries, the war's impact on Germany itself, and an explanation of the Nazi philosophy. These and other books gave the American public another perspective of the war and its Axis enemies, in addition to what it was receiving from the movies, radio, and other media formats.

Japan

Germany was not the only Axis power; another was Japan. Wherever the Japanese were fighting—in the Aleutian Islands off Alaska's coast, China, Southeast Asia, or the Pacific—books took the American reader there. Books described a people who had recently come out of feudalism and imported into their old civilization those aspects of Western civilization that helped their country become a powerful military state. Books like Jesse F. Steiner's *Behind the Japanese Mask* (1943) described various aspects of Japanese culture, including its views of marriage and morals, and its education that taught Japanese youth that they were superior to other people because of their "divine descent from the gods." Readers could also learn how five great families, including Mitsui, Mitsubishi, and Sumitomo, controlled about one-half of Japan's industry and shipping and how they acquired their wealth, in addition to profiting from Japan's wartime activities in Asia.

One of the more interesting books about Japan, *How Japan Plans to Win*, was written in 1940 by Kinoaki Matsuo and published in the United States in 1942. Matsuo, a Japanese naval officer, predicted that Japanese aggression would be launched suddenly while his country was conducting diplomatic negotiations with the United States. He also suggested that Japan consider conquering India after the fall of Singapore and Australia after the fall of New Guinea.

Books allowed the reader to travel to the battlefields where American forces were encountering this Far Eastern enemy and could hear the Japanese war cry: "Go to hell, Babe Ruth, American, you die!" One island that epitomized the horror and fierceness U.S. forces faced in fighting the Japanese in the Pacific was Tarawa atoll in the Gilbert Islands. Betio, an islet at the southwest tip of Tarawa atoll, was less than one square mile of sand, coral, shattered palm trees, and an airfield which the American Marines captured in November 1943, at a cost of 3,000 casualties, including 931 missing or dead. In his book, *Tarawa: The Story of a Battle* (1944), Robert Sherrod, a correspondent for *Time* and *Life* magazines, describes the battle in which the Marines held a 20-foot-wide beachhead while the Japanese shot at them from dugouts only 30 feet away. The book told vividly what war is all about. On the third night of the battle, the Japanese admitted defeat by making their customary suicide charge and on the fifth day, except for a few well-hidden snipers, corpses were rotting everywhere in the sun. Sherrod methodically counted group after group of bodies.

> Nearby there are a dozen half-Japs whose life had been flicked away by a flame thrower . . . A little further on, there are fifty more dead Japs—they seem to be thicker on this end of the island . . . Scattered around a big blockhouse and what apparently had been a power plant there are at least 150 more who had been hit by a variety of weapons: some are charred, others have their heads blown off, others are only chests or trunks. Only one of them appears to be a suicide.[26]

Elsewhere, Sherrod saw dozens of Japanese who had shot themselves with their own rifles or blown themselves to pieces with hand grenades.

Such battles were not only being fought in the South Pacific. Readers could follow the war northward to the Aleutian Islands off the coast of Alaska in Keith Wheeler's *The Pacific is My Beat* (1943) and Howard Handleman's *Bridge to Victory* (1943). They could read of the capture of Attu Island, which characterized the Japanese will to fight, their undying compromise not to surrender. The fight climaxed in May 1943 when Colonel Yosuyo Yamasaki knew there was no hope left and gathered together his remaining forces, about 1,000 men. The wounded who could not walk were given the choice of death by pistol or morphine. The remainder—those who were well, the walking wounded, and a few civilian employees—were given weapons, which even included bayonets nailed to sticks. Screaming and overcome with the fear of death, the Japanese threw themselves at the American forces, wreaking much havoc. The Japanese died quickly and in the end only twenty-eight were captured.

This was the enemy. Whether in the snows of the Aleutians or the jungle heat of the South Pacific, they fought to the bitter end. Their tenacity in battle raised many questions, particularly, why did the Japanese soldiers fight to the death? Part of the answer was found in a pamphlet published by the Intelligence Bureau of the Japanese War Office, which stated that Japan "views the nation as an organic substance forming a happy whole with the Emperor as the nucleus, a living body which grows and develops eternally." . . . "A Japanese private explained that when a Japanese soldier enters the army, he gives his soul and body to the Emperor. 'No longer is his ego his own; it is the Emperor's. He is now one in a great endless force reaching back to the era of his god-ancestors and forward to the infinite perfection of his Emperor's godlike idealism.' The Japanese soldier accomplishes his ideal only in death; he was not complete until his spirit rested in the military shrine in Tokyo."[27]

Once the war was over, what was to be the fate of Japan and its role in the postwar world? Books addressed these issues as well. Owen Lattimore, editor and historian, in *Solution in Asia* (1945) warned that the Japanese attacks at Pearl Harbor, Singapore, and Hong Kong had ended the age of Western Imperialism. Ideas would comprise the competition in the Orient. Lattimore predicted that if America's ideals did not assure a better life for the inhabitants of this part of the world, and if the French and Dutch colonialists did not understand the meaning of their awakening, then the peoples of the Orient would become increasingly attracted to the ideology of Communist Russia and through its ideas rather than a conspiracy would the Soviet Union demonstrate its power. Willis Lamott, who taught in Japanese schools for almost two decades, expressed the view in *Nippon: The Crime and Punishment of Japan* (1944) that Japan would always be a menace to the world as long as the Emperor was identified with the concept of divinity—an idea that had to be abandoned if the Far East was to remain stable. William C. Johnstone expressed another view of postwar Japan in *The Future of Japan* (1945). He believed that Japan had to be completely disarmed, prevented from resuming aggression once the war was over, and built into a peaceful democratic nation after the Japanese had been chastened by military defeat. The author believed that only a democratic Japan would truly be a safe Japan. In the hindsight of history, each of these books foresaw the future—the Emperor lost his divinity; Japan became a democracy and world economic power; and the Soviet Union's communist ideology prevailed in many lands in Asia.

Italy

Italy, the third Axis partner, was not only the weakest militarily but also had the fewest books published about it. However, one book, *The Remaking of Italy* (1942), written by Pentad, a pseudonym for four Italian refugees and a British friend, raised many political questions about the country. Written before Italy surrendered in 1943 and joined the Allied cause, the authors raised the issue as to whether Italy had made a fatal mistake in allying itself with Germany rather than England and whether Italy should reverse its course at the first opportunity. In deed and thought, the authors thought that England was always a more faithful friend than Germany, which they portrayed as Italy's steadfast enemy. They wanted to see Italy abolish the monarchy and become a federal republic; they also opposed the monopoly of big business, state regimentation, and "certain reactionary elements of the Roman Catholic Church."[28] They proposed that Italy should ally itself with England and France in the future—an alliance long since realized.

Contemporary Books about the Allies

Russia

Just as there were many books written about America's enemies who in the postwar world became its allies, there were also many books published about its allies, some of whom became its enemy in the aftermath of the war. One of these, of course, was the Soviet Union. Books told the story of this nation from many perspectives. Some like Walter Duranty's *USSR: The Story of Soviet Russia* (1944) traced the history of the country from the arrival of Lenin in Petrograd in 1917 up through the war years. Others took readers to the colossal battles for Smolensk, Leningrad, and Moscow. Still others like Aron Iugov's *Russia's Economic Front for War and Peace* (1942) looked at the Soviet Union from an economic perspective, discussing its finances, living standards, industrial and ag-

ricultural development, the organization of its collective farms, and domestic and foreign trade at the beginning of the Soviet-German war.

Russia at war was more than just the story of a country whose inani-
mate boundaries could be seen on a map or whose history could be read
in the cold type of a page. Russia at war was also the story of a people
and their suffering on the most personal of levels. Maurice Hindus, an
American, wrote about the Russian people in *Mother Russia* (1943) after
he returned to the Soviet Union and interviewed the inhabitants of several liberated villages. He found that "what impressed them was not
only the brutality of the Germans but also their blind passion to defile
and destroy. Books were the first object that attracted them, after barn-
yard fowls: they used the Russian classics to fill mudholes or keep fires
going. At the Tolstoy homestead, they refused to gather firewood. 'We
don't need it,' a German doctor said. 'We'll burn everything connected
with the name of Tolstoy.' School houses were set afire or used for sta-
bles. Everything that contributed to the well being of the inhabitants
was next destroyed, often at the cost of the Germans' own comfort
levels. . . . Soon the Russians began to hate not only fascists but the
whole tribe of German invaders . . . 'Kill the German!' said an article in
Komsomolskaya Pravda. 'Kill the German!' is the plea of your old
mother. 'Kill the German!' is the plea of the girl you love. 'Kill the German!' whispers the grass of your native land now drenched in blood.
But along with this physical hatred for the Germans went a love for
everything Russian—the people, the trees, the wheatfields, the land itself. There was a new growth of regional pride, with the people of each
province boasting that it was the best in the Soviet Union . . . A quotation
from Stalin was printed on a war poster, beneath a portrait of General
Kutuzov, who defeated Napoleon: 'Let the valorous example of our great
ancestors inspire you in this war.' Newspapers talked of the old national
heroes: Kutuzov . . . and Alexander Nevsky . . ."[29] Like the United States
and other countries Russia also knew how to use the media to wage war
and kill the Germans.

China

China was another ally about which much was written. Like Japan,
China was part of the mysterious Orient about which Americans knew
very little. Some books like Kwok Ying Fung's *China: A Portrait Survey*

of China and Her People (1943) told of the diversified nature of modern Chinese life through its art and architecture, religion, industry, and the everyday life of its people. In *Resistance and Reconstruction* (1943), Chiang-Kai-shek, China's wartime leader, published a collection of his most important speeches and statements made between July 1937 and January 1943. He described the progressive and reactionary forces operating within China during this period. He also rejected the idea that the world's major powers should rule the region and noted that China was not going to impose its own imperialism in Asia in place of Western imperialism. His book spoke of the acute internal tensions and strains that were threatening Chinese unity—how opposition political parties, including the Communists, opposed the one-party rule of the Kuomintang (the political party that controlled the Chinese National Government). The diverse groups opposed to the Kuomintang hoped that Chiang-Kai-shek would become the leader, not of one party, but of a united democratic nation that would ensure that the age of Western imperialism in Asia was over.[30]

Other books also discussed China's political problems, the growth of guerilla warfare within China, the nature of Chinese unity since 1936 and its rifts since 1939 as well as presenting a study of the national government and its leadership. In *The Making of Modern China* (1944), Owen and Eleanor Lattimore seemed to sum up China's dilemma at the time. They noted that politically and economically China was still a revolutionary country confronted with revolutionary issues. They noted that "the Kuomintang, as the party that controlled the government, has yet to make the great historical decision—whether it will champion the interests of the people as a whole, or itself submit to the domination by the landlords. . . ."[31] Postwar history between 1945 and 1949 demonstrated which political party—the Communists or the Kuomintang—had the support of the Chinese masses in their struggle for control of the country.

David Nelson Rowe, a member of the Institute of International Studies at Yale University, discussed in *China Among the Powers* (1945) the speed and the means by which China could become a great industrial and military power in the postwar world and help the other great powers maintain the world's security. Noting that the country was a vast territory without any adequate communications and regional in its loyalties—many provinces being semi-independent with little sense of national unity—the author wrote of a China that had no central government by the end of the war. He stated that some acceptable regime had to unite the country, both physically with a modern transportation system and conceptually with a nationalistic ideology. Rowe believed that the peasants were attracted to the Chinese Communists not because they represented a new ideology but rather a revolt against the harsh conditions under which the peasants had to live. Rowe concluded that the Communists' program could not be ignored if China was to be a stable country. He seemed to suggest that the Kuomintang oligarchy could be slowly replaced or controlled under America's guidance and that Chiang-Kai-shek could serve as a symbolic leader to unite the country behind the development of an industrial military power, while reforms to improve the living conditions of the people were being carried out. Rowe recommended that the United States do the job. He proposed that the United Nations treat Japan so harshly that it could not become a military threat again. He further proposed that the United States maintain its military power through a peacetime draft and build and maintain numerous bases on the islands captured from Japan in the South Pacific and near China. He also believed that the United States should keep troops in Korea and other United Nations should supplement them. In brief, Rowe argued that America should build a kind of military Great Wall to protect China while helping her build up her military and industrial power. As postwar history demonstrates, his suggestions were somewhat prophetic except that the mainland China which began building a military industrial complex was Communist; the Nationalist Chinese resided on the island of Formosa (Taiwan) where they received America's assistance for their own military and industrial development.

France

France was an American ally under enemy occupation. Many books were written about its fall and the reasons for it, but one of the best was *The Gravediggers of France: Gamelin, Daladier, Reynaud, Pétain and Laval: Military Defeat, Armistice, Counter-Revolution* (1944). The book was written by Pertinax, André Geraud, a correspondent of the *London Daily Telegraph*, the *Baltimore Sun* and the *North American Newspaper Alliance*. Pertinax wrote about the history of France from the outbreak of the war to the return of Pierre Laval in April 1942—a history arranged around the principal personages of the tragedy. These included General Maurice Gustav Gamelin, the general who was prepared to re-fight World War I and who was utterly incapable of adapting to the strategy of the blitzkrieg of 1939–1940; Edouard Daladier, the premier who failed in his attempts to rally his people or arouse in them a will to win; Paul Reynaud, Daladier's successor as premier, who came into office too late to turn the tide of battle and save France from German occupation and too easily acceded to those who preferred an armistice rather than continuing the fight from Africa and with the French fleet; Philippe Pétain, the elderly Marshal whose servile vanity, a deep distrust of Democracy, and the desire to command induced him to become the Hindenburg of France; and Pierre Laval the convinced fascist who, in serving the interests of the Germans, presided over the disintegration of Vichy, France, into a police action against his own countrymen. Pertinax did not believe that treachery in its strictest meaning assumed an important role in the defeat of France. Rather, the author blamed petty treachery that arose from the neglect and apathy of leaders, great and small, who forgot their public trust or else believed that they could discharge it by performing their routine duties. That kind of treachery was often observed.

As far as the future of France was concerned after the fall of its puppet government, Albert Guérard, who wrote *The France of Tomorrow* (1942), believed his country had no future as a great power. In his opinion, France's only hope was to become part of a United Europe without national armies or custom duties or currencies—a Europe consisting of fifty or sixty small federated states in which France, like Germany, would lose her political existence but in which French culture would flourish—an idea whose concept was not too distant from some aspects of today's European Common Market.

The War at Home

Many books were being published about the United States as well. Some dealt with its conduct of the war abroad whereas others described the economic, political, and social impact the war was having on the home front. While America was waging war on the Axis nations, Americans were waging war on each other in the name of race. The classic book on race during the war years was Gunnar Myrdal's *An American Dilemma: The Negro Problem and Modern Democracy* (1944). Examining the black problems in America, Myrdal, a Swedish sociologist, wrote that "America is free to choose whether the Negro shall remain her liability or become her opportunity." It is a moral choice and it is "fateful not only for America itself but also for all mankind."[32] Myrdal believed that the American creed must prevail for the world to sustain its hope in democracy, or the American deed must prevail and the faith in human goodness be destroyed. The American deed was defined as the prejudicial belief that the black was physically and culturally inferior as evidenced by sickness, death, and crime rates; for this reason, the South should keep the blacks in their place and the North would remain generally indifferent. America had two choices—its creed or its deed.

Adding her own comments in a collection of speeches and articles entitled *American Unity and Asia*, Pearl Buck wrote:

> If democracy did not win, the white people would have to make themselves into a great standing army, highly trained, constantly prepared to keep colored people subdued, and there could be no greater slavery than that necessity. It is possible, in this grave moment, that in such a place as Australia there might be white people made slaves by their conquerors, just as white people now are slaves in certain countries and no less slaves because their rulers are other white men. The issue today is not one of race, colored or white. It is freedom.[33]

Buck's comments applied to all races. Books such as Carey McWilliams's *Prejudice: Japanese Americans—Symbols of Racial Intolerance* (1944) were also addressing the bigotry directed toward such peoples as Japanese-Americans. The Nisei who were American citizens found themselves interned in camps within the continental United States simply because, as some authors believed, of the vicious and untruthful campaigns carried out by business propagandists and prejudiced newspapers in years past.[34] "Why treat the Japs well here?" asked a column in a chain of Western newspapers at the time. "They take the parking positions. They get ahead of you in the stamp line at the post office. They have their share of seats on bus and streetcar lines. Let 'em be pinched, hurt, hungry, and dead up against it. . . . Personally I hate the Japanese."[35]

Racial prejudice was only one kind of war being waged within the

United States. Another was sabotage. In *Sabotage! The Secret War Against America* (1942) Michael Sayers and Albert E. Kahn wrote of a worldwide plot to keep America out of the war, and, if that failed, to destabilize America both materially and psychologically to prevent her from winning it. Although they could not cite the number of physical disasters that resulted from sabotage rather than carelessness, the authors asked, "How about certain mysterious forest fires, many of them in the immediate vicinity of lumber yards or shipbuilding plants working for the navy? . . . How about all the fires and explosions in defense plants? . . . How about the mystery of the shifting cargoes which wrecked eight ships carrying lend-lease supplies to Russia? Eight ships in eight weeks, all loaded by the same stevedoring company. . . ."[36] Sayers and Kahn also wrote about Nazi psychological sabotage perfected to be more subtle, pervasive, and dangerous than its physical form. They told how the Nazis decided to employ anti-Semitism and opposition to President Roosevelt's New Deal to direct their attack on American unity and morale. For example, George Sylvester Viereck, who "was one of [the Nazi's] principal agents, . . . wrote speeches for American Senators, sent out millions of pieces of anti-Semitic, pro-Axis propaganda under Congressional frank, and in general did his work so well that Berlin gladly paid him at least $39,000 a year for his services."[37] This book reminded readers that saboteurs not only could be foreign aliens but also American citizens who either through physical or psychological destruction could advance the enemy's cause.

Other books analyzed how the threat of war became a reality. In *How War Came: An American White Paper from the Fall of France to Pearl Harbor* Forrest Davis and Ernest K. Lindley defended the actions and policies of the U.S. State Department in trying to hold the Nazis in check and keep America out of the war. They noted that in January 1941, based upon Polish and Chinese intelligence sources, the State Department warned Russia that Germany would attack Russia in June 1941. British Prime Minister Winston Churchill sent Russia the same warning. Russia chose to ignore both warnings, possibly because Joseph Stalin knew that German army leaders opposed such an attack and because he thought he could prevent it.

Davis and Lindley also wrote about sixty conversations Secretary of State Cordell Hull had with Japan's envoys before the attack on Pearl Harbor. At the time, it was a new story. The authors believed that Admiral Kichisaburo Nomura was trying sincerely to avoid war between the United States and Japan; however, he could not promise that Japan would withdraw from China or break her alliance with Germany. The other Japanese envoy, Saburo Kurusu, had a more specific mission. Contrary to popular belief at the time, he was not sent to deceive the United States as the Japanese fleet sailed toward Pearl Harbor; Kurusu's purpose was to present the terms of surrender. "The United States, he said, must abandon China, drop the embargo, supply oil to Japan, and help her to acquire raw materials from the Indies. In return for all this, the Japanese would agree not to press southward beyond Indo-China and would withdraw from that country when and if the Chinese yielded."[38] The Japanese demands were so disproportionate to their promises that they seemed to constitute an implied threat: If the United States did not meet the Japanese demands, it could reap the consequences. When Secretary Hull rejected the Japanese terms on November 26, 1941, he knew war was coming, but he knew it only emotionally, not as a reality; however, he warned his War Cabinet colleagues that if they were not careful the Japanese "might stampede the hell out of our scattered forces."[39] Hull's warning was not heeded, because no one—not the Secretary of State, not the Secretary of War, not the Secretary of the Navy, not the American public—could believe that the most powerful nation in the world was actually being given an ultimatum by a tiny island nation in the Pacific. The rest is history.

Looking Beyond the War

The books Americans read during World War II covered the war from many perspectives. They allowed readers to visit enemy countries as well as those of their allies, spoke about enemy leaders as well as those of the United Nations, brought readers to scenes of battles, great and small, and let them see war's humor as well as its pathos. As they learned about the war and the times they were living through, the public could experience many different emotions from a variety of books. But, how was the war to end? What was going to happen to the world after the war? These questions lead to another category of books published during the war—the strategy and peace proposal books.

In *Defense Will Not Win the War* (1942), former Lieutenant Colonel

W. F. Kernan warned America not to fall into the trap of making Japan its primary enemy rather than Germany. Kernan believed that the war would be settled on the battlefields of Europe, the Atlantic, and the Mediterranean and if the United States concentrated on Japan, Hitler would be granted his wish of keeping American forces away from the European theater of war. In *Strategy for Victory*, Hanson W. Baldwin of the *New York Times* warned Americans that total war required a total response. It could not be won by sea power, air power, or land power alone. It could not be won by offense alone or defense alone. America's single hope was to use all of its armaments and all of its strategies to achieve victory. As history has demonstrated, the policies these authors advocated were the strategies the United States adopted to gain victory.

Some wartime books proved to be quite prophetic about the postwar world. For example, in *Time for Decision* (1944), Sumner Welles, the Undersecretary of State from the late 1930s until 1943, believed that Russia ought to be guaranteed frontiers for its own security and had the right to establish a federal regionalism in Eastern Europe, but it had to consist of independent sovereign states. He also proposed that "the best solution in the Near East is the abandonment of the British mandate in Palestine, to be replaced by a Jewish-Arab autonomous state within a Near Eastern federative system. . . . that the solution in the Far East lies in applying the international-trusteeship principle to Korea, Burma, French Indo-China, and the island peoples of the Southwestern Pacific, with India and the Dutch East Indies being granted some form of freedom or autonomy in accordance with the commitments already made by Great Britain and Holland. . . . 'the German menace' can be ended if the Allies adopt a policy of continuing control over German armaments and the German economy, if Central Europe's communications and power development are internationalized, if Germany is politically partitioned, and if a world organization is created within which the Germans, thus, controlled, policed and cut up can move toward a decent partnership with other nations."[40] The world organization would consist of an overall United Nations Executive Council, a World Court, a World Congress, and a Securities and Armaments Commission. As heads of their respective regions, the United States, Russia, Great Britain, and China would dominate the council. Each region would decide for itself how it would make force available to maintain peace in its area. If the regional system could not settle a controversy, the world organization would invoke force. But the use of such force would require the unanimous consent of the Great Powers. In other words, a veto could stop such action.[41]

Although these recommendations were made in 1944, Mr. Welles's vision of the postwar world did come true in several respects. Russia and her eastern bloc allies Poland, the German Democratic Republic (East Germany), Hungary, Rumania, and Czechoslovakia formed the Council of Mutual Economic Cooperation (their equivalent of the European Economic Community) and the Warsaw Pact (their equivalent of the North Atlantic Treaty Organization), which lasted until the fall of Communism in the early 1990s. The Jewish state of Israel was established but not as a Jewish–Arab autonomous state. The various islands that composed the Dutch East Indies such as Sumatra, Java, and Bali received their independence after the war and formed the Republic of Indonesia. India was granted independence from the British Empire. Only a few islands in the Pacific came under American mandate. Finally, some aspects of Welles's plan for a world organization achieved reality with the establishment of the United Nations and the World Court, although his regional power concept of the Big Four powers never materialized.

In another look at the postwar world, Walter Lippmann, the distinguished columnist, predicted in *U.S. Foreign Policy: Shield of the Republic* (1943) that the Atlantic community in the future would consist of the Americas and the western fringe of Europe, especially England and France. In the postwar world America's new frontier would not stop on its East Coast but rather on the Rhine River. In the late 1940s America became a member of the North Atlantic Treaty Organization (NATO) along with England and France and other European countries.

In *One World* (1943), based on his trip around the world in 1942 Wendell L. Willkie, presidential candidate of the Republican Party in 1940, appealed for self-government among the people of the Near and Far East and for an end to imperialism everywhere. As he wrote in one passage, "It is all very well to say as some people said to me in Cairo and Jerusalem that 'the natives don't want anything better than what they have.' That is the argument that has been used everywhere for centuries against the advancement of the underprivileged by those whose conditions make them satisfied with the status quo."[42] Or in admiring Russia's success at the time, he stated: "The best answer to Communism is a living, vibrant, fearless democracy—economic, social and political. All we need to do is stand up and perform according to our professed ideals. Then, those ideals will be safe."[43] In the postwar world, France, England, and the Netherlands did give various countries in the Far and Middle East their independence, and by the early 1990s Communism collapsed as a way of government in the Soviet Union and Eastern Europe. Democracy continues to grow and flourish in various parts of the world.

Another prophetic view of the postwar world, particularly in Europe, was presented by Albert Guérard in *Europe: Free and United* (1945). He foresaw a World Commonwealth of Regional Unions in which the European nation would assume its rightful position if certain conditions could be fulfilled: England had to rise above empire and insularity and, in Guérard's opinion, abandon her role as a manipulator of continental power balances and join the European union; Russia had to cease being suspicious of the West and allow a united Europe to exist, without Russia; and a European solution of the German problem had to be devised, without German dominance of the Union. Guérard noted that Germany must be absorbed not isolated. The Europe that would emerge from his plan would be a rich community of autonomous cultures to which a customs union, a federal banking system, a common currency, and common social legislation gives cohesion. Today the European Economic Community is striving toward many of these goals.

At the same time, other authors such as Major George Fielding Eliot in *Hour of Triumph* argued that Germany and Japan should be dismantled, indefinitely occupied and partitioned because of their criminal nature as nations. Others like Harold G. Moulton and Louis Marlio in *Control of Germany and Japan* argued that these countries should be reintegrated into the community of nations to make this one world.

Reflection

These were the books Americans were reading on the home front—books about themselves, their enemies, their Allies, or the world of tomorrow. They represent only a fraction of the books published during World War II. In part, books were among the most important rebuilding elements in a devastated world because all nations—the victors, the vanquished, and the liberated—had to learn once again how to live with each other. Books contributed to the bridges of understanding among the different peoples of the world for achieving this goal.

It has been stated before and will be stated again and again because it is a truth found at the core of World War II: This conflict consisted of many battles, but its most important was that for the minds of men. Upon the outcome of this war rested the future course of civilization. Books not only were used as weapons and ammunition in this battle but also they were the best of weapons and the best of ammunition. They dispensed knowledge and ideas that helped guide the United States to victory. Whether it was a work of fiction or semifiction, or a book about politics, economics, social concerns, war strategy, military battles large and small, or self-help—whatever the subject, a book was probably available, which could help Americans survive the wartime environment and make them understand why and how they had to win so that they would never have to fight another war again. Despite the darkness of the hour, books provided an unparalleled counter-attack when the enemy attacked America's way of thinking. They provided the public with a belief in a better tomorrow without which life during the World War II would have been quite empty and unbearable. A poet said it best when he once wrote "But somehow the poor old Earth blunders along. . . . Gets to port as the next generation will witness." It certainly can be said that the books published during this international upheaval helped the old Earth along its way.

Notes

1. "Ideas for Americans at War Spread by Council of Books," *Publishers Weekly*, December 25, 1943, 2300.

2. "Book and Author War Bond Committee Reports," *Publishers Weekly*, February 24, 1945, 924–25.

3. As quoted in "Book Reading in 1943," *Publishers Weekly*, January 1, 1944.

4. Ibid., 28.

5. As quoted in Malcom Cowley, "The War Against Writers," *New Republic*, May 8, 1944, 631.

6. Ibid.

7. Ibid., 632.

8. William Rose Benét, "Writers and the Fighting Spirit," *Saturday Review of Literature*, November 14, 1942, 12.

9. William Rose Benét, "War Morale and the Writer," *Saturday Review of Literature*, July 4, 1942, 4.

10. Ibid., 3.

11. Ibid.

12. Norman Cousins, "The War Against Hindsight," *Saturday of Review of Literature*, April 15, 1944, 28.

13. Harrison Smith, "War and Literature," *Saturday Review of Literature*, September 20, 1941, 8.

14. As quoted in Malcom Cowley, "William L. Shirer Speaking," *New Republic*, June 30, 1941, 893–94.

15. Ibid.

16. Ibid., 894.

17. Malcom Cowley, "Inside Germany," *New Republic*, September 7, 1942, 289–90.

18. Ibid., 290.

19. Graham B. Hovey, "This Is Ernie Pyle's War," *New Republic*, December 11, 1944, 804.

20. Ibid.

21. Ibid.

22. Ibid., 805.

23. Herbert Lyons, "Bill Mauldin's Book," *New Republic*, June 18, 1945, 848.

24. Guenter Reimann, "Inside Germany," *New Republic*, August 10, 1942, 182.

25. Ibid.

26. As quoted in Malcom Cowley, "Rattling Around the War," *New Republic*, March 20, 1944, 383.

27. As quoted in Malcom Cowley, "Notes on the Enemy," *New Republic*, November 23, 1942, 685.

28. G. A. Borgese, "The Remaking of Italy," *New Republic*, April 13, 1942, 499.

29. Malcom Cowley, "Russian Turnabout," *New Republic*, June 14, 1943, 800–801.

30. Kate L. Mitchell, "China Today," *New Republic*, October 4, 1943, 463.

31. Ralph Bates, "Recent Books on China," *New Republic*, April 3, 1944, 474.

32. J. Saunders Redding, "The Negro: America's Dilemma," *New Republic*, March 20, 1944, 384.

33. As quoted in Eleanor Roosevelt, "The Issue of Freedom," *New Republic*, August 3, 1942, 147.

34. Carroll Kilpatrick, "Two Battles: One Front," *New Republic*, August 3, 1942, 147.

35. "This Fabulous Century 1940–1950," (New York: Time-Life Books, 1969), 201.

36. Varian Fry, "Sabotage: The Two Faces," *New Republic*, September 12, 1942.

37. Ibid.

38. Malcom Cowley, "The State Department Story," *New Republic*, August 31, 1942, 260–61.

39. Ibid., 261.

40. Max Lerner, "The World of Sumner Welles," *New Republic*, July 31, 1944, 135.

41. Ibid.

42. "Willkie Sees the World," *Commonweal*, April 30, 1945, 45.

43. Ibid.

Chapter Eight

CARTOONS
How They Fought the War

DURING THE SECOND WORLD WAR, America's Arsenal of Democracy consisted of many weapons to maintain the nation's morale and fight the Axis powers. One of the most imaginative was the cartoon, which appeared in many media formats, including comic books, newspapers, radio, movies, and posters. Of the various formats, the most popular was comic books and newspaper strips with such heroes as Superman, Batman and Robin, Captain Marvel, Captain America, Joe Palooka, and Smilin' Jack. On the home front, these characters sold war bonds, promoted salvage drives, organized Victory Garden Clubs, combatted intolerance and absenteeism at work, warned against overoptimism in the global conflict, kept the nation alert to the dangers of sabotage, argued for an international police force in the postwar world, and recruited men and women as blood donors, for industry, and the armed services. By December 1945, 20 million comic books were being sold on the newsstands every month. In addition, 1.5 billion copies of four-or five-panel comic strips were circulated each week in daily newspapers. Only two of the nation's 2,300 major daily newspapers—the *New York Times* and the *Christian Science Monitor*—did not publish comic strips.[1] The pervasiveness and popularity of the comic strip made it a vital medium of communication during the war.

Comics and Culture

Even before the United States officially entered the war, the influence of the comic strips was noticeable and varied. They affected America's

213

eating habits, fashions, language, and other aspects of everyday life. "Blondie" gave the nation the mountainous and precarious Dagwood sandwich. "Bringing Up Father" with Maggie and Jiggs, a newly rich Irishman, inspired the development of Dinty Moore restaurants, which specialized in his favorite dish, corned beef and cabbage. The glamour girls of the future who appeared in "Flash Gordon" popularized the upswept hairdo and the bare midriff playsuit. Sad Sack, the luckless hero of Sergeant George Baker's comic strip, had a leading theatrical role in *Hi, Yank!*. Krazy Kat inspired a ballet; Barney Google inspired the song "Barney Google with the Goo-Goo-Googly Eyes" and the expression, heebie-jeebies. Other comic books characters added such expressions to the language as "let George do it" (Jiggs), "jeep" (Popeye), "time's-a-wastin" (Barney Google) as well as many other phrases such as hi, doc, O.K., hot dog, darn, holy mackerel, nope, wow, double cross, Sh-h, huh, and hotsy totsy.

The comics even had an impact on politics. When Joe Palooka, boxing's heavyweight champion of the world, enlisted in the Army in 1940—the first comic strip character to put on a military uniform—President Franklin D. Roosevelt personally thanked Ham Fisher, the comic strip's creator, for making the prewar draft in 1940 more acceptable to the public.

The American public was so absorbed in the lives of the comics' characters that the country seemed to become one large family. When Little Orphan Annie lost her dog Sandy in 1933, Harold Gray, her creator, received the following telegram: "Please do all you can to help Annie find Sandy. We are all interested," signed, "Henry Ford."[2] When Blondie became pregnant in 1941, Chic Young, her creator, offered some prize money for the newborn's name; along with 400,000 suggestions (Cookie won) came a great deal of advice on how to raise the baby. When Smilin' Jack was lost in the Pacific, agitated readers urged Pan American Airways to send out a rescue plane. When Milton Caniff, creator of "Terry and the Pirates," killed off the beautiful Raven Sherman in 1943, telephone calls tied up newspaper switchboards; flowers were sent to the funeral; and 450 students at Chicago's Loyola University met at dawn for a minute of silent mourning, facing the Far East (the comic strip's setting).[3]

Comics Do Their Part for the War Effort

The contribution of comic strip heroes to the war effort was suggested by *Newsweek* when the magazine noted that

if the United Nations ever recruited a task force of these and other American comic book heroes to fight the Axis powers, the war would have ended overnight. Given a free hand, Barney Baxter and Smilin' Jack would have knocked the [German] Messerschmidts and [Japanese] Zeros out of the skies. Don Winslow of the Navy and Alley Oop would have rid the seas of German and Japanese submarines. Joe Palooka and Snuffy Smith would have defeated the Axis land armies, while on the home front Little Orphan Annie, Secret Agent X-9, and Superman would have polished off the spies and saboteurs.[4]

By July 1942, fifty of these comic strip heroes had begun to do their part in helping defeat the enemy.

While Superman kept fairly busy rounding up fifth-column members in the United States, Little Orphan Annie served "as a Colonel of the 'Junior Commandos' who [collected] scrap and [sold] War Stamps. Inspired by the idea, children around the country . . . organized Junior Commando units." When Annie asked children to help their war-working mothers with housework, millions of children sprang to their brooms.[5] In Boston alone, 15,000 Junior Commandos suddenly appeared to help their mothers with household chores.[6] Annie helped our country's defense in other ways as well. Just thirteen days before Nazi spies actually landed on American shores from Nazi submarines in June 1942, Annie and her pal, Panda, blew up a German U-boat to thwart a similar landing.

Meanwhile, Smilin' Jack, "a lieutenant in the Air Force Ferrying Command, [was] flying bombers across the ocean to our Allies," and Barney Baxter (operator of a Devil Cat aircraft factory), "by a streak of cartoonist good luck, . . . bombed Tokyo . . . simultaneously with [Lieutenant Colonel] Jimmie Doolittle's squadrons [in April 1942]." However, Barney Baxter was not alone in the Pacific. Wash Tubb's friend, Captain Easy, "assigned by Army Intelligence to the Philippine back country to keep alive the fight for freedom [was] blowing up enemy ships and exposing Japanese propaganda of Asia for Asiatics." On the other hand, "Alley Oop—the caveman from prehistoric Moo—[was] cruising the Pacific Ocean in a captured Nipponese submarine with his buddies Foozy, King Guz, and the renegade scientist, Oscar Boom. While tinkering with the sub's gear, Alley accidently torpedoed a Jap cruiser."[7]

As already noted, Joe Palooka was the first comic strip character to put on a military uniform when he enlisted in the Army in 1940. Upon Joe's entrance, Knobby Walsh, his boxing manager, too old to enlist, got a job in a defense plant. Never late or absent himself, Knobby immediately began to expound on the wartime evils of absenteeism, tardiness, and changing jobs. Meanwhile, Joe's mother, generally a quiet person, mounted her pen-and-ink soapbox and gave other American mothers a terrific scolding about being so afraid and critical of Army camp soldiers who might be interested in their daughters. In no uncertain terms, she told American mothers that the boys at the new military camps were just like other boys, no different from their own sons—"just tired, homesick kids who badly needed a little sistering and mothering." Also serving in the same service was Snuffy Smith, the lovable little mountaineer who made hilarious shambles out of Army life and held an unusual wartime distinction. His dialogue was so super-military that the Army imitated him. "Yardbird" (meaning the rawest recruit) and other Snuffy Smith expressions became part of every soldier's vocabulary.[8]

Some Americans took these comics quite seriously. Until becoming a soldier, Joe Palooka was boxing's heavyweight champion of the world. Always a clean fighter, Joe, to the shock of his fans, shot a Nazi in the back in the course of battle. Ham Fisher, Joe's creator, had to come to his hero's defense by reminding readers that real soldiers are not polite in combat, and Joe had the same rights they did. As Joe fought the Nazis, Tillie the Toiler joined the WACs (the Women's Army Corps) and influenced many other young women to do so. Buzz Sawyer also did his part by reenlisting in the U.S. Navy at its request to plead various causes before the public and in Congress.

But our wartime comic heroes did more than participate in adventure stories or help out in various war drives on the home front. They also delivered messages to raise the morale of America's fighting men and those they left behind. An excellent example is a talk Colonel Flip Corkin delivered to Terry Lee in "Terry and the Pirates"—a message that was published in the *Congressional Record*, an excerpt of which follows:

Well, you made it . . . You're a flight officer in the Air Forces of the Army of the United States . . . Those wings are like a neon light on your chest . . . I'm not going to wave the flag at you—But some things you must never forget . . .

Every country has had a hand in the development of the airplane—But after all, the Wright brothers were a couple of Dayton, Ohio, boys—and Kitty Hawk is strictly in North Carolina . . . The hallmark of the United States is on every aircraft . . .

So you find yourself in a position to defend the country that gave you the weapon with which to do it . . . But it wasn't just you who earned those wings . . . A ghostly echelon of good guys flew their hearts out in old kites to give you the know-how . . .

And some slide rule jokers sweat it out over drawing boards to give you the machine that will keep you up there shooting . . . I recommended you for fighter aircraft and I want you to be cocky and smart and proud of being a buzz-boy . . .

But don't forget that every bullet you shoot, every gallon of gas and oil you burn was brought here by transport pilots who flew it over the worst terrain in the world! You may get the glory—but they put the lift in your balloon! . . .

And don't let me ever catch you being high—bicycle with the enlisted men in your ground crew! Without them, you'd never get ten feet off the ground! Every grease monkey in that gang is right beside you in the cockpit—and their hands are on the stick, just the same as yours . . .

You'll get angry as the devil at the Army and its so-called red-tape . . . But be patient with it . . . Somehow the old eagle has managed to end up in possession of the ball in every war since 1776—so just humor it along . . .

Okay, sport, end of speech . . . When you get up in that "wild blue yonder" the song talks about—remember, there are a lot of good guys missing from mess tables in the South Pacific, Alaska, Africa, Britain, Asia and back home who are sorta counting on you to take it from here! Good night, kid![9]

As Terry leaves Colonel Corkin, he passes a sign that says: "This way to Tokio! Next stop U.S.A."

In various ways, comic heroes, books, and strips went to war. In their own fashion, they were an indispensable part of America's Arsenal of Democracy. They not only went to war in the strips, but comics themselves also literally went to war as their popularity among the armed forces attests. Comics were published in various regional editions of the Army's newspaper, *Stars and Stripes*, and in more than 1,200 service newspapers throughout the country. At Army post exchanges, comic books outsold by a ratio of ten to one the combined purchases of *Life*, *Reader's Digest*, and *Saturday Evening Post*. A survey released in 1945 by the Market Research Company of America revealed that of the men in training camps in this country, 44 percent read comic books regularly and another 13 percent occasionally.[10]

A Controversial Educational Tool

During the war years, comics not only sought to entertain and lift morale, they also sought to educate the readers whether they were in the military or not. The armed forces used a character named Private Pete and his colleagues to explain basic training programs to servicemen and to teach them how to read.

Comic books were also used during the war to educate the nation's children, but the controversy of using comics for such purposes was serious and furious. The fears with which America's older generation viewed comics and their influence upon the young in the early 1940s is illustrated by this editorial excerpt that appeared in the *Chicago Daily News* on May 8, 1940:

> Save for a scattering of more or less innocuous "gag" comics and some reprints of newspaper strips, we found that the bulk of these lurid publications depend for their appeal on mayhem, murder, torture and abduction—often with a child as the victim. Superman heroics, voluptuous females in scanty attire, blazing machine guns, hooded "justice" and cheap political propaganda were on every page . . . badly drawn, badly written and badly printed—a strain on young eyes and young nervous systems.[11]

But this was mild commentary compared with the following criticism:

> There are only two ways to meet this problem: one is to shut your eyes to it, and the other is to open your arms to it. In terms of their generation, all that is said about comic magazines by parents who confine themselves to the daily or Sunday funnies is true. It was bad enough when four pages

became eight and when eight came out in color. But to be able to sit down and read sixty-four pages of colored comic books—for ten cents—and then read sixty-four more on a swap, and finally become a child of this feebly vicious material, certainly seems like a goalless excess of decadence. This is a sub-hell where the devil himself is disciplined.[12]

Despite such criticisms, especially those that equated comics with "trash," about 6,000 schools by the end of 1943 were using comic books as supplementary texts.[13] The industry was able to calm the fears of parents and educators about its products by establishing advisory groups of clergy and educators to maintain the quality of comic books on as high a level as possible. As a result, schools were able to use comics to teach such subjects as English, Spanish, and social studies. There was even a series in which classic books like *Ivanhoe* were reduced to comic book form, while Sunday school children were studying a comic book called *Picture Stories from the Bible*, featuring such stories as Noah, Moses, and Jonah. Comics also covered such subjects as geography, science, history, and biography. The advocates of comics argued that these publications increased children's language skills and vocabulary, gave them a sense of adventure denied them in real life, and taught them moral values in regard to the law and that crime does not pay. The magnitude of the potential influence of comics in American society was underscored by a 1943 survey that revealed that 95 percent of children between eight and eleven years of age, 84 percent of adolescents between twelve and seventeen years, and 35 percent of adults between eighteen and thirty years of age read comic books on a regular basis.[14]

Comic book critics argued that comics would crowd out more desirable reading, hinder children from developing a sense of the real world because of their indulgence in the fantasy worlds of comics, and interfere with their development of language skills because of the reliance on pictures rather than the written word. It was feared that children would develop the bad reading habit of sliding over words they did not know.[15] Perhaps, Josette Frank, staff advisor to the Children's Book and Radio Committee of the Child Study Association of America, stated one of the more definitive and authoritative conclusions on the comic book debate during the war years:

Hop Harrigan, flying his streamlined plastic plane or tracking down a sabotage plot, is much closer to home than Ulysses doing battle for Helen

of Troy—though many children do enjoy both. Today's children want
their heroes to rush in and conquer today's villains—gangsters, saboteurs,
foreign spies . . .

We at the Child Study Association have a deep abiding faith in children.
I believe that we may safely accept our children's likes and dislikes for
what they are—a stage in growth—provided we also help them grow
toward wider horizons. I believe that, along with their other reading, we
can safely let our children read comics."[16]

Thus the comic book debate waxed and waned during the war years,
but the desire of children to see their comic heroes aid in the war effort
was not lost on the creators.

Superman, Super Hero

Of all the superheroes who appeared in comics during the war years,
the one who revolutionized an art form and industry and inspired the
creation of other comic superheroes was Superman. Perhaps the best
way to illustrate the impact of the comic superhero in a society at war is
to look at the significance and influence of Superman on children and
adults alike.

Superman first appeared in *Action Comics* in June 1938. After his
publication, the comic book industry was never the same again. In the
previous thirty-eight years, the comic industry had gone through two
phases. The first lasted from about 1900 to 1920 when comics were
meant to be funny. For example, in 1907 the *San Francisco Chronicle*
introduced a humorous strip called "A. Mutt," which was changed in
1909 to "Mutt and Jeff" when Mutt, who began as a sportsman-hustler
and evolved into a harassed husband met Jeff, a dwarflike man, in a
mental hospital. Jeff had introduced himself as James L. Jeffries, retired
heavyweight champion of the world. Another humorous strip, introduced
in 1913, was "Bringing Up Father," with Jiggs and Maggie. In England,
Jiggs's favorite food of corned beef and cabbage became tripe and on-
ions, in China, rice, in Italy, spaghetti, and in Mexico, hot tamales. The
second phase of America's comic book evolution began hesitatingly in the
early 1920s with the introduction of pathos and human interest. By
about 1930, leading comic strips stopped trying to be humorous and
became adventure strips. In 1921, Frank King's "Gasoline Alley" began

the trend toward straight storytelling when he converted his funny strip into a pictorial life of a character named Skeezix Wallet. This strip became so popular in its portrayal of the average American life that during World War II when a columnist reported that Skeezix who had joined the Army Ordnance Branch was going to be wounded by a Japanese bullet, the public responded with fury. In fact, one newspaper, the *Pittsburgh Post-Dispatch*, felt compelled to assure its readers in front page headlines that Skeezix was safe. Then, in 1924, Little Orphan Annie—who never grows up—began her series of unfunny adventures.

In 1938 Superman appeared and represented a radical departure from the previously accepted standards of storytelling and drama. Although not the first of the fantastic strips (Tarzan, for example, in 1929 was earlier), Superman became an overnight favorite of the public. Within a few years, Superman was everywhere in the nation's culture. After his first appearance in *Action Comics*, he became a newspaper strip (1938), went on radio in the United States (February 12, 1940) and Canada—for the first time listeners heard "Up in the sky! Look! It's a bird! It's a plane! It's Superman!"—and began appearing in Paramount Studio animated cartoons in 1941. Superman became a television series in the 1950s, full-length movies in the 1970s and 1980s, and a new television series in the 1990s. During the war years, rare was the child who did not have Superman dungarees, or a Superman Krypto-Raygun, or certificates, cards, or buttons of a member of the Superman Club of America. A Superman Day was held at the 1939 New York World's Fair and, during World War II, an Army Tank Corps was named after him. His success in such comic magazines as *Action Comics* and *World's Finest Comics*—a 15-cent, ninety-six page magazine, which its publishers claimed to be the largest selling comic book quarterly—led to the development of many other comic book superheroes like Batman and Robin and Wonder Woman.[17]

By 1945, comic books were still evolving as a pictorial story-telling art form. They were not meant to be humorous nor were they primarily concerned with dramatic adventure. As with Superman and other superheroes, the emotional appeal of comics at this time was based on wish fulfillment.

Created by Joe Shuster and Jerry Siegel, two Cleveland, Ohio, high school seniors, Superman was distinctly different from the comic strip heroes who preceded him. Superman represents the tradition of Homer, the Greek poet— Achilles with or without a vulnerable heel, Hector who defends his home town against foreign invaders, and Ulysses who cleverly accomplished the downfall of his enemies by the exercise of superhuman wisdom.[18] Superman (with his blue jersey and tights, red trunks, buskins and a flowing red cape) has all the attributes of a hero God. He is as handsome as Apollo, as strong as Hercules, and as swift as Hermes. As a "savior of the oppressed and the helpless," he is like a protective deity.[19] His motivating traits are "super courage," "super goodness," and "super justice." His mission in life is "to go to the rescue of persecuted people and deserving persons."[20] Superman never risks danger; by definition he is always superior to every kind of menace. He is invincible and invulnerable. He can leap over skyscrapers in a single bound (an eighth of a mile in any direction), fly through the air, crush rock or steel in his bare hands, scale buildings like a fly, lift and smash tremendous weights, repel knives or bullets, swim faster than fish, catch munitions with his bare hands, render people unconscious by pressing an appropriate nerve at the back of their neck, eavesdrop on a conversation within a hundred yards with his super sensitive hearing, see through objects with X-ray vision, and blow out fires with his breath.

Superman and the superheroes who followed satisfied our human longing to be stronger than all opposing obstacles and fulfilled the universal desire to see wrongs righted, the underdogs beat their oppressors, and good triumph over evil. In these various qualities, Superman was far different than his predecessor comic heroes and was the standard against which subsequent superheroes who followed were measured and compared.

So who is this Superman whose "Up, Up and Awa-ay!" is like a second name. To those who may still be unaware of his origins and background, a brief explanation may be of interest. Superman is the sole survivor of a planet named Krypton, the home of a super race, which was suddenly destroyed by earthquakes. Split seconds before the planet's demise, Jorl-l, the great Kryptonian scientist, put his firstborn whose name was Kal-El into a rocket ship, and launched him into interplanetary space. Some 3 billion light years away, the rocket ship safely landed on a roadside near Metropolis, U.S.A., where a passing motorist found him and brought him to an orphanage.

When Superman is seen next, he has grown to super manhood and is a young man about 25 years old. But as his readers know, Superman has a dual personality. Part of the time the world knows him as Clark Kent, a mild-mannered reporter for the *Daily Planet* newspaper who tends to shy away from unpleasantness. But when evil doings arise, he ducks into privacy, gets rid of his glasses and blue suit, and emerges bold as truth, in the gaudy outfit of Superman. This dual identity allows Clark Kent to give his newspaper some extraordinary scoops on Superman's latest feats. Most of Superman's coups are brought off on behalf of Lois Lane, the *Daily Planet*'s attractive reporter, whose nose for news is constantly landing her in trouble.[21]

Super War Effort

Even before America's official entrance into World War II, Superman's influence was felt overseas. In a special strip drawn for a magazine, Superman's creators had him demolish the Siegfried Line (a line of German defensive fortifications facing the French Maginot Line), seize Hitler and Stalin by the napes of their necks and whisk them off for judgment before the League of Nations. Under orders from Joseph Goebbels, the German Minister of Propaganda, *Das Schwarze Korps*, the official newspaper of Hitler's Elite Guards (the *Sturmtruppen*), virulently attacked Superman as a Jewish-American plutocrat with a well-known infamous record and insisted that his creators, Shuster and Siegel, were Jewish as it continued its counter-blast: "The clever creator of Superman is a Colorado beetle [*sic*] . . . He stinks."[22]

Superman's contribution to the war effort cannot be minimized. Three months before the Battle of Midway in June 1942, the Navy Department gave a high-priority rating to the shipment of Superman comic books to that island's garrison. Being the superhero that he is, Superman presented his creators with a very serious dilemma. World War II was not going to end overnight, but Superman could probably accomplish a total victory if given the chance. Yet in view of his unquestioned patriotism, Superman could not stay out of the war. Therefore, Superman's creators had Superman called up for military induction; during his physical examination, Superman mistakenly read an eye chart in an adjoining room with his X-ray vision and was rejected for military service. This situation did not prevent Superman from catching spies in the United States during the war.

The punishment Superman administered to our enemies could take many forms because he is a superhero with high morals. He is "never allowed . . . to destroy property belonging to anyone except the villain, and then when it is absolutely unavoidable . . . Superman never kills anyone and never uses a weapon other than his bare fists."[23] He can knock a villain silly or scare the wits out of him by tossing him into the stratosphere or destroy an enemy plane in full flight. People usually get killed only by their own doing, as when the villain hits Superman on the head with a crowbar only to have the crowbar rebound to shatter his own head.

Superman's view of the Axis powers may have been summarized in one of his many soliloquies about his own personal enemy, the arch villain, Lex Luthor: "So Luthor is still alive and plotting the downfall and subjugation of present-day civilization! The world will never be safe until that fiend is destroyed—and somehow I've got to accomplish it."[24]

Superman and American Children

Superman not only came to the assistance of Lois Lane and the helpless and oppressed peoples of the world in fiction, but he also was of invaluable assistance to children in the real world during the war years. From the viewpoint of educators, Superman performed meaningful duty for children. He could be found in the public schools and libraries. More than one public library increased its circulation of good books for children with a poster announcing: "Superman says: Read a Good Book Every Week." Children then could obtain a list of good books Superman suggested, such as *Treasure Island, Twenty Thousand Leagues Under the Sea, Tom Sawyer, The Prince and the Pauper*, or *Pinocchio*. In addition, the book list contained a special message from Superman to the children:

> An alert mind is as important as a sound and healthy body. It is only with this combination of powers that you boys and girls of America can grow into sturdy, upstanding citizens. One swell way of cultivating your mind is to read good stories. Your library has many books you will enjoy and I have selected a few of them that I know you will like particularly well. They are packed full of adventure, thrills, excitement and fun. Ask your librarian for one today and get into the habit of reading.[25]

Superman not only encouraged children to read books written by others, but by the spring of 1942 was the subject of a Superman workbook that more than 1,500 classrooms were using as a teaching aid for English grammar.[26] In addition to picture stories, the workbooks contained vocabulary exercises. As a result of the success of Superman as a classroom educational device, the Superman strips began to include a certain percentage of words that were above the average child reader to increase the scope of children's vocabulary.

Super Critics

Despite all his positive activities, Superman, like other comic strip characters during the war, had his share of critics and controversy. To some critics, Superman was more than just a figment of someone's imagination. At a time when the Axis powers and fascism seemed on the rise, Superman symbolized the ideal of Friedrich Wilhelm Nietzsche, the nineteenth-century German philosopher.

Despite Superman's admirable defense of right and justice, his method of achieving such ends greatly concerned his critics. According to Fred Latimer Hasdel, Superman never acted by using the law but was always above it. The implication was that Superman depicted the idea that the laws of the land were inept and the police ineffective and that justice could only be realized by abandoning the traditional methods of law and order and resorting to a superman. Hasdel asked, was this not the solution of many Germans to extricate themselves from their troubles? Might not it be the inclination of many Americans if our democratic processes should appear to be too slow or ineffectual? Hero worship combined with contempt for law and order, according to this reasoning, was potentially—if unconsciously—fascist. Fascist rule could therefore develop in the United States if the people should seek a hero who could cut through our governmental system with the avowed objective of defending that very democracy which, in fact, would be destroyed.[27] Years after the airing of this debate, the American Republic still endures and its fascist enemies of World War II have disappeared from the face of the earth.

While some critics opposed the concept of Superman on ideological grounds, others had psychological reasons. In the wake of this debate, new comic strip characters were born. From the psychological viewpoint, William M. Marston, a professional psychologist and creator of Wonder Woman, thought that blood-curdling masculinity was the worst offense of comic books. The male hero lacked various qualities such as love and tenderness, which are essential in any child's development. If the child's ideal became a super*man* who used his extraordinary powers to help the weak, love—the most essential ingredient in human happiness—would still be missing. It is smart to be strong. It is big to be generous. However, according to the comics' rules of masculinity, it was not manly to be tender, affectionate, and alluring. For example, rarely by so much as a word or a glance was tender passion suggested between Superman and Lois Lane. For one thing, Superman had shyly confessed that he would never embrace a girl, lest he inadvertently crack her ribs.[28] The obvious remedy was to show that such qualities as tenderness, affection, and allure are proper for little girls. As a result, girls were given their own superhero to admire—Wonder Woman who has all the strength of Superman with all the attraction of a good and beautiful woman. While Superman never kills, Wonder Woman saves her worst enemies and reforms their characters. By 1943, Wonder Woman became the latest formula in comics—super strength, altruism, feminine love and allure, all combined in a single character. She even became a great favorite of men who saw in her character masculine strength blended with her other qualities. Girls as well as boys now had their own comic heroes whom they could emulate.[29]

Government Wartime Comics

While societal debate over the value of comic books and strips was never ending during the war, there was no debate within the federal government. As a tool for propaganda, the federal government found comic books to be a very useful tool. For example, the federal Office of Inter-American Affairs sponsored the creation of comic-style pamphlets in Spanish and Portuguese; *Heros Verdaderos* (True Heroes) spoke about the achievements of Americans at war. *Nuestro Futuro* (Our Future) was a frank anti-Nazi publication in comic book style that illustrated the issues at stake in this global conflict. Distributed in the Americas, these comic-style publications proved to be very popular reading matter.[30]

The single cartoon also assumed a very important role in the public and private sectors of our society. The U.S. Office of War Information (OWI) had a cartoon character named Kid Salvage who had plenty of work to keep himself busy. One week he even stopped a man from hanging himself—just to salvage the rope. Kid Salvage and other cartoon characters, which OWI commissioned from various artists, both amused and educated the public about such issues as meat rationing, sharing automobiles to save rubber and gasoline, the need for women in industry, salvaging grease fats and scrap metal, and other wartime conditions brought about on the home front.

Each week OWI issued several cartoons and one serious drawing which were then printed in hundreds of daily newspapers and almost 2,000 factory periodicals. Cartoonists who did not work directly with OWI received weekly letters that discussed impending government drives and suggested sketch ideas that could contribute to the success of the government's efforts. The government then reaped the benefits of its mailings as its ideas began to appear in editorial cartoons and in magazine and newspaper comic strips throughout the country.

The Tokio Kid

The government was not alone in using cartoon or comic strip characters to increase wartime production. Private industry was also involved. Beginning in March 1942 when the Dutch East Indies had just fallen to the Japanese, General Douglas MacArthur and his forces were trapped on Corregidor and there appeared to be no stopping the Japanese advances through Southeast Asia. At the same time, the Japanese began to infiltrate American factories, but not to the benefit of Japan. They were all versions of one character—Douglas Aircraft's gargoylelike cartoon, "The Tokio Kid." His appearance was quite graphic. Holding a dagger dripping with blood in one hand, The Kid wore a small cap, the top of which was emblazoned with an emblem of "The Rising Sun," and round-rimmed glasses; he had an apelike forehead, slanted narrow eyes, elongated buck and fanged teeth, a drooling mouth, and pointed ears.

The message The Kid delivered to American workers was quite simple: When they faltered on their production efforts, perhaps by breaking tools, they were making the Japanese quite happy and were helping them win the war (which was the situation at the time the first cartoon appeared.) The Tokio Kid proved to be so popular that hundreds of other companies adopted him, and the U.S. Treasury Department began using The Kid in 1942 to sell war bonds. The Kid helped out in community scrap drives. In Santa Monica, California, a reproduction of The Kid was erected on a downtown street corner by artists of the Douglas Aircraft Company. There with his motto, "Tokio Kid Say Rubber Scrap not Good for Jap," in the spring of 1942 residents tossed their rubber drive contributions through The Kid's gaping mouth into a hidden receptacle. Beneath the mouth's opening was an American slogan: "Slap the Jap in the Yap."[31]

The Tokio Kid delivered many kinds of messages between the time he first appeared in March 1942 and the last time Douglas Aircraft published him in February 1944. One message read: "Wash up early, rush out door, give Jap time, to win the war." Another stated: "Much waste of material make so-o-o-o happy, thank you." Or still another: "Broke up tools, waste for scrap, just like bullets make for Jap, thank you." The Kid's contribution and that of Douglas Aircraft to help win the war was inestimable for what began as one idea in one American company spread throughout the land as a unified war effort.

The Japanese victories during the first half of 1942 were quite evident when the first of these caricatures was created, and the survivability of the democracies was being questioned. At this time, the racist caricature of The Tokio Kid was not unusual. Comic books were also portraying the Japanese as snarling monsters with bright yellow skin, leering eyes, cavernous jaws, and fangs for teeth.[32] The reasons were quite simple. America's hatred for its enemies, especially the Japanese, was probably more intense than that of any other war in which it had fought. The scope of the Nazi's inhumanity toward the conquered people of Europe would not come to light until the war began to end, but at the war's beginning, Americans had already seen and heard of the atrocities the Japanese had committed against their enemies during the 1930s. This knowledge, combined with the Japanese attack on Pearl Harbor and the treatment of American prisoners in the Philippines and elsewhere, created a portrait that fueled the intense hatred toward the Far Eastern enemy. As part of the communication media, comic books, comic strips, and posters were one of the means available for Americans to vent their hostility.

War Posters

Poster art had various functions during the war. According to O. W. Riegel, propaganda analyst for OWI, "the function of poster art is to make coherent and acceptable a basically incoherent and irrational ordeal of killing, suffering and destruction that violates every accepted principle of morality and decent living."[33] While OWI was the primary war poster-producing agency, other federal agencies, the armed services, and private organizations printed posters by the thousands as a cheap method to enlist public participation in the war effort and promote home front production, conservation, and sacrifice. As Archibald MacLeish, Director of the Office of Facts and Figures, forerunner OWI, stated: "The principal battleground of this war is not the South Pacific. It is not the Middle East. It is not England, or Norway, or the Russian Steppes. It is American opinion."[34]

Posters used two psychological strategies during the war. On one hand, World War II posters appealed to America's nobler emotions by imbuing Americans with a national sense of pride that they were engaged in a global struggle for what is right. Their bright and cheerful colors, often red, white, and blue, instilled feelings of patriotism, confidence, and a positive outlook. On the other hand, posters were also created to shock the American public out of any complacency that they may have harbored about the conflict. Some posters presented visually grim unromantic views of the war—its human costs in terms of wounded soldiers, corpses, graveyards, and monstrous enemies. Other posters sought to convince Americans, though separated from actual warfare by great distances, that they were within arm's reach of the enemy—in immediate danger—their backs against the wall, living in the shadow of Axis domination.[35]

Many posters went beyond the emotions of suspicion and fear to evoke terror and hatred by transforming the enemy into something subhuman like apes, dogs, snakes, and vicious racial stereotypes. Dehumanization of the enemy was not new in propaganda; it was one method to rationalize the irrational destruction of human life.[36]

In appealing to the viewer's darker impulses by fostering feelings of suspicion, fear, and even hate, the posters had a simple message. After showing people who had fallen victim to the enemy, they warned Americans that they stood next in line. If nothing else, poster art with its diverse messages contributed toward unifying the home front in the war effort and, when combined with comic books, cartoons, and other visual media, helped shape and influence public opinion and behavior in ways that corresponded to the government's goals at home and abroad.

A Patriotic Medium

It was not accidental that comics or cartoons or even posters were used to convey war messages. Newspaper comic strips, for example, reached more people than anything written by reporters, editors, and columnists. By 1945, surveys by the Gallup Poll and others found that comic strips—daily and Sunday—had a reading public, including children and adults, of between 60 and 70 million. It was a truism in the newspaper business that comics, next to the news, sold the papers.[37]

The comic book artists have several weapons at their disposal for conveying messages to the public—namely wit and humor, the striking effects delivered by pictorial representation and a loyal audience. Humor is the delight of the propagandist because it can so easily disarm the most logical of critics. Pictures are invaluable because they create more lasting images than the printed word. The nature of serial comics induces the reader to return to the same strip.

In addition to finding comics to be enjoyable, interesting, easy to read, exciting, amusing and suspenseful, readers found that comics represented an unbroken continuity from the past to the present. The comic strip characters are like old friends the reader may have followed from childhood to adulthood. Readers often resist new comics because the characters are strangers. For readers, whose lives may have a sameness day after day, comics give them a sense of participation in a broader, more interesting society. The comics of World War II unified a nation—its readers shared a common experience and felt a sense of belonging and identification. As children grew up, comics taught them common concepts, doctrines, attitudes, and sentiments. Although never asking to be taken seriously, comics mirrored life in many of the issues or problems they addressed whether it was in a serious or humorous manner. The comics never strayed from the basic beliefs of their readers or the tastes or manners of the times. With these various attributes, the comics were able to build loyal followings and with a continuous readership, the ideas expounded in the comics had a better chance of taking hold than if the reader or listener only saw or heard them fleetingly elsewhere. Comics— the daily and Sunday strips, and the comic books—emerged during the war years as an American institution, a major medium of communication and an influence in society-at-large.

The old saying, "Let me write the people's songs and I care not who makes their laws," might well have read during World War II, "Let me draw the people's comic strips . . ."[38] Through their humor, pathos, and adventure strips, comics helped define and bring understanding to the problems Americans faced as individuals and as a nation. For example, some comic book stories were purported to be based upon secret files, preceded by the legend: "Now it can be told." Comics greeted World War II with a display of public patriotism. Superheroes competed with each other to be seen with the president, to be officially thanked for selling war bonds, apprehending spies, or opening up a second front. The August 1943 issue of *Detective Comics* featuring Batman contained the following patriotic message:

> Rat-at-ta-tat! Rat-at-ta-tat! Hear the drum roll? Twee! Twee! Twee! Hear that shrill of a fife? It's a call brother—it's a call to join the parade! You, too sister . . . you're in on this! Get in step! Get in step! For here they come! The butcher, the baker, the girl riveter, the man machinist, the farmer, the banker, housewife, school kid!
>
> Everybody's marching . . . marching behind the Minute Man. $o buy tho$e war bond$! Buy tho$e war $tamps! Get in step! Get in step with Batman and Robin as they go marching on to victory with . . . the Bond Wagon.

While the comic book superheroes may have been the fictional product of the human imagination, the effect of their words and their deeds were very real in American life. They turned away from fighting bank robbers and mad scientists toward blond, short-cropped Germans who spoke with thick accents and were not very smart or Japanese who were often portrayed with fanged bicuspids, a great deal of drooling, and with little subtlety in their torture techniques. The comics helped reinforce many deeply held beliefs about the meaning of life in wartime America and the relationship of individuals to other individuals and to society as a whole. Although the comic book and comic strip heroes may not have been able to defeat the Axis powers overnight, their tangible contributions to the war effort certainly helped hasten its end and the world's new beginning.

Notes

1. William M. Marston, "Why 100,000,000 Americans Read Comics," *American Scholar*, Winter 1943, 35.

2. J. Claire Mattimore and Hannibal Coons, "The Fighting Funnies," *Colliers*, January 24, 1944, 24.

3. Fred Rodell, "Fifty Years of the Comics," *Reader's Digest*, March 1945, 72–73.

4. "War in the Comics," *Newsweek*, July 13, 1942, 60–61.

5. Ibid.

6. Mattimore and Coons, 24.

7. "War in the Comics," 60–61.

8. J. Claire Mattimore and Hannibal Coons, 24, 44.

9. Ibid., 24.

10. Harvey Zorbaugh, "Comics-Food for Half-Wits?," *Science Digest*, April 1945, 30.

11. As quoted in "Superman Scores," *Business Week*, April 18, 1942, 55.

12. Lovell Thompson, "How Serious Are the Comics?," *Atlantic Monthly*, September 1942, 128.

13. "Escapist Paydirt," *Newsweek*, December 27, 1943, 55.

14. Ibid.

15. Ruth Strang, "Why Children Read the Comics," *Elementary School Journal*, February 1943, 336–37 and M. Katharine McCarthy and Marion W. Smith, "The Much Discussed Comics!" *Elementary School Journal*, October 1943, 100–102.

16. "Issues Relating to the Comics," *Elementary School Journal*, May 1942, 642.

17. "The Comics and Their Audience," *Publisher's Weekly*, April 18, 1942, 1478.

18. Marston, 38–39.

19. Slater Brown, "The Coming of Superman," *New Republic*, September 22, 1940, 301.

20. John Kobler, "Up, Up and Awa-a-y! The Rise of Superman, Inc., " *Saturday Evening Post*, June 21, 1941, 15.

21. Ibid., 70, 73.

22. Ibid., 15.

23. Ibid., 74.

24. Ibid., 74.

25. Mary R. Lucas, "Our Friendly Enemy," *Library Journal*, October 1, 1941, 827.

26. "The Comics and Their Audience," 1479.

27. Fred Latimer Hasdel, "Propaganda in the Funnies," *Current History*, December 1941, 367.

28. Kobler, 74.

29. Marston, 43–44.

30. "Escapist Paydirt," 55.

31. "Eats His Words," *Douglas Airview News*, June 1942, 19.

32. Margaret Frakes, "Comics Are No Longer Comic," *Christian Century*, November 4, 1942, 1349.

33. As quoted in Stacey Bredhoff, *Powers of Persuasion: Poster Art from World War II* (Washington, D.C.: National Archives, 1994), 29.

34. Ibid.

35. Ibid., 33.

36. Ibid., 28.

37. Zorbaugh, 25.

38. Hasdel, 368.

Chapter Nine

ADVERTISING
How We Sold the War at Home

AFTER THE JAPANESE ATTACK on Pearl Harbor, America's future seemed very grim. Our principal adversaries, Germany and Japan, were considered two of the strongest nations in the world. Our battlefronts extended across two oceans. Our Allies were under attack in distant lands. Our Navy had been scattered and sunk. Our Army and Air Force could not compare to the military might of the Axis powers. America was cut off from vital materials to build up its strength. Yet, almost four and one-half years later at war's end, America had produced one of the most formidable and destructive fighting forces the world had ever seen. One of the elements that had helped to transform America's industry and military into such a force by 1945 was the advertising industry; its role cannot be minimized. Advertising executives knew how to reach many millions of people at minimum cost and maximum speed, how to gain and hold the public's attention, and how to enlist the indispensable support of the public to whom it appealed. Advertising's influence was everywhere—on radio, in magazines, on billboards, in newspapers, on buses, and in bus and train stations.

When America entered World War II, the role of advertising in wartime was not clear. The industry's position was precarious and there was concern that government itself would enter advertising and place restrictions on commercial activities. The business community feared that the nation's conversion to a wartime economy would lead to either restricted production of consumer goods or no production at all. Under such conditions, would a firm that could not advertise be forgotten by the public and out of business when the war ended? Without products to promote, what would happen to the advertising industry? Some members of the industry believed that advertising's biggest job lay ahead; they were convinced that advertising could assume a responsible role in the war and business firms could keep their names before the public in new ways.

The War Advertising Council

The advertising industry viewed the government's position as trying to sell a product without an effective sales force. The industry believed that it could do a better job than government in telling the American public what total war meant in terms of conservation and increasing sacrifice. Representatives of the advertising industry came to Washington to provide government with the missing sales force. But conditions at the war's beginning were chaotic. No one knew which government department to approach, what the government wanted to publicize, or who would pay the advertising bill. There were no priorities. No one was in charge of making definitive decisions about what to publicize. While some government officials thought the advertising industry could be helpful, others looked upon the industry as "soap salesmen" whose talents were not required for the war effort.[1]

Despite all this confusion, rebuff, and chaos, the advertising industry believed that coordinated action with the government would be necessary. A few days after Pearl Harbor, the industry established a new organization "to mobilize the power of advertising for victory"—its name, the Advertising Council (later changed to the War Advertising Council) and its slogan, "A War Message in Every Ad."

The War Advertising Council was a nonprofit voluntary organization that represented all elements of the industry, including advertisers, advertising agencies, and such media as radio, newspapers, and magazines. The group obtained its financing from its sponsoring organizations and some individual contributions; it provided its services free to the government and the American public. Its purpose was to locate meaningful work for the advertising industry during the war, plan and organize that work, persuade hundreds of organizations and individuals to donate advertising space and ability without charge, and obtain government support for its efforts.[2] The council considered war advertising different than commercial, defining it "as advertising which induced people through information, understanding and persuasion to take certain actions necessary to the winning of the war."[3] This excluded "brag advertising" in which a company or industry boasted of its accomplishments or the achievements of its products in winning the war, or "political" advertising that advanced certain ideas regarding private enterprise.

More than 400 advertising agencies volunteered their services to the council during the war without receiving any compensation for their efforts. The council only acted upon the request of the Office of War Information's Bureau of Campaigns (though not all bureau programs were council campaigns) and on projects requiring national publicity. In addition to working with the Office of War Information (OWI), the advertising group also assisted the Office of Economic Stabilization, the Office of Price Administration, the War Manpower Commission, and other government agencies that needed its services. The council's work required and involved exasperating effort in overcoming prejudices and misconceptions about the industry it represented. Some government officials believed that journalists or literary writers could present the government's needs to the public better than advertising personnel whose industry, in their opinion, did not champion the facts but gave consumers dubious, nonsensical, frivolous, and unbelievable information.

Beginning in January 1942, the advertising industry had to operate under a censorship code from the Office of Censorship which extended its press and radio censorship code to this group. The code banned information on troop, ship, and plane movements; fortifications; the weather (except under certain conditions); transportation of munitions; specific information on war contracts; shipyards including their number, size, character, location, or launchings; new or secret military designs; and existing or new factory designs for war production. The previous items could not be mentioned in advertisements without official government approval. In practice, the Army, Navy, the Office of Production Management, and other war agencies continued to censor their own output of information. But all advertising copy that referred to the Army and Navy or that contained photographs of Army and Navy subjects had to be referred for review to the public relations bureau of that particular service. The military services reminded advertisers that they could not present the Army or Navy or its personnel in any unfavorable light; could not say or imply that the Army or Navy prefers, approves, or uses the product advertised to the exclusion of competing products; could not include in their advertisements any misleading or otherwise objectionable features; and could not divulge secret, confidential, or restricted information.[4]

Wartime advertising not only could curb or direct the consumption of goods and services, but also inspire and educate the public about the issues of the day. A good example of such advertising was a U.S. government war message prepared by the War Advertising Council about inflation and entitled "Squeeze that Money Brother . . . It's Mine Too!" In this ad, a soldier fighting somewhere overseas is talking to a home front worker who is counting his week's pay:

Sure, that Saturday night pay envelope's bulging. But let me tell you something, brother, before you spend a dime . . . *That money's mine too!*

I can take it. The mess out here. And missing my wife and kid.

What I *can't* take is you making it tougher on me. Or my widow, if that's how it goes. And brother, it *will* make it tough—if you splurge one dime tonight. You're making money. More money than there's stuff to buy. Money that can sock the cost of living to kingdom come—if you blow it! So hang on, till the job's done. On to every last dime—till the squeal means a hole in the seat of your pants!

You're working . . . and *I'm fighting* . . . for the same thing. But *you* could lose it for both of us—without thinking. A guy like you could start bidding me right out of the picture tonight. Any my wife and kid. There not being as much as everybody'd like to buy—and you having the green stuff. But remember this, brother—everything you buy helps to send prices kiting. Up. UP. AND UP. Till that fat pay envelope can't buy you a square meal.

Stop spending. For yourself. *Your* kids. And mine. That, brother, is sense. Not sacrifice.

Know what I'd do with that dough . . . If I'd the luck to have it?

I'd buy War Bonds—and, God, would *I* hang on to them! (Bonds buy guns—and give you four bucks for your three!) . . . I'd pay back that insurance loan from when Mollie had the baby . . . I'd pony up for taxes cheerfully (knowing they're the cheapest way to pay for this war) . . . I'd sock some in the savings bank, while I could . . . I'd lift a load off my mind with more life insurance.

And I wouldn't buy a shoelace till I'd looked myself square in the eye and knew I couldn't do without (you get to knowin'—out here—what you can do without.)

I wouldn't try to profit from this war—and I wouldn't ask more for anything I had to sell—seeing we're all in this together.

I've got your future in my rifle hand, brother. But you've got both of ours, in the inside of that stuffed-up envelope. You and all the other guys that are lookin' at the Main Street shops tonight.

Squeeze that money, brother. It's got blood on it![5]

Through this message the U.S. government was telling the American public how inflation begins, the effect that rising prices can have on the standard of living, what Americans could do to control inflation, how the public could best direct its monies to help out in the war effort, and what the war was like for those fighting overseas and the risks they had to endure to preserve America's way of life, including possibly losing their own. The message reminded the American public that fighting World War II was basically a joint partnership—between those shouldering arms overseas and those shouldering wartime responsibilities on the home front.

Commercial Advertising in a Wartime Economy

In the beginning, advertising, especially by firms with war contracts, consisted of vulgar boasting, false self-praise, and dangerous complacency. These characteristics diminished but never really disappeared as the war continued. Before World War II, powerful and persuasive advertisements enticed people to purchase various goods and services, making Americans conscious of bad breath, body odor (B.O.), dish-pan hands, and coffee nerves. When the war began, advertisers were not sure what they should be doing. Companies with goods to sell wanted their products to have a "war angle"; firms with no products to sell wanted to keep their prestige in tact. The automobile industry was ordered by the federal government in 1942 to cease the manufacture of new automobiles for the duration of the war. Instead, the industry converted its assembly lines into war production and manufactured tanks, jeeps, aircraft, and other weaponry of battle. Some companies printed messages of general interest and of public concern; others described phases of the defense program in which they were participating. Still other organizations encouraged a more economical use of their products or described

the usefulness of products that were not available as yet to anyone except
the government.

The government helped stimulate wartime advertising by allowing a
firm to deduct from its income taxes a reasonable amount of advertising
expenses as a business expenditure. The U.S. Treasury Department decided what was a "reasonable amount." Businesses that did not have
civilian goods to sell knew that the government would not be amenable
to large amounts of money being spent to advertise items that were no
longer being produced. Businesses still manufacturing civilian goods also
knew that the Treasury Department would not look with favor on advertising that encouraged people to spend and, perhaps, spur inflation. As a
result, through its tax regulations the government had an indirect impact
upon the advertising practices of private industry during the war years.

Exploiting the War Effort

As far as the private sector was concerned and as the following examples illustrate, advertisers used many kinds of approaches to associate
their product with the war or to speak or boast about their role or contribution to the war effort. Thus, Nash-Kelvinator Corporation in an ad,
"Not Alone . . . ," spoke about the 2,000 horsepower engine it was
building for the Navy's Corsair fighter and how the engine would give
the aircraft the edge over any known Axis plane. According to the advertising copy, the company's motivation was not just to make America
supreme in the air through its engines and propellers, but the manufacturer also noted that it was giving its all because America's sons were up
there. The advertising copy then concluded, "Listen! In the roar of their
engines—you can hear the beating of our hearts." Meanwhile, the Food
Machinery Corporation boasted of how its heavily armed amphibious
vehicle, the Water Buffalo, designed in cooperation with the U.S. Navy
Bureau of Ships, helped win victory in nearly every American invasion,
spearheading attacks, swimming through seas, charging over coral reefs
and beaches, and destroying enemy fortifications in the Pacific theater of
war. The advertiser claimed that this vehicle went where no other boat
or vehicle could go as it tirelessly moved troops, guns, ammunition, and
the wounded.

But according to some advertisers, machinery was not the only reason
for America's wartime victories. For example, a Royal Crown Cola ad-

vertisement told of a Marine who had killed forty-two Japs (captured thirty more) but between battles, while other Marines remained nervous and tense, he was able to play solitaire. The advertisement noted that while the Marine was just as tense as his friends, he had learned how to relax; that secret allowed him to return to battle thinking quicker and fighting harder. But the advertising copy concluded, Americans have known that secret for a long time and when they have a moment for a break, they choose a frosty bottle of cola. That is why, Royal Crown Cola noted, millions prefer its cola for a lift and fresh start.

Soft drinks did not offer the only way to relax in wartime America. Smoking was another. An advertisement of Camel cigarettes stated that steady nerves were the order of the day not only for U.S. paratroopers getting ready for a jump, but for all Americans as well. The advertisement suggested that the folks on the home front take a tip from those on the fighting front and make the paratrooper's favorite cigarette theirs as well. But the advertiser was not partial to any particular branch of the service. In another ad, Camel cigarettes noted that in the Navy "belay" means stop, "chop-chop" is hurry up, "stew" refers to a commissary officer, and Camel cigarettes are the Navy man's favorite smoke. Meanwhile, when the diversion of chemicals to the war effort caused Lucky Strike cigarettes to change the color of its packs from green to white, the manufacturer told the public that Lucky Strike green has gone to war.

Advertisers sought to boast of their product's quality in other ways as well. The Cast Iron Pipe Research Association in discussing the quality of its construction product pictured the parting of a soldier and his girl. As she implores, "Promise to take care of yourself," he responds "don't worry, I'm as strong as cast iron pipe." Yet many of those who departed also returned home wounded. The National Dairy Products Association recognized this situation by stating in its ad, "When the wounded come home," that, in addition to the healing skills of doctors and nurses, dairy products also assumed a vital role in the medical treatment of the wounded. In the advertisement, an unnamed medical officer, whose unnamed medical ship treated 4,039 South Pacific casualties and lost only 7, reported: "Ice cream was served the patients every day as a food medicine. It helped build both strength and morale. To those wounded men, ice cream nearly represented home and civilization." The advertiser then concluded the copy by stating that the company knew that the home front would willingly share its ice cream and other dairy products like milk with the returning casualties—even if it meant doing with a little less—at the same time it reminded the public that milk is nature's most perfect food.

While the war required the American home front to make many sacrifices such as in its standard of living, some advertisers, in associating their products with the war, reminded the public that the wartime situation did not necessarily mean that Americans had to completely neglect their personal appearance. One advertiser stated: "Introducing Volunteer . . . new nail polish shade for fingertips on and off duty . . . It's a deep red, stirring as the times, bright as courage." Another advertiser described the product, "Courage, as . . . a fragrance attuned to the times . . . as stirring as martial music . . . reflecting the gallant spirit of today."[6]

The previous examples became known as "brag ads." Some businesses went to such lengths in even claiming success for victories on the battlefield that C. R. Larrabee, the president of *Printer's Ink*, one of the leading publications of the advertising industry, stated:

> With bull-headed cynicism utterly out of keeping with the times, some advertisers continue to use themes and tricks which were unpleasant enough in prewar days but seem outrageous today.
>
> Others try to climb aboard the wartime bandwagon using a theme for products that are remotely, if at all, related to our victory.
>
> A few are still so unimaginative as to think that the public will believe that without their product the war might be lost.
>
> To all these may be added the advertisers who insipidly congratulate themselves because they are doing no more and no less than what any patriotic citizen should be doing.[7]

Even servicemen vented their anger toward these kinds of ads, such as the one that informed readers that a particular airplane would go higher, fly faster, dive quicker, and generally perform better than any other airplane in the world. Yet, American pilots knew better, as one stated:

> I have been flying this plane for two months. I have been in many fights. Those things in there just aren't true. She's not bad for some things, but I have seen too many fellows get killed. Our squadron has done well, but it is because we figured out ways and means of out thinking the Luftwaffe.[8]

Public Service Advertising

By the end of the first year of the war, many organizations began to cease their "brag advertising" and began describing their efforts more positively. Some began noting the work they were performing for the government, while reminding the consumer that they would be serving the public efficiently and enthusiastically once the war was over. Others honestly tried to raise public morale by speaking of Army and Navy exploits. Still, other ads displayed the Army-Navy "E" pennants that flew over their plants and thanked their employees in the ads for its award. The military services awarded these pennants as recognition to those businesses that made distinguished industrial contributions to the defense effort. Other ads displayed the War Savings Flag (the Minuteman of the American Revolution encircled by a field of stars), which flew over a plant and signified that 10 percent of a company's gross payroll was voluntarily being invested in war bonds. Other businesses urged the public through their advertisements to collect scrap, conserve gas, and reduce the number of long-distance telephone calls.

Support for the Troops

Like the U.S. government, private business also sought out the War Advertising Council to create meaningful public service messages. One excellent example is the former New Haven Railroad, which published an advertisement to explain to its passengers that the inconvenient delays they were experiencing were necessary because of the wartime priority to move troops. The ad was later displayed in newspapers throughout the country and has become one of the most anthologized Ad Council advertisements of all time. The ad is called "The Kid in Upper 4" and reads:

It is 3:42 A.M. on a troop train.
Men wrapped in blankets are breathing heavily.
Two in every lower berth. One in every upper.
This is no ordinary trip. It may be their last in the U.S.A. till the end of
    the war. Tomorrow they will be on the high seas.
One is wide awake . . . listening . . . staring into the blackness.
It is the kid in Upper 4.

Tonight, he knows, he is leaving behind a lot of little things—and big ones.

The taste of hamburgers and pop . . . the feel of driving a roadster over a six-lane highway . . . a dog named Shucks, or Spot, or Barnacle Bill.

The pretty girl who writes so often . . . that gray-haired man, so proud and awkward at the station . . . the mother who knit the socks he'll wear soon.

Tonight he's thinking them over.

There's a lump in his throat. And maybe—a tear fills his eye. *It doesn't matter, Kid*. Nobody will see . . . it's too dark.

A couple of thousand miles away, where he's going, they don't know him very well.

But people all over the world are waiting, praying for him to come.

And he will come, this kid in Upper 4.

With new hope, peace and freedom for a tired, bleeding world.

Next time you are on the train, *remember the kid in Upper 4*.

If you have to stand enroute—*it is so he may have a seat*.

If there is no berth for you—*it is so that he may sleep*.

If you have to wait for a seat in the diner—*it is so he . . . and thousands like him . . . may have a meal they won't forget in the days to come*.

For to treat him as our most honored guest is the least we can do to pay a mighty debt of gratitude.[9]

Through this advertisement, the public was once again reminded of the respect it should show a serviceman who might be leaving home for a very long time, the kind and significance of the memories he was harboring, the emotions evoked by his parting, and that in a world torn apart by war, many people in many lands were hoping that his arrival would bring them peace and freedom. In essence, the ad reminded the public that the sacrifices it was making such as in regard to transportation were insignificant compared to the enormous burdens and responsibilities a serviceman was experiencing and enduring during these troublesome times.

But what happened when the serviceman reached his destination? Ads reminded the public of his possible fate. One ad, "By His Deeds . . . Measure Yours," that appealed to the public's emotions showed an American soldier lying dead on a foreign battlefield and the advertiser asked the public to measure their deeds against that of the soldier who gave his life for his country. The advertiser reminded the public that while it was not pleasant to have a peaceful life disturbed by wartime restrictions, needs, and activities, it wasn't pleasant to die either. The ad pointed out a direct connection between home front activities and the probability of saving a serviceman's life overseas. The copy stated that if the public did everything it could to hasten victory as fast as possible, it could save the lives of some men who would otherwise die because the war lasted too long. The ad concluded: "Think it over. Till the war is won you cannot, in fairness to them, complain, or waste or shirk. Instead, you will apply every last ounce of your effort to getting this thing done . . . In the name of God and your fellow man that is your job."[10]

Other advertisements stressed different themes such as conservation in a wartime economy. An ad entitled "Which comes first—Your second helping? or our second front?" addressed the issue of food shortages by reminding the public that if it wanted the war to be won quickly and carried to the enemy with a vengeance, that desire would require a second fighting front which, in turn, would need food—not only for American servicemen but also for our allies. The ad then asked the public whether it wanted more meat for itself or enough meat for them. An extra cup of coffee at breakfast or a full tin for a fighting soldier. The advertisement concluded by stating that the meat, coffee, and sugar that the public was not receiving was up at the front lines fighting on the public's behalf and asked "Would you want to have it otherwise?"[11] As another example, Kimberly-Clark Corporation stressed the importance of paper conservation and how paper was contributing to the waging of the war, from its use as cartons for shells, as fins for bombs, as camouflage, as helmet linings for soldiers in the tropics, and as boxes for food and medical supplies. The company then urged the public to use less paper to reduce its shortage on the home front and to turn in all wastepaper for the war effort (excepting waxed, oiled or tarred).

Perhaps a lipstick manufacturer best summed up the whole concept of what was required to win World War II. The advertisement noted that its lipstick would not build morale because that was made from sterner stuff. It would not help a fighting man because his courage is his own. It would not preserve the American way of life because we had to work and fight for that. All its lipstick would do, according to the ad, was to make someone look prettier. The manufacturer concluded the ad by

stating, "If it's Victory you want—and that's what we all want—
BETTER BUY WAR BONDS!"[12]

Editorial Opinion

In addition to the brag ads and those boosting public morale, some
companies used advertisements to express personal viewpoints for some
special public or private interest. If ads could urge the public to buy war
bonds or accept rationing, why not use ads to convince the public to
support isolationism or the status quo or other ideas while keeping a
corporate name before the public at so cheap a price. In arguing for the
preservation of the prewar enterprise system, one company stated that it
believed "in the American dream, in the resourcefulness of private enterprise and personal initiative, in the power of free men to serve a high
statesmanship as well as the profit motive."[13] *Advertising Age* cited a
speech by Homer McKee, an advertising firm's vice president, who said,
in part, "the people must be told that if they hurt free enterprise, they
hurt the girl who works in the laundry, the cab driver, the white-collared
clerk, the widow who, with trembling hands, clips coupons to hold body
and soul together."[14]

Nash-Kelvinator Corporation expressed this idea of prewar laissez-
faire in an advertisement entitled "When the Last Bomb Goes
Home . . ." in which an airplane bombardier who is overseas expresses,
in part, what America has come to mean to him. He states that it is a
country where he and his parents can live the way they have always
lived, where there is work to do and no one is ashamed to do it, where
neither his ambitions nor his opportunity are limited, and he is able to
go as far as his ability can take him. The ad concludes: "Whatever you
do, don't change that, ever! I know now that's what I'm fighting for."[15]
Thus, some businesses began to use advertising as a primary weapon to
sell social, political, and economic ideas when they no longer could advertise products and services they once delivered.

A Better Tomorrow

On the other hand, when companies did advertise goods and services,
some went overboard as to what lay ahead in the future. General Electric
envisioned a home constructed of plastic and glass with a two-car ga-

rage, electric eye door openers, an automatic garbage disposal, and a kitchen that would practically shop for the family. Durez displayed a helicopter that could fit into a front yard, and another business envisioned cheap and roomy automobiles with motors in the back. The boldness and imaginativeness of this kind of advertising excited a country weary of war and offered it hope of a higher living standard once the war was over.[16]

During this period, the country was using up goods at a terrific rate. No one could calculate with any reasonable degree of accuracy the normal exhaustion of material wealth on a daily basis. Every day, roofs were wearing out, paint was eroding, carpets were wearing thin, upholstery was becoming threadbare while electric irons, toasters, refrigerators, stoves, washing machines, vacuum cleaners, furnaces, automobiles, and other necessities of everyday living needed to be replaced. Thus any kind message that spoke about a better tomorrow was wholeheartedly received by the American public.

Using the Airwaves

War Messages

One of the major forms of media that advertising used to deliver its messages was radio. Initially, government and the War Advertising Council did not know how to use the airwaves to present important war messages to the public. On occasion, the government sent advertisers a message that was to be aired exactly as it was written, and often its style was not suitable for the program. Other times, several government agencies would request the same air time. Working with the War Advertising Council, OWI developed a Radio Allocation Plan under which radio stations, networks, and advertisers all agreed upon a certain amount of time each week for presenting war messages to the public. OWI then decided which messages should be broadcast and established a system of priorities based on the relative importance of each. The advertisers and radio stations were then given fact sheets from which the program producer could develop the message. Various programs, whether for adults or children, even developed stories or themes around a war message such as rationing, or buying war bonds.[17] How did these messages sound? Well, a Marine recruitment message simply stated:

Men, join a career. Enlist in the United States Marines and get action. Help build to victory now, for yourself, for your home, for this land we love. There is a Marine recruiting station in every corner of the country. See the officer in charge and get the latest information on joining the fighting Leathernecks. Do it now and know the pride of service with the United States Marines.[18]

In 1943, an OWI program, "Soldiers of Production," reminded the country:

Friends, American men and women are doing a lot but they can and must do more to help shorten the war. More than ever it is important and imperative that every one of us recognize his personal responsibility in helping to win the war—that every one of us stick to his war useful job in spite of real and aggravating obstacles. That's our way of licking the Axis if we can't shoulder arms.[19]

The influence of radio advertising was dramatic. On May 27, 1943, the War Advertising Council published the results of a few radio campaigns:

• Candidates for Marine officers schools increased 40 percent after two weeks of national radio promotion, June 8–21, 1942.

• Shoe rationing—in 1942 this campaign was so secret that the Office of War Information called it the Oyster Campaign. To avoid a run on shoe stores, the campaign had to be announced on Sunday at 3:00 P.M. Because Sunday newspapers were printed on Saturday night, they could not be used. Radio not only had to tell the public that shoes could not be purchased without rations, but also had to inform shoe store owners and managers that they could not open on Monday. Very few instances of shoe dealers not hearing the report were reported.

• V-Mail (letters on very thin paper, one sack of V-mail equaled 65 sacks of regular mail)—in 1942 a week before the radio campaign, the postal service handled 500,000 V-mail letters. During the third week of the campaign, 1,250,000 V-mail letters were mailed—a 116 percent increase. In May 1943, the increase was between 150 and 200 percent.[20]

The presentation of war messages and advertising's contribution to their development was of inestimable value to the war effort. The country discovered what a powerful and positive force radio and advertising could be when they combined their efforts toward public service.

The Plug-Uglies

The war message was not the principal radio advertising. More common were commercials for consumer products. Advertisers used various approaches to establish product identification in the public's mind and many were tastefully done. Sometimes the product was pleasingly woven into the content of the story like Johnson Wax on the "Fibber McGee and Molly" program; sometimes humor was added to the commercial as in the case of Jack Benny's advertising of Jello; other times the sponsor's name was included in the show's title ("Fitch Bandwagon"); and many commercials were in the form of jingles that consumers could easily remember whether the advertiser was promoting soap detergents like Super Suds, Rinso, Tide, or Duz; or shampoos like Fitch, Halo, or Lustre Cream; or soaps like Lava, Ivory, or Lifebuoy. However, some of these advertisements tied into the war effort, and listeners considered them in such poor taste they named these commercials the "plug-uglies." Such a commercial might read: "BC for headaches—the Germans are attacking Sevastopol—get quick soothing relief in handy 10 cent, 20 cent . . ."[21] Or a news program might begin with Esso telling the radio audience that its brand of gasoline was the best ever dispensed from the dealers' tanks, and continuing with news about fierce bloody fighting on the Russian front. Esso then would remind the audience to try its gasoline for smooth driving, signing off with the words "Happy motoring!" Edwin Hill, speaking for Amoco gas, remarked, "Cheer up, ladies, the Big Bad war isn't going to deprive you . . ."[22] In promoting Barbasol shaving cream, newscaster Gabriel Heatter (whose airtime signature was "Ah, yes, there's good news tonight . . .") told his audience, "Ah, man, get yourself a tube," then proceeded to state how many Russians were lying dead on the battlefield while Russian teenagers were carrying out sabotage, and concluded with "Send a soldier a tube . . ."[23] Even the print media began to tie their advertisements into the carnage of war. When Hitler's military forces began their quick thrust through Belgium and Holland in 1940, the word *blitzkrieg* (lightning war) became part of the English language. In short time, retailers began using the word to advertise goods at bargain prices—"Blitzkrieg on every article in our great stock" or "Now for a blitzkrieg on values."[24]

The plugs offended listeners by using graphic descriptions of bodily processes to sell a product. No matter what kind of radio program was being aired, its audience could listen to such commercials as

"If you don't feel good, try Carter's Little Liver Pills. They wake up the flow of one of your most vital digestive juices . . . Doctors say your kidneys contain 15 miles of tubes. Doan's Pills will help flush out poisonous wastes . . ."[25]

Listeners were quick to vent their anger. Sponsors received such comments as "We are to win the war by using gum. Anybody's will help but So-and-So's will win the war quicker. Isn't that disgusting?" Or "We come back from a week's field maneuver and what hits us in the face but the B.O. foghorn? We all know we smell; let them lay off. Anyway, any soap will get results."[26] The public's reaction against distasteful radio commercials became so widespread that by the war's end in 1945, several radio stations such as the NBC-affiliated KSD of the *St. Louis Post Dispatch* newspaper began to forbid the broadcast of "middle commercials" in their news broadcasts and to stop news programs from being sponsored by advertisers who sold palliatives for bodily aches and pains, stomach acidity and gas, body odors, bad breath and, in the words of the *St. Louis Post Dispatch*, "a thousand and one equally revolting subjects."[27] Other radio stations began to stop the practice of radio commercials made before and after station identification breaks—announcements known in the trade as "hitchhikers and cow catchers." So why did advertisers sponsor commercials of such poor taste? Simply stated, the war presented advertisers with a far greater audience for their money than could be attracted in prewar days because millions of anxious people were tuned in for news of the war.

Moral Dilemmas of Wartime Advertising

The advertisements, regardless of their media placement, raised fundamental questions on the home front. How could any business executive have the effrontery to base his sales campaigns on world killings and suffering? Or if he had the effrontery, how could he believe that the public would be persuaded to use a product that was advertised in such a manner? Even more importantly, commercial advertisements had the potential of harming the war effort at home.

The American consumer was caught in the middle between what the government war messages and the commercial "plug-uglies" were saying. On the one hand, the government urged the American public to sacrifice while, on the other hand, advertisers urged them to buy. The government urged Americans to forgo needless expenditures while advertisers urged them to buy products they did not need. War messages urged the listeners and readers to contribute to the nation's war effort while the "plug-uglies" called upon consumers to think only of themselves. At a time when it was necessary for people to live simply and frugally, some advertisers had Americans thinking of luxuries, comforts, and self-interest. One appeal canceled the effects of the other. Fortunately, these contradictory appeals did not harm the nation's overall war effort on the home front.

On balance when advertising's record of "plug-uglies," "brag ads," and those espousing a particular social or political viewpoint were measured against those messages that made a laudatory and significant contribution to the war effort, then the role of the advertising industry was indispensable. As a result of the work of the War Advertising Council, billions of dollars of war bonds were sold to the public with such slogans as "Back the Attack with War Bonds" or "You've Done Your Bit, Now Do Your Best." When millions of Victory Gardens were needed, a canning company headlined an ad: "Wanted: 1,000,000 Competitors."[28] As a result of this and similar advertising efforts, the Department of Agriculture stated that in one year Americans planted 20 million Victory Gardens, which produced 8 million tons of food worth $500 million.[29]

Advertising agencies also conducted tremendous campaigns against inflation as the War Advertising Council developed a symbol of a hand pushing down prices and plugged it with the slogan "Use It Up, Wear It Out, Make It Do, Or Do Without." To remind the troops of the value of their equipment, the council developed the slogan "Take Care of Your Equipment and Your Equipment Will Take Care of You." War messages were so widespread that by the end of the summer of 1944, 50 percent of the advertisements on billboards were such pronouncements.[30] In saluting the War Advertising Council and those who worked with it, the War Bond Division of the Treasury Department stated:

> Not a single penny of taxpayer's money goes into this huge advertising program for time and space. All radio time and every line of advertising space is made possible by patriotic businesses and individuals—by the advertisers, agencies and media men of America.[31]

Despite public complaints about the advertisements that appeared in the various media, a majority of the public approved of the manner in which the industry presented public service messages. A poll published in the spring of 1943 revealed that the public thought that advertising was doing a good job in explaining how rationing worked (63 percent), in selling war bonds (82 percent), in delineating the objectives of the war (55 percent), and encouraging the planting of Victory Gardens (56 percent).[32]

By 1944 the War Advertising Council had developed in cooperation with the government more than 90 home front advertising campaigns. In the first year of the war, the council was instrumental in arranging $250 million worth of free advertising—100 times the amount donated during all of World War I. In 1943, the value of this mighty stream of war messages rose to $352 million. By the middle of 1944, the amount of donated advertising space that was linked to home front campaigns approached $400 million, or more than a million dollars a day.[33] By war's end, the total value of donated advertising space and time exceeded $1 billion, and advertising had participated in more than 100 home front campaigns.

In its annual report of 1945–1946, the War Advertising Council assessed its accomplishments from January 15, 1942, to August 14, 1945—1,307 days—when the organized power of advertising was given the job of telling the American people what had to be done to hasten victory. The influence of advertising on our society was quite pervasive during this time. Its activities encompassed war bonds, food, the armed services, civilian nurses, conservation and salvage, labor, fund-raising, and civilian services. The advertising industry helped to account for the following wartime achievements: more than 800 million war bonds were sold. Four million workers were recruited to ease labor shortages on farms and in food plants. Fifty million Victory Gardens were planted during the war and in 1944 the home production of Victory Gardens accounted for 40 percent of all the fresh vegetables consumed by civilians. Army and Navy nurse requirements were met without a draft, and hundreds of thousands of women became nurse's aides and took home nursing courses. Salvage efforts collected 538 million pounds of waste fats, 23 million tons of paper, and 800 million pounds of tin. Campaigns focused on worker recruitment, antiturnover, and antiabsenteeism. Red Cross and National War Fund quotas were met. Millions of men and women were recruited as blood donors, auxiliary police and firefighters, ration board workers, and other volunteer civilians. All this from an industry that only a few years before had been attacked by some in our society who wanted advertising eliminated because it added to the costs of the goods and services and, therefore, represented a financial burden to the consumer.[34]

Advertising presented various faces to the public during the war years. Perhaps, a speech delivered by Paul West, president of the Association of National Advertisers, in 1942 influenced its wartime role. In discussing advertising's responsibilities during this national emergency, he noted that in a war economy advertising had to continue to inform the public about products that were still available for sale. Furthermore, he stressed that advertising had a responsibility for telling the public about changes in the quality and appearance of a product as a result of the war. Advertising also had an obligation for stimulating plant morale, fostering better employee relations, and encouraging better workmanship while supporting wartime activities so that the public, industry, and the war effort all benefited. While noting that advertising could speak about postwar product developments, West condemned advertising that was done just for boastful purposes or that could not demonstrate a useful function.[35] These guidelines were observed, to a greater or lesser degree, throughout the war. Although public criticism of the way advertisements were presented was justified in regard to the brag ads, the industry did make positive contributions to the war effort as reflected by its public service messages. It may be that its influence in helping win the war can never be measured. How can the value of an endeavor that enhances motivation be weighed? Perhaps one answer is that at war's end America as a nation endured, as did its personal freedoms. To the extent that the advertising industry contributed toward preserving America's way of life, advertising must be considered a credit and not a debit to the war effort on the home front.

Notes

1. Raymond Rubicam, "Advertising," an essay in Jack Goodman ed., *While You Were Gone: A Report on Wartime Life in the United States*. (New York: Simon and Schuster, 1946), 424.

2. Ibid., 425.

3. Ibid., 431.

4. "Censor Over Ads," *Business Week*, January 24, 1942, 51.

5. A United States war message prepared by the War Advertising Council; approved by the Office of War Information; and contributed by the Magazine Publishers of America, as it appeared in the *Atlantic Monthly*, March 1944.

6. Charles Neider, "Advertise for Victory," *Nation*, May 29, 1943, 772.

7. "Advertising in Wartime," *New Republic*, February 21, 1944, 233.

8. Ibid., 234.

9. An advertisement prepared for the New Haven Railroad by the War Advertising Council.

10. "By His Deeds . . . Measure Yours," as it appeared in the *New Republic*, February 22, 1943, contributed by the Magazine Publishers of America.

11. "Which comes first—Your second helping? or our second front?," *New Republic*, June 14, 1943, contributed by the Magazine Publishers of America.

12. Harry Lorin Binsse, "This Is the Army," *Commonweal*, July 1942, 304.

13. Neider, 771.

14. As quoted in Neider, 771.

15. Neider, 771.

16. "Advertising in Wartime," 235–36.

17. Rubicam, 430.

18. "World War 2," Sounds of History: American Radio Mobilizes the Home-front, National Archives, Washington, D.C., 1980.

19. Ibid.

20. J. Harold Ryan, "Radio Public Service in Time of War," (Washington, D.C.: National Association Broadcasters, July 27, 1944), 9–11. (a speech)

21. Robert Littell, "Radio's Plug Uglies," *Reader's Digest*, August 1942, 2.

22. Jesse R. Sprague, "Slaughter, Sponsored by—," *New Republic*, October 6, 1941, 434–35.

23. Ibid., 435.

24. Ibid.

25. Littell, 2.

26. "Report on Plug Shrinkers," *Reader's Digest*, October 1942, 59.

27. As quoted in "Plug Ugly Time," *Business Week*, February 24, 1945, 82.

28. Don Wharton, "The Story Back of War Ads," *Reader's Digest*, July 1944, 104.

29. John Carlyle, "How Advertising Went to War," *Nation's Business*, November 1944, 77.

30. Wharton, 105.

31. Carlyle, 76.

32. "Advertising at Work," *Business Week*, June 19, 1943, 96.

33. Wharton, 103.

34. Carlyle, 76.

35. "More Advertising in Uniform," *Business Week*, November 21, 1942, 127.

Chapter Ten

WORLD WAR TWO
A Turning Point

WORLD WAR II WAS THE first and, hopefully, the last truly global war. Encompassing all lands, seas, and air, the war has dwarfed any conflict since the dawn of civilization. For millions of people, it will always be *the* war, an event in their lives that no other historical episode can rival. The war not only transformed America's role in the world for the remainder of the twentieth century—and possibly beyond—but also changed American society permanently. The war years saw the establishment of big government, big business, growth in labor unions and agriculture, rapid advances in science and technology, and an explosive growth in the size of the armed forces. For many people, World War II is a dividing line. Events are remembered as happening before the war or after. The media not only chronicled the events of the war, but were among the many instruments the United States used to hasten the victory.

Decades after the morning of December 7, 1941 changed the role of America in world history, there continues to be interest in the circumstances and reasons for the Japanese attack on Pearl Harbor. History notes that Japan's attempt to secure domination over China in the late 1930s was frustrated, yet Japan's ruling cliques were unable to approve withdrawal. Beginning on July 24, 1941 through a treaty with Vichy France, Japan occupied the rest of French Indo-China after her initial invasion on September 22, 1940. Now Japan was one step closer to the oil fields of the Dutch East Indies, the rubber of Malaya, subsequent self-sufficiency, and her New Order in Asia. On July 25, 1941, President Roosevelt froze all Japanese assets in the United States and finally embargoed the shipment of certain raw materials like oil to Japan. By August 1st, all Japanese-American trade had stopped.

In view of the latter circumstances, Japanese leaders were confronted with difficult decisions. With only a two-year supply of oil on hand, Japan could begin to withdraw from her gains in Asia and lose face. However, her military who had seized and were responsible for Japan's expansionist foreign policy didn't want to lose face as well as possibly power at home. Japan's other choice was to move south and seize the oil fields of the Dutch East Indies. The country's Army leaders argued that unless Japan began an invasion of the Dutch East Indies before the end of 1941, the shortage of oil would rule out such a move forever. The capture of the oil wells intact would require a surprise assault—not just on the Dutch East Indies but also on Malaya and the Philippines as well. Having captured the oil, Japan would then be faced with the problem of bringing it back to Japan without the British Royal Navy based at Singapore or the massive American fleet based at Pearl Harbor stopping this transport. Japanese leaders believed that if war came and Japan was to fight in a conventional way, the country had little hope of winning. The idea arose to strike a simultaneous blow against the American fleet at Pearl Harbor as the war started. Meanwhile, Japan's leadership extended the deadline from mid-October to the end of November for its diplomats to negotiate an end to America's oil embargo.

However, the oil embargo negotiations were not proving fruitful, and Japan, still cut off from its oil supply, began to fear the economic consequences. In the ensuing crisis in her domestic political affairs, the various groups who shared power could not compromise. On October 17, 1941 Prime Minister Prince Fumimaro Konoye, a moderate who wanted to avoid war with the United States, resigned. Thereupon, Lieutenant General Hideki Tojo, the war minister, became the prime minister at the invitation of Emperor Hirohito and formed a new pro-war Cabinet. These extremists saw Germany's victory as a certainty and wanted to share in the spoils. The strategy they envisioned assumed that Britain and Russia would be defeated; one or two blows would crush American power in the Pacific; and a defense line could then be established which would hold against American attacks. These, they thought, would come slowly and with little strength since they viewed Americans as soft and weak-willed. The Japanese assumed that after these attacks had been repulsed, the United States would then be willing to negotiate for peace.[1]

In Washington, in November, the Japanese and Americans discussed a possible last-minute pact for the Japanese to evacuate southern Indo-China and for the United States to lift its freeze on Japanese assets and its oil embargo on Japan. The Japanese foreign minister rejected the American proposal. The attack on Pearl Harbor was probably more successful than the Japanese had originally envisioned and the rest is history.

On the evening of December 7, 1941 listeners tuned to WOR-Mutual in New York heard the author, Vincent Sheean, state, in part:

> Shall we pretend, as I have heard so-called experts pretend on radio, that this thing is easy? . . . Let us get ready for a series of shocks.[2]

The shocks did come. In December 1941, Guam, Wake Island, and British Hong Kong surrendered to the Japanese. During 1942, Manila fell, Singapore surrendered, and the Japanese occupied the Dutch East Indies. In North Africa, the Germans seized Tobruk and threatened Alexandria and the Suez Canal. In Russia, the Germans entered Stalingrad and were poised to capture the oil in the Caucasus. By the end of 1942, the outcome of the war looked very grim, even as America engaged in its first offensives on Guadacanal in the South Pacific and in the deserts of North Africa.

As each day passed, people at home began to hope that victory would be ours and not the enemies' as radio broadcast the following news bulletins:[3]

June 1942—
> Please stand by for this special news release.
> Japanese neared Midway on June 3rd hoping to launch an all out knockout blow on that pair of coral atolls, shortly after dawn on June 4th. They were roundly defeated during the ensuing three days.

January 1943—
> It's ten o'clock and here is the news you've been waiting for. Franklin D. Roosevelt and Winston Churchill have met on the soil of Africa, at Casablanca. There, not far from the noise of war, they drew up battle plans for 1943—plans designed to bring about the unconditional surrender of Germany, Italy, and Japan.

July 10, 1943—
> Hello the OWI in New York, this is Allied Force headquarters in North Africa. The Allies tackled this morning the hardest job of the war when

following a terrific pounding, our infantry landed on the soil of Sicily, supported by the Allied naval forces who had previously coordinated their work with the Air Force in bombing the coast.

November 1943—

This is Sergeant Roy Maple, a Marine Corps combat correspondent with the initial Marine landing parties on the now Jap-held island of Bougainville. Dawn is about to break as we stand ready to attack. The Marines are ready to land.

June 5, 1944—

Ladies and gentlemen, the President of the United States.

My friends, yesterday on June 4, 1944, Rome fell to American and Allied troops. The first of the Axis capitols is now in our hands. One up and two to go.

July 21, 1944—

This is July 21, 1944, six o'clock in the morning. American Marines are this morning landing on Guam Island in the Marianas, liberating territory seized by Japanese fascists immediately following Pearl Harbor two and a half years ago.

August 24, 1944—

Bells are ringing tonight in Paris—in a liberated Paris—a Paris that for the first time since 1940 is free from oppression.

October 20, 1944—

A few moments ago, we heard on our monitoring system the word that we could release a flash that the Philippines have actually been invaded. It is now 7:30 P.M. Eastern Wartime.

March 24, 1945—

Supreme Headquarters has announced that General Hodges' First United States Army has crossed the Rhine. Elements reached the Rhine and crossed to establish a bridgehead on the east bank, somewhere south of Cologne. This means that the battle for the penetration of inner Germany has begun.

April 12, 1945—

President Roosevelt is dead. The President died of a cerebral hemorrhage. All we know so far is that the President died at Warm Springs in Georgia [John Charles Daly on CBS].

May 8, 1945—

4:25 Eastern Wartime, Bob Hight reporting. In a little over an hour and a half, the last German forces in Europe will lay down their arms and the fighting will officially be over—the end of nearly six years of war for many Allied troops. Here at home, as in the rest of the Allied world, the day has been spent in celebration and in prayer at the end of the European war. Only a few war plants closed down, however, and, for the most part, workers stayed on the job. In Philadelphia, the Liberty Bell was rung. And in New York at 8:30 tonight the torch on the Statue of Liberty will be relighted for the first time since Pearl Harbor. Bob Hight reporting, this is CBS, the Columbia Broadcasting System.

August 9, 1945—
Good evening from the White House in Washington. Ladies and Gentlemen, the President of the United States.
My fellow Americans, the British, the Chinese and the United States governments have given the Japanese people adequate warning of what was in store for them . . . The world will note that the first atomic bomb was dropped on Hiroshima, a military base. If Japan does not surrender, bombs will have to be dropped on her war industries and unfortunately thousands of civilian lives will be lost. I urge Japanese civilians to leave industrial cities immediately and save themselves from destruction.

September 1, 1945—
We are on the Pacific fleet flagship, the U.S.S. *Missouri*, in Tokyo Bay for the signing of the surrender of Japan—three years, eight months, 25 days since the attack on Pearl Harbor . . . [Note: As a result of the time differences between countries, the day of surrender was September 2, 1945 in Japan.]

In World War II, the distinction between soldier and civilian became blurred as civilians in many countries fought in underground resistance movements, as propagandists, saboteurs and collaborators, that is, as soldiers without uniforms.[4] Like their military counterparts, the soldiers without uniforms also sacrificed their lives and in so doing allowed others to carry on their cause as surely as those who invaded enemy lands with all the weaponry of battle.

It was a war of unimaginable savagery. Reports about the decapitation and torture of prisoners of war and the bayoneting of captured civilians by the Japanese were not unusual. The Japanese were not alone in their savagery. Japanese prisoners were subjected to inhumane treatment. As Herman Wouk said of Ensign Keith in the *Caine Mutiny*: "Like most of the naval executioners of Kwajelein, he seemed to regard the enemy as a species of animal pest."[5] It seemed as if everyone had succumbed to the savagery of war. On Okinawa alone, only a few weeks before the atomic bomb was dropped on Hiroshima, 123,000 Japanese and Americans were killed. "Just awful" was the comment, not of a pacifist, but of General Douglas MacArthur.

World War II was a conflict in which military leaders became their nation's heroes. Decades after the war's conclusion, America still continues to honor and celebrate their names with the Patton Tank, the Spruance class destroyer, the *Nimitz* and *Eisenhower* aircraft carriers. The country remembers such phrases as "I shall return," General MacArthur's reference to the Philippines; "Old Blood and Guts," the nickname of General George S. Patton; and "Nuts," the reply Major General Anthony McAuliffe gave in response to a German surrender ultimatum at Bastonge, Belgium, during the Battle of the Bulge in December 1944. Americans have not forgotten the Normandy invasion on D-Day, the battles at Stalingrad, El Alamein, Monte Cassino or at Corregidor, Midway, Okinawa, Iwo Jima, Guam, Guadacanal, or Tarawa, some of whose memories are honored as the names of U.S. naval vessels.

World War II was a war in which the media were used for making public appeals, which did not hesitate to impugn the character of any American citizen who chose not to participate in the war effort, whether the activity involved buying war bonds, voting in elections, giving blood, or making material sacrifices. For example, one night a radio program called the "Manhattan Merry-Go-Round" aired the following announcement:

> Tonight our Manhattan Merry-Go-Round program is brought to you for one purpose—to ask you to start buying more war bonds now and to keep on buying. All of us know that our men now are engaged in deadly conflict raging overseas. They're fighting to drive back the Germans and crush the Japs. To help them do this as soon as possible and to keep the casualties as low as possible we, at home, must do our part to the fullest—to the point of sacrifice. For one thing, we must buy more war bonds regularly, and we must hold onto the ones we already have. Remember, you and I when we buy war bonds are only lending our dollars, while our men at the front are giving their lives, if need be. So do your duty. Start buying more war bonds tomorrow as in as large amounts as you possibly

can. At this critical hour, no man or woman who is able to do so and who fails to buy war bonds is worthy of the name, American.[6]

Or the night in 1942 when a radio program called "This Is Our America" aired a public service message urging Americans to vote in an upcoming election. The message appeared at a time when divisiveness toward the war effort persisted, as some newspapers and other publications caused a segment of the public to question whether its leaders deliberately maneuvered the country into the conflict. The announcement noted that there were Quislings or incompetents in office, and the public was responsible for originally electing them. The message went on to state that as public officials, American fascists were deliberately slowing down the war effort, causing casualty lists to grow, and unnecessarily adding 5,000 more people each day to the rolls of the dead. In asking the public to elect an honest, fighting Congress, the announcement challenged voters to prove that they were proud to be Americans by registering for the election, reviewing the names of the candidates on the ballot, and defeating those who were doing untold damage to the war effort. The message noted that in a world of concentration camps and flying swastikas, the right to vote was a rare privilege for which the armed forces of the United Nations were sacrificing their lives to preserve; it boldly added that any American who would not cast a vote at a time like this would be a traitor to the cause of Democracy. This radio message was not the only warning about the enemy within. Newspapers attacked other newspapers they believed to be sowing dissent in a society that had to be united for war; movies spoke about the issue. Magazines of such different political hues as *Life* and the *New Republic* wrote about American groups who tried to arouse hatred and bigotry among their fellow citizens and turn American against American during this national emergency.

World War II was an international conflict of such dimensions that its implications for the future of mankind are still unfolding. In committing their resources toward ending this conflict and hastening the homecoming of our armed forces, the media presented many faces to the public. They were informative, instructive, exposing, secretive, functional, responsible, irresponsible, provocative, embarrassing, divisive, unifying, uplifting, and entertaining. To illustrate the diverse roles they assumed, let us examine some of the major characteristics of World War II and the media's role and response.

World War II was a war of genocide and racism. The Germans were called the "Krauts" or the somewhat milder name, "Jerries," and Japanese the "Gooks", the "Nips"—a shortened version of *Dai Nippon*, the Japanese word for Japan—and much worse. Even before the attack on Pearl Harbor, most Americans viewed the Japanese as less than human. Various events reinforced these feelings such as the Japanese attack on Nanking—then capitol of China—in 1937, an event known today as the "Rape of Nanking." It was estimated that Japanese soldiers raped thousands of women, killed hundreds of thousands of people, and destroyed one-third of the city by fire.

To unite our country against the savagery and barbarism of the enemy, our comic books and poster art caricatured them, our music ridiculed them, and some of our movies stereotyped them. *The Battle of China*, a film produced by Lieutenant Colonel Frank Capra in cooperation with the U.S. Army Signal Corps for the *Why We Fight* series, said it another way: "In 4,000 years of continuous history, the Chinese never waged a war of conquest. They are not that sort of people," the direct implication being that the opposite is true of the Japanese. Consequently, it is not surprising that Americans viewed Japan rather than other nations in the Far East as *the* Yellow peril and just as evil as Nazi Germany.

Although Americans understood little or nothing of Eastern philosophy, they did understand the meaning of genocide—a policy carried out through an elaborate bureaucracy of the Nazi government, which exterminated not only Jews but members of other religious faiths, handicapped persons, gypsies, political dissenters, and conquered citizens. The media were not errant in warning the public of such possibilities. As early as 1941, William L. Shirer's *Berlin Diary: The Journal of a Foreign Correspondent, 1934–1941* told about the German "mercy" killings of mentally handicapped persons. On October 19, 1942, the National Broadcasting Company (NBC) aired Edna St. Vincent Millay's epic poem, "The Murder of Lidice" which spoke about the fate of the inhabitants of that village at the hands of the Nazis. Newspapers carried stories of the Nazis' treatment of the Jews during the war. But all these warnings were insufficient to change the policies of the U.S. government in its prosecution of the European war. As a result, the Holocaust in all its guises continued and many millions died.

World War II was a war of imperialism—an effort by the Axis powers to divide up the world for their own interests. Italy fought to seize the western Balkans and the Mediterranean (or *Mare Nostrum*, meaning "Our Sea" in Latin). Japan's rhetoric about "the Greater East Asia Co-Prosperity Sphere" scarcely hid its aspirations in China, Southeast Asia, and the western Pacific. Those who surrounded Hitler quarreled about the control of a permanent empire of slave laborers numbering in the millions over whom the Nazis would stand guard while preserving the Thousand-Year Third Reich. Like the Germans, the Japanese and Italians were equally determined to retain full control over their spheres of influence as well.

Books, films, and radio tried to educate Americans about this aspect of the war. *The Nazis Strike*, another film of the *Why We Fight* series, noted that the Germans have a "passion for conquest." According to Hitler, "We have a sacred mission. Today we rule Germany, tomorrow the world." The Nazi-produced films *Baptism of Fire* and *War in the East*—showing the annihilation of Poland and distributed in Belgium, Holland, and the Balkans before the blitz of 1940—did nothing to dispel such notions of world conquest from the public's mind. Books and magazines spoke about the imperialist aims of the Axis powers and their plans for the world, including the United States, if they won the war. Radio broadcast book discussion programs such as "Words on War" and the "Radio Reader." Contemporary authors even discussed the significance of imperialism in the postwar world if the United Nations won the conflict. In 1945, Owen Lattimore in *Solution in Asia* wrote that Western imperialism died in the Far East when the Japanese attacked Pearl Harbor, Singapore, and Hong Kong. He warned the West that if the democratic ideals of the United States did not promise a better life to Asian peoples and if the Dutch and the French did not understand the awakenings of these populaces, then the communist ideology of Russia would appeal to them and through ideas rather than a melodramatic conspiracy the power of the Soviet Union would begin to ascend.

World War II was a war of ideology, a struggle in which the liberal democracies confounded political groups on the extreme Right and Left who had long been predicting victory for totalitarianism as the wave of the future. The concepts and policies of appeasement, defeatism, and isolationism were cast aside as the British fought for national survival, Americans for security and a better world, and the Free French for honor, patriotism, and life itself. Franklin D. Roosevelt and Winston

Churchill proved that governments which have the solid support of their people could operate fairly and relatively openly in a wartime environment; that civil liberties and legislative processes need not cease; and that civilian leaders could devise strategy without constant arguments with the military. They both showed that unified democracies could wage war successfully without ceasing to be democratic.[7] World War II was the kind of war about which Winston Churchill once remarked, "I have only one purpose, the destruction of Hitler . . . If Hitler invaded hell, I would at least make a favorable reference to the Devil in the House of Commons."

Here too, the media played an important role in trying to explain the significance of the ideological differences between the Axis powers and ourselves. The U.S. Office of War Information (OWI) through films, short-wave radio broadcasts, publications, and other media delivered such messages to foreign audiences, though not always successfully. On the home front, radio, movies, and publications tried to explain the significance of war and what was at stake if the United Nations won or lost. Advertisements tried to perform the same tasks through the simplicity of their copy. The theater presented such productions as *The Moon Is Down* or *A Bell for Adano* to portray the differences between fascism and democracy. Radio broadcast programs of public affairs discussions, dramatizations such as "This Is War!" and commentaries by distinguished news analysts about the issues. Newspapers, while adhering voluntarily to a government censorship code, were not constrained in their editorial comments about the war. Some presented opinions that could divide a nation, while others published editorials that helped unify the country and point out the fallacies of the divisive positions. Using a multitude of resources, the media made an effort to help the public understand the ideological differences between the democracies and the fascists, although they were not always successful in speaking with a singular voice or viewpoint.

It was a war of science and technology. When the conflict began, some of Germany's opponents were still using strategy and armaments dating back to World War I such as the Maginot line fortifications in France and the cavalry in Poland. When the war ended six years later, the technological and scientific advances in weaponry, medicine, chemistry and other areas changed the world and continue to do so. The United States organized its scientific resources under the direction of Vannevar Bush and the Office of Scientific Research and Development (OSRD). This agency coordinated the work of scientists who labored on government contracts in universities and private laboratories. During the war, scientists invented or improved upon such technologies as radar, flame throwers, amphibious assault boats, long-range navigational aids, submarine detection devices, and radar bombsights. OSRD also worked on the development of DDT (dichloro-diphenyl-trichloromethane), which protected American troops from typhus outbreaks in North Africa and Italy, and warded off malaria, making life more tolerable for American forces in the Pacific jungles. The most dramatic advance made under the guidance of the OSRD was the development of the atomic bomb, which ignited the Atomic Age. American, Canadian and British scientists cooperated in building this weapon. Here again, the media played an informative role in these various areas.

Companies that advanced the war with the products they created and manufactured for the government spoke openly of these scientific advances, whenever their revelations did not violate national security. Advertising promised the public that a multitude of products or derivatives being developed for the war effort would be available once the war was over. At the same time, the newspapers, radio, and comics could also guard our national security with utmost scrupulousness. One example relates to the development of the atomic bomb. On June 23, 1943, the U.S. Office of Censorship sent the following confidential message to all radio stations and daily and weekly newspapers:

> The Codes of Wartime Practices for the American Press and Radio Broadcasters request that nothing be published or broadcast about new or secret weapons . . . experiments. In extension of this highly vital precaution, you are asked not to publish or broadcast any information whatever regarding war experiments involving:
>
> > Production or utilization of atom smashing, atomic energy, atomic fission, atomic splitting or any of their equivalents.
> >
> > The use for military purposes of radium or radioactive materials, heavy water, high voltage discharge equipment, cyclotrons.
> >
> > The following elements or any of their compounds: polonium, uranium, ytterbium, hafnium, protactinium, radium, rhenium, thorium, deuterium.[8]

From that date in June 1943 to August 6, 1945, when President Harry S. Truman announced the dropping of the first atomic bomb on Hiroshima, Japan, the U.S. Office of Censorship kept a constant vigil against any mention of the bomb's development. Whenever a vague reference to an experiment was discovered, a courteous letter was sent at once to the author explaining the importance of avoiding discussion of the experiment. Even comic strips picturing great scientific advances were cautioned lest they accidently come too close to the truth. The result of all this secrecy was that the test of the new weapon in the New Mexican desert three weeks before its use against Japan failed to arouse any undue journalistic interest. The flash was seen at a great distance, but the Army passed it off as an explosion of a remote ammunition dump. By voluntarily adhering to the country's censorship code, the nation's press generally was able to keep thousands of items of information that could endanger the country's security out of print and off the airwaves.

The media also maintained secrecy about large-scale invasion plans. In November 1942, a great fleet of American ships landed thousands of troops and tons of supplies on the North African coast. The first large-scale invasion in the Western theater of war proceeded with marked success. "Operation Torch" came after months of careful and extensive planning, the assembly and routing of thousands of men, vast equipment, and an enormous ship convoy. Yet, like the invasion of Europe itself a year and a half later on June 6, 1944 at Normandy, France, this project was kept secret from the public and was known to the enemy only when the ships appeared off the invasion coast.

In the field of wartime medicine, advances were made using blood plasma to treat the wounded, and medical scientists found a method to produce large quantities of penicillin to cure a wide spectrum of illnesses, ranging from pneumonia to venereal disease to blood poisoning. Posters and advertisements hailed these achievements, while government agencies produced films such as *VD Hygiene*, to teach people, especially in the armed services, how to protect themselves from contracting various diseases.

When World War II began, most airplanes were flying at about 200 miles per hour and by war's end Germany was introducing jet planes that flew through European skies at 500 miles or more per hour. In addition to the jet plane, the Germans made great progress in the field of missiles and rockets. Their V-1 and V-2 missiles were the first guided missiles used in wartime and were the forebears of the rockets that have carried humans into outer space. The helicopter was introduced during the war. Modern warfare also required that communications be improved among military units. So science developed for U.S. forces the radio telephone which police, ambulance teams, taxi drivers, and others use in peacetime. The development of television continued during the war years, and its influence on the media around the world is still evolving.

World War II was also a war of changing world power. Germany was beaten, its size reduced, its provinces occupied, its desire for world power checked and, perhaps, eliminated. At the end of the war, Japan also had lost its empire and domination of East Asia. Great Britain and France emerged from the war weakened monetarily and politically, their population and economic resources clearly were insufficient for upholding their great power status; in the postwar world their colonies sought and gained independence—sometimes obtaining their freedom with bloodshed and other times without. Russia and the United States emerged from the war as superpowers. Both nations were able to recover from serious defeats in 1941 and 1942 to develop enormous military and economic strength, to extend that strength over great distances, to maintain unity at home and an alliance filled with ideological rivalries. Each nation had performed a unique mission in the war; the Russians by "ripping the guts out of the German Army" (Churchill's phrase) on the Eastern Front and America by achieving the same end against the Axis powers on the Western Front and in the Pacific.[9] For a moment in time, two rivals—capitalism and communism—were submerged by an alliance between nations whose greater goals were survival and saving the world from the New Order of the fascist powers.

That World War II was a war of changing power relationships and that a new international political order would emerge from its conclusion should not have surprised anyone who read books or listened to radio commentary or public affairs discussions during the war. Books had forecast that in the postwar world America's eastern frontier would not stop on its East Coast but rather at the Rhine River; how Japan and Germany should be treated upon their defeat; the development of the European Economic Community; the establishment of a United Nations organization, and the death of imperialism in various parts of the world, and the emergence of independent nations out of its demise; and what democracy must do to withstand the competitive ideology of communism, and to bear witness to communism's demise—all of which did transpire.

It was a war of machines, hence speed, maneuverability, and surprise. Striking hard was linked to striking fast; *blitzkrieg* (meaning "lightning war") became part of the vocabulary; and powerful forces could emerge from the sky or sea as at Normandy. Combining overwhelming firepower with the maneuverability of the tank, airplane, and carrier task force gave wartime offensives a breadth quite dissimilar from the war of attrition fought in the trenches of World War I. Both sides suffered bad defeats during the course of the war: the French in 1940, the Italians in Greece and Libya, the Russians in mid-1941, the Americans at Pearl Harbor, the British at Malaya, the Japanese at Midway Island, and the Germans at Stalingrad. Despite these tremendous setbacks, their armed forces did not break.[10]

The role of the media was indispensable in helping to produce the machinery of war, recruit personnel for the armed services, coordinate the offensives of the Allies who spoke different tongues, and keep elements of the offensives a surprise. The armed services produced films, which they distributed to war factory workers to show them how their efforts were indispensable to the war effort and to maintain their morale. Comic book characters as in "Joe Palooka" and poster art urged Americans to stay on the job, keep up production, and reduce work absenteeism. Films, recorded in different languages, allowed the Allies to coordinate their attacks with each other, train their own armed forces, and teach them how to repair and maintain the American equipment they were being sent.

On the home front it was a war of social change. Songs like "Rosie the Riveter" or "They're Either Too Young or Too Old" reminded the Americans of the changing role of women in our society and the desolation they felt as men went off to war. Rose Franken's play *Soldier's Wife* addressed the issue of what would happen when loved ones were reunited after the war was won—after each had experienced totally different life styles at home and in war-ravaged lands—and the implication of these differences for their relationships.[11] In many instances, the war led to a nation's soaring divorce rate.

William N. Robson through his "Open Letter on Race Hatred" aired over the CBS alerted the country to the dangers of existing racism as the country fought to eradicate the perpetrators of similar intolerances overseas. Books such as Gunnar Myrdal's *An American Dilemma: The Negro Problem and Modern Democracy* and Pearl Buck's *American Unity and Asia* gave fair warning to the American public of the consequences of racism in America and other societies if these issues were left to simmer and were not resolved. At the same time, while some were using the media to denounce racism, others were using it to foster and support racism, if in their view of national security it was warranted. Such was the situation when newspapers and eminent columnists like Walter Lippmann in 1942 supported the government's incarceration of West Coast Japanese-Americans in internment camps in the United States and, yet, the social blindness brought by racism, intolerance, and prejudice could not stop thousands of Japanese-Americans, blacks, Jews and other minority groups from serving their country with great distinction in the armed services or as civilians in private life.

World War II was a war without exhilaration or glory for most countries, although Americans still tend to regard it as a time of national purpose, filled with the glamour of heroism and crusading zeal. The media reinforced America's views of the war in many ways. In the world of fantasy, Hollywood through its films had America defeating its enemies against impossible odds when in reality, at the war's beginning, the odds of America and its allies winning the conflict were slim. Cartoon characters like Superman and Little Orphan Annie were vigorously destroying our enemies and promoting patriotism at home. Our music was both patriotic and uplifting, for example, "We'll Be Singing Hallelujah Marching thru Berlin."

Perhaps America's purposefulness was inspired, in part, by President Roosevelt when he addressed the Congress on January 6, 1941, and delivered his "Four Freedoms" speech. At a time when Western Europe lay under Nazi domination, the president presented a vision in which American ideals of individualized liberties were extended throughout the world. In this speech, Roosevelt articulated the ideological aims of the war when he stated:

> We look forward to a world founded upon four essential human freedoms. The first is freedom of speech and expression—everywhere in the world. The second is freedom of every person to worship God in his own way—everywhere in the world. The third is freedom from want—everywhere in the world. The fourth is freedom from fear—anywhere in the world.[12]

Thus, with confidence in its own morality and principles, the United States once again helped save the world from a terrible tyranny. However, a Norwegian freedom fighter expressed the other side of war when he noted: "Though war can bring adventures which stir the heart, the true nature of war is composed of many innumerable tragedies, of grief, waste and sacrifice, wholly evil and not redeemed by glory."[13]

It was a war of incalculable destruction—both human and physical. Historians cannot even begin to measure its human and physical costs. World War II claimed more lives than any other war in history. Of the more than 55 million deaths, civilians were estimated to constitute about one-half, most of whom died from bombings, massacres, forced migrations, epidemics, and starvation. Damage to important industries, transportation, and housing in World War II was far greater than in World War I. Bombings, artillery fire, and street fighting devastated such cities as Berlin, Budapest, Coventry, Dresden, Frankfurt, Hamburg, Hiroshima, Nagasaki, Leningrad, London, Manila, Milan, Nagoya, Rotterdam, Stuttgart, Tokyo, and Warsaw. The war left millions of people in Europe and Asia without adequate food, shelter and clothing, without fuel, raw materials, and money. The war caused large populations to migrate. Millions had to flee their homes because of race, religion, or political beliefs or were sent as slave laborers to isolated areas. At the end of the war, many became displaced persons. In some countries, whole groups of people were uprooted.

Newsreels and documentary films bore witness to the human and physical devastations of World War II. Newspapers and magazines described the destruction of other peoples in other lands by the Axis powers. Nothing, however, prepared the world for the magnitude of human destruction that was to be discovered at war's end. No one was prepared for Edward R. Murrow's personal witness to the crimes against humanity, as he described the sights, sounds, and smells of the Buchenwald concentration camp upon its liberation in early 1945.

> Permit me to tell you what you would have seen and heard had you been with me on Thursday. It will not be pleasant listening . . . For I propose to tell you of Buchenwald. It's on a small hill about four miles outside of Weimar and it was one of the largest concentration camps in Germany. And it was built to last . . . Now let me tell this in the first person for I was the least important person there, as you shall hear.

. . . There surged around me an evil-smelling horde. Men and boys reached out to touch me . . . death had already marked many of them but they were smiling with their eyes . . . and [I] asked to see one of the barracks . . . I was told that this building had once stabled 80 horses. There were 1,200 men in it, five to a bunk. The stink was beyond all description . . . 242 out of 1,200 [died] in one month. As I walked down to the end of the barracks there was applause from the men too weak to get out of bed. It sounded like the hand clapping of babies. They were so weak . . . As we walked out into the courtyard, a man fell dead. Two others, they must have been over sixty, were crawling towards the latrine. I saw it but will not describe it. In another part of the camp, they showed me the children. Hundreds of them. Some were only six. One rolled up his sleeve, showed me his number; it was tatooed on his arm . . . The others showed me their numbers. They will carry them till they die. An elderly man standing beside me said, the children, enemies of the state. I could see their ribs through their thin shirts . . . We crossed to the court-yard. Men kept coming up to speak to me and to touch me. Professors from Poland. Doctors from Vienna. Men from all Europe. Men from the countries that made America.

. . . I asked to see the kitchen [the hospital]. It was clean. The German in charge had been a communist . . . had been at Buchenwald for nine years. He showed me the daily ration, one piece of brown bread about as thick as your thumb. On top of it a piece of margarine, as big as three sticks of chewing gum. That and a little stew is what they [internees] received every twenty-four hours . . . about 6,000 [prisoners] died during March . . .

Dr. Heller, the Czech, asked if I would care to see the crematorium. He said it wouldn't be very interesting because the Germans had run out of coke some days ago and had taken to dumping the bodies into a great hole nearby.

We proceeded to the small courtyard . . . there were two rows of bodies stacked up like cordwood. They were thin and very white. Some of the bodies were terribly bruised, though there seemed to be little flesh to bruise. Some had been shot through the head but they bled but little. All except two were naked . . . all that was mortal of more than 500 men and boys lay there in two neat piles . . . It appeared most of the men and boys had died of starvation. They had not been executed. But the manner of death seemed unimportant. Murder had been done at Buchenwald. God alone knows how many men and boys have died there during the last 12 years. Thursday I was told there was more than 20,000 in the camp. There had been as many as 60,000. Where are they now? . . .

I pray you to believe what I have said about Buchenwald. I have reported what I saw and heard. But only part of it. For the most of it I have
no words. Dead men are plentiful in war, but the living dead, more than
20,000 of them in one camp. And the country round about was pleasing
to the eye and the Germans were well fed and well-dressed . . . If I have
offended you by this rather mild account of Buchenwald I am not in the
least sorry . . .[14]

To see in film, or hear in words from a safe distance thousands of miles
away could never be the same emotional or searing experience that
troops and journalists encountered—no matter how much the media
might have attempted to portray it, but at least they tried.

It was a war whose significance, decades after its conclusion, began to
erode from the knowledge of the world's newest generations. In 1981,
on the fortieth anniversary of the attack on Pearl Harbor, an Associated
Press-National Broadcasting Company poll revealed that about one out
of six adult Americans did not know the significance of Pearl Harbor,
while 9 out of 10 Americans who were 10–24 years old at the time of
the attack did.[15] Perhaps this is a natural effect of time on historical
events; in 1944 Norman Cousins, editor of the *Saturday Review of Literature*, cautioned writers about this possibility:

. . . a correct understanding of history sometimes can mean the difference
between war and peace. It was precisely the misunderstanding of one
disaster that helped bring on another for the generation after the last war.
For misunderstanding, like war itself, has effects and causes.

Does anyone doubt that there is a danger of another period of misunderstanding tomorrow that may invite yet another catastrophe. The cost
of this war in blood and wealth will be high. Mistakes will be made in the
winning—many of them inevitable and insignificant, taking the size of
the job into account. The reconversion to a peacetime economy will be
rough; the dislocations and physical adjustments may be deeper and
broader than most of us had anticipated. The ideals that had such a
genuine ring when they first sounded early in the war may sound hope-
lessly remote and tinny tomorrow.

These will be the effects of war. Will the next generation recognize that
those effects, horrible and complex and sweeping though they may be,
represent actually a comparative luxury alongside what might have been?
Will the next generation have any idea of what the might and menace of
Nazi Germany were after the fall of France? Will it have any idea of the

bristling peril surrounding this nation the night of December 7, 1941? Or will it content itself only with the effects washed up by that struggle for survival, becoming cynical and jaded at precisely the time when a virile and progressive approach to world problems will be most urgently needed? And if the next generation turns sour, will the ferment help produce another war?

This does not mean that today's readers are to be brushed aside, for the broad, general, integrated stories of this war which can be so useful for tomorrow have their own usefulness today. It is just that, so far as the next generation is concerned, the type of writing we have been talking about here will go a long way toward taking the astigmatism out of hindsight.[16]

Well, the leaders of the governments of the world who were born before or at the time of Pearl Harbor certainly did not forget the lessons of World War II. The Soviet Union armed itself so as never to be weak again, as the country remembers its 27 million dead who suffered at the hands of the Nazi might. America, remembering her sons who died at Pearl Harbor and fighting the might of the Axis powers, vowed never to be the victim of a sneak attack again. Israel remembers the six million Jews who died at the hands of the Nazi might and has vowed that its people will never be exterminated again. While nations arm themselves to avoid and to attain psychological and military security, the world becomes a little less secure and a little more uneasy, especially as some of the smaller countries attempt to develop their own arsenals, particularly those based on a nuclear capability. Governments still remember the lessons the Axis powers taught the world in World War II—they taught their lessons very well.

So how did World War II finally end after all of its carnage? Well, it ended twice. World War II first ended in Tokyo Bay on the deck of the American battleship, U.S.S. *Missouri*, on September 2, 1945 when General Douglas MacArthur, the Supreme Allied Commander, began the conclusion of the surrender ceremony (the Japanese forces of Southeast Asia surrendering to the British on September 12) with a prayerful wish: "Let us pray that peace be now restored to the world and that God will preserve it always." Then, General MacArthur officially ended the ceremony and the Second World War, the greatest cataclysm in the history of mankind, with just four simple words: "These proceedings are closed."

Then World War II ended on Boston's Lorna Road and countless other Lorna Roads in cities, towns, villages, and hamlets across the country with firework displays, playing bands, waving flags, and many other untold celebrations. For my family watching the firework displays from the front porch of the Waters' family home on Lorna Road, World War II ended with my mother saying, "Thank God! Thank God, it's all over!"

Notes

1. U.S. Budget Bureau, "United States at War," Washington, D.C., 1946, 510.

2. WOR-AM, New York, N.Y., December 7, 1941.

3. "World War 2," Sounds of History: American Radio Mobilizes the Homefront, National Archives, Washington, D.C., 1980.

4. Leonard Bushkoff, "The War that Changed the World," *Washington Post*, September 2, 1979, C5.

5. As quoted in Paul Fussell, "Hiroshima: A Soldier's Story," *New Republic*, August 22 & 29 1981, 29.

6. "Manhattan Merry-Go-Round," National Broadcasting Company, New York. (date unknown)

7. Bushkoff, C4.

8. Byron Price, "Report on the Office of Censorship," U.S. Office of Censorship, Washington, D.C., November 15, 1945, 41.

9. Bushkoff, C5.

10. Ibid.

11. Rosamond Gilder, "Escape to Mama," review of *Soldier's Wife* by Rose Franken, *Theatre Arts*, December 1944, 699–700.

12. As quoted in Stacey Bredhoff, *Powers of Persuasion: Poster Art from World War II*, (Washington, D.C.: National Archives, 1994), 8.

13. Bushkoff, C5.

14. Edward R. Murrow, Columbia Broadcasting System, April 15, 1945.

15. "Poll Finds 1 in 6 Unsure of Attack's Importance," *Washington Post*, December 6, 1981, C1.

16. Norman Cousins, "The War Against Hindsight," *Saturday Review of Literature*, April 15, 1944, 28.

BIBLIOGRAPHY FOR CHAPTER SEVEN

Baldwin, Hanson W. *Strategy for Victory*. W. W. Norton: New York, c. 1942.

Baynes, Norman H. *The Speeches of Adolph Hitler, April 1922–August 1939*. 2 vols. Oxford University Press: London and New York, 1942.

Buck, Pearl S. *American Unity and Asia*. John Day Company: New York, 1942.

Davis, Forrest, and Ernest K. Lindley. *How War Came: An American White Paper, from the Fall of France to Pearl Harbor*. Simon and Schuster: New York, 1942.

de Jong Louis and Joseph W. F. Stoppelman. *The Lion Rampant*. Querido: New York, 1944.

Duranty, Walter. *USSR: The Story of Soviet Russia*. J. B. Lippincott and Company: New York, 1944.

Eliot, George Fielding. *Hour of Triumph*. Reynal and Hitchcock: New York, 1944.

Fung, Kwok-Ying. *China: A Portrait Survey of China and Her People*. H. Holt & Company: New York, 1943.

Géraud, André. *The Gravediggers of France: Gamelin, Daladier, Reynaud, Pétain and Laval: Military Defeat, Armistice, Counter-Revolution*. Doubleday, Doran and Company: New York, 1944.

Goffin, Robert. *White Brigade*. Doubleday, Doran and Company: New York, 1944.

Guérard, Albert L. *The France of Tomorrow*. Harvard University Press: Cambridge, 1942.

Guérard, Albert L. *Europe: Free and United*. Stanford University Press: Palo Alto, 1945.

Gunther, John. *Inside Europe; again completely revised*. Harper & Brothers: New York, c. 1940.

Hagen, Paul. *Will Germany Crack? A Factual Report on Germany from Within*. Harper & Brothers: New York, 1942.

Handleman, Howard. *Bridge to Victory: The Story of the Reconquest of the Aleutians*. Random House: New York, 1943.

Heiden, Konrad. *Der Fuehrer: Hitler's Rise to Power*. Houghton Mifflin Company: New York, 1944.

Henri, Ernst. *Hitler over Russia? The Coming Fight between the Fascist and Socialist Armies*. Simon and Schuster: New York, 1936 (Translated by Michael Davidson).

Henri, Ernst. *Hitler over Europe*. Simon and Schuster: New York, 1934 (Translated by Michael Davidson).

Hindus, Maurice G. *Mother Russia*. Doubleday, Doran and Company: New York, 1943.

Hitler, Adolph, *Mein Kampf.* Stackpole Sons: New York, 1939.

Ingrao, Charles W. *The Hessian Mercenary State: Ideas, Institutions, and Reforms*. Cambridge University Press: New York, 1987.

Iugov, Aron. *Russia's Economic Front for War and Peace*. Harper & Brothers: New York, 1942.

Johnstone William C. *The Future of Japan*. Oxford University Press: New York, 1945.

Kai-shek Chiang, *Resistance and Reconstruction*. Harper & Brothers: New York and London, 1943.

Kernan, William Fergus. *Defense Will Not Win the War*. Little, Brown and Company: Boston, 1942.

Krueger, Kurt. *Inside Hitler, from the German of Kurt Krueger, M.D.* Avalon Press Inc.: New York, 1941.

Lamott Willis. *Nippon: The Crime and Punishment of Japan*. John Day Company: New York, 1944.

Lattimore, Owen. *Solution in Asia*. Little, Brown and Company: Boston, 1945.

Lattimore, Owen. *The Making of Modern China*. W. W. Norton & Company: New York, 1944.

Lewis, Sinclair. *Babbitt*. Harcourt, Brace and Company: New York, c. 1922.

Lippmann, Walter. *U.S. Foreign Policy: Shield of the Republic*. Little, Brown and Company: Boston, 1943.

Matsuo, Kinoaki. *How Japan Plans to Win*. Little, Brown and Company: Boston, 1942.

Mauldin, Bill. *Up Front*. H. Holt and Company: New York, 1945.

McWilliams, Carey. *Prejudice: The Japanese-Americans—Symbols of Racial Intolerance*. Public Affairs Committee Inc.: New York, 1944.

Mitchell, Margaret. *Gone with the Wind*. Macmillan: New York, 1936.

Moulton, Harold G. and Lewis Marlio, *The Control of Germany and Japan*. Brookings Institution: Washington, D.C., 1944.

Myrdal, Gunnar. *An American Dilemma: The Negro Problem and Modern Democracy*. Harper & Brothers: New York, 1944 (2 volumes).

Pentad. *The Remaking of Italy*. Penguin Books: New York and Harmonsworth, Middlesex England, 1941.

Pyle, Ernie. *Brave Men*. H. Holt and Company: New York, 1945.

Rowe, David Nelson. *China Among the Powers*. Harcourt, Brace and Company: New York, 1945.

Sayers, Michael and Albert E. Kahn. *Sabotage! The Secret War against America*. Harper & Brothers: New York, 1942.

Sherrod, Robert. *Tarawa: The Story of a Battle*. Duell, Sloan and Pearce: New York, c. 1944.

Shirer, William L. *Berlin Diary: the Journal of a Foreign Correspondent, 1934–1941*. A. A. Knopf: New York, 1941.

Smith, Howard K. *Last Train from Berlin*. A. A. Knopf: New York, 1942.

Snow, Edgar. *Red Star over China*. V. Gollancz, Ltd.: London, 1937.

Snow Edgar. *Battle for Asia*. Random House: New York, c. 1941.

Steinbeck, John. *Grapes of Wrath*. Viking Press: New York, c. 1939.

Steiner, Jesse. *Behind the Japanese Mask*. MacMillan: New York, 1943.

Thompson, Paul W. *Modern Battle: Units in Action in the Second World War*. Penguin Books: New York, 1942, c. 1941.

Welles, Sumner. *The Time for Decision*. Harper & Brothers: New York, 1944.

Wheeler, Keith. *The Pacific Is My Beat*. Books Inc.: New York, 1943.

Willkie, Wendell L. *One World*. Simon and Schuster: New York, 1943.

Winsor, Kathleen. *Forever Amber*. MacMillan: New York, 1944.

INDEX

About the Author

Jordan Braverman is a freelance writer and columnist. A graduate of Harvard, he also has graduate degrees from Yale University and Georgetown University's School of Foreign Service.

His writings, commentaries, and columns have appeared in the *Baltimore Sun*, the *Washington Star*, the *Congressional Record*, *U.S. News and World Report*, and other publications. His newspaper columns have been entered for nomination for the Pulitzer Prize. He received the Editor's Choice Award in the North American Poetry Contest (1994) and has been published in the poetry anthologies, *Echoes of Yesterday* and *Best Poems of 1995.*